Endorsements

I am not into medical protocol, cannot understand medical equations, but have had more than my share of life-threatening medical events. So I do know the difference between health and sickness. I have happily chosen health over sickness. Jackie and the information in this book have been a part of my pursuit in implementing that decision.

I am fairly certain that this book and its author represent a major breakthrough in the protocol of achieving and preserving good health.

Everybody who is searching for the keys of overall happiness and good health should read this book!

A happy and healthy octogenarian,

Jack Taylor
Melbourne, Florida
President of Dimensions Ministries
Author of 13-plus books
Broadman's best-selling author

Jacquelyn Sheppard has taken a complex subject that is difficult to explain, and using easy to read and understand language she has written a well-documented explanation of that subject. She has an excellent command of her material, and her handling of the subject matter is to be commended. It is definitely a book that will help someone understand a new biochemical concept of the human body.

Norman G. Marvin, MD
Former assistant professor
The Department of Family Practice
University of Kansas Medical Center
Member, American Academy of Family Physicians
Member, American Medical Association

Jackie Sheppard is in the business of changing lives through her amazing nutritional research and counsel. We are so grateful she has put this together in her book, *Silent Takeover*. Filled with life-changing insights, this book will open your eyes to ways of bringing healing to your body and mind. We believe God will use this book to restore the health He has provided for us in natural, God-given ways.

Dave and Kim Butts
Founders, Harvest Prayer Ministries
Chairman of America's National Prayer Committee

As Christ's body, we are called by our Lord to minister to those who are sick and broken. Jesus commissioned His disciples to go forth with His Good News and "heal the sick." This is a vital aspect of the gospel. In *Silent Takeover*, Jackie Sheppard offers well-researched insight, wisdom, and tools to respond to and care for those with emotional, mental, and addictive disorders. Most significantly, the final chapters powerfully explore how prayer, worship, and community can make a life-changing difference to respond to these challenges in practical ways. Armed with this knowledge, the Church (and that means you and me) can become beacons of hope and healing for those who suffer among us. Read this timely and provocative guide and join God's army of healers.

Dr. Dick Eastman
International President
Every Home for Christ

Jackie Sheppard has given us an eye-opening view of how the human spirit, mind, and body interact. *Silent Takeover* is filled with research that challenges the status quo of how we have traditionally dealt with mental and emotional issues. Whether you are struggling with any of those issues or you know someone wrestling with them, I commend *Silent Takeover* to you. It will direct you on a path of mental and emotional wellness.

Sammy Tippit
Author and international evangelist

This book, like everything Jackie Sheppard sets her mind to accomplish, is a work of wisdom.

Penelope Edwards-Conrad M.D.
Integrative neurologist

Jacquelyn Sheppard's book *Silent Takeover* gives an eye-opening look into the hidden dangers of seemingly innocuous elements in our environment. Our brains are not separate from our bodies. Foods, sound, and light affect the production of chemicals in our bodies that affect the way we think and behave. Depression, anxiety, and addiction often have a physical as well as spiritual root. Jackie has been researching information for years and wants to help those who have been hijacked so they can regain good health in both body and mind.

J. Lee Grady
Former editor, *Charisma* Magazine
Director, The Mordecai Project

In this book you will be privileged to accompany Jackie on a journey of discovery. She raises questions that will challenge you to think outside of the conventional boxes and adopt the heart of learner. You will better understand the amazing ways in which nutrition, human choices, spirituality, and physical disciplines all are woven together in a rich integrated tapestry of life. She will do so by raising persistent questions, sharing personal testimonies, reflecting on exquisite parables, and unpacking thought-provoking research. I encourage you to embark on this journey of discovery with her.

David Hamilton
Vice President for Strategic Innovation
University of the Nations
Youth With A Mission

silent
takeover

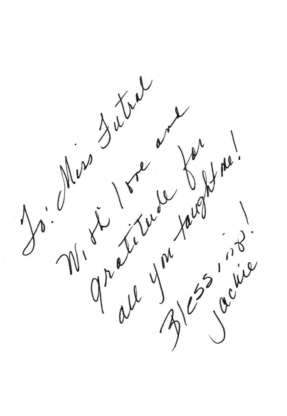

To: Miss Futrul

With love and
gratitude for
all you taught me!

Blessings!
Jackie

silent takeover

How the Body Hijacks the Mind

OVERCOMING

Emotional, Mental, and Addictive

DISORDERS

Jacquelyn Sheppard

DESTINY IMAGE® PUBLISHERS, INC.
P.O. Box 310, Shippensburg, PA 17257-0310
"Promoting Inspired Lives."

This book and all other Destiny Image and Destiny Image Fiction books are available at Christian bookstores and distributors worldwide.

Cover design by: Eileen Rockwell

For more information on foreign distributors, call 717-532-3040.
Reach us on the Internet: www.destinyimage.com.

ISBN 13 TP: 978-0-7684-0924-6
ISBN 13 eBook: 978-0-7684-0925-3

For Worldwide Distribution, Printed in the U.S.A.
1 2 3 4 5 6 7 8 / 20 19 18 17 16

Dedicated to my wonderful family:

My husband of 51 years, Glenn,

Our three children, their mates, and our eight grandchildren.

Tre' and Tori, Aidan and Elena.

Krista and Mark, Arianna, Hudson, and Hunter.

Trent and Bronwyn, Mire'a, Blaze, and Petra.

I love and admire all of you for how you live your lives
and all you are doing to make the world a better place.

And

To all of my students along the way who caused me
to look deeper than the surface in life.

To the Reader

Silent Takeover is intended to "whet your appetite" and to hopefully cause you to delve deeper into the complex issues affecting emotional, mental, and addictive disorders.

It's impossible to cover such a broad and emerging field in a book intentionally designed to be short and easily read and understood.

I am not a doctor, nor have I been trained in the medical field. This information is for educational purposes only.

Acknowledgments

I want to thank my non-official science editors, Jere White, Lena Misener, Rich Sauter, and Dr. P. Edwards Conrad for reading and editing *Silent Takeover* for me. Not only do they have brilliant minds, advanced knowledge, and training in science, but also they live exemplary lives. I am very grateful for their help and for being my friends.

And to my family, who gave me the time to write and who have pushed me for years to make the time to write—thank you for believing in me and for your strong words of encouragement. You kept me going. To Trent, thank you for the hours you spent poring over the pages again and again, helping me refine my words so that the message would, hopefully, be clear. To my eight grandchildren, I never have enough time with you, and I missed you more than words can say these past months when I was "locked in the dungeon" to write. Thank you for understanding. To my niece by marriage, Leah Barnett—through the years, you have continued to believe in my writing and have encouraged me to persevere. Your words have sunk deep into my heart and kept me believing that my writing was worthy enough to be published. Thank you.

To *Destiny Image Publishers* for giving me the opportunity to publish my book. Sierra, Ronda, John—I appreciate every word of encouragement and every effort you have made to bring this book to the readers. May thousands of lives be changed because you opened the door and helped me walk through it.

In addition, I want to thank Rob Pyles and his family for kindly offering my son and me a place to write on Cape Cod. It was there that the falling snow brought the book into focus and convinced me to press through on this book.

And, I want to thank my husband's cousin, Cindy Gilbert, for offering my husband and me her lovely home on St. Simon's Island, Georgia. As I revised and finished the book, my soul was refreshed by the gentle spirit of the island and the sea.

Contents

Preface

As we look at the human race throughout the span of time, I believe it is safe to say that every single one of us can be viewed as a miraculously complex and completely unique individual. As a counselor, I have come to learn that everyone has a story; some people are genetically predisposed toward certain psychological or biological issues, while others experience certain life events that can have an incredible impact on that person's life, either positive or negative or a blend of the two. Quite often in the field of mental health, there seems to be a "one size fits all" approach that falls short of truly looking at the whole person, and all too often they are swallowed up by the system or they slip through the cracks. In my quest to become a better counselor, I knew that I wanted to help others in a multifaceted way—I wanted to help the whole person. In simplified terms, my goal is to look at a person's health in the following areas:

- Biological health

- Psychological health

- Emotional health

- Relational health

- Spiritual health

- Financial health

In most of these areas, there is ample training and plenty of resources available for those who work in the mental health field, but I found that in many ways training was limited in the area of biological health, unless I wanted to seek out specific training in the medical field. Even then, there was no guarantee that it would increase my knowledge in regard to a biological basis of behavior or teach me how to take a wellness approach rather than a system of mitigating symptoms. That being said, I felt my options were limited and my hands were tied.

That all changed in 2011, when I met Mrs. Jackie Sheppard and she began to share some of her experiences, wisdom, and research. I was completely captivated by her level of knowledge in the field of cellular health as it relates to learning and behavior, and I have learned a wealth of information from her over the past four years. I am ecstatic that this book is being released, as it will equip so many of us who are in the mental health field with understanding and an ability to help others in a much more effective manner. I encourage you as the reader to dig into the information contained in these pages, and then go out and share what you've learned with those who are searching for answers, because in my heart I believe we are all counselors.

Sean Ruthrauff, MA
Executive Director
New Leaf Counseling Center
Kansas City, Missouri
www.NewLeafCounselingCenter.com

The Road That Led Me Here

My interest in how the body affects the mind, will, and emotions covers five decades. A book cannot contain a lifetime of learning. *Silent Takeover* is an attempt to pass on some of what I've gained along the way. I am not a doctor and offer this information to you as education and not medical advice.

I was born in 1943 into a health-conscious family. Our great-grandmother was a "granny woman" and blacks and whites came to her when there was sickness or a pending birth. She died of pneumonia contracted while crossing a freezing creek on her way to deliver a baby on a cold Georgia night. The story always captivated me—imagining the buggy and horse, which we were told she'd push as fast as possible on the way to a birth…or imminent death.

On the other side of the family, I remember my other grandmother mixing a terrible broth of "weeds" in the spring that I had to drink. No one dared mention being sick; if the dark green drink didn't cure you, calomel or castor oil were next. Most often, I was the recipient of these terrible cures because I was "sick all the time." At six weeks of age I had whooping cough. In those days, many infants did not survive whooping cough. My parents were told I would be susceptible to respiratory illnesses, and I cannot remember a school year when I wasn't feverishly ill with colds, sore throat, and deep chest congestion.

Removing my tonsils did little good. The hemorrhage that followed left permanent stains in my uncle's new car as he rushed me to the hospital. Nephritis, hepatitis A, chicken pox, and three kinds of measles followed. At age ten, it was influenza meningitis. I was in a coma for three days and was allergic to the only treatment at the time—sulfa drugs. The doctors gave my parents no hope for my recovery. A church held all-night prayer for me, and I awakened from the coma and began the long recovery.

Four years after that, a tumor was removed from my breast. Five years later, an appendectomy. The following year, mumps. I was hospitalized often during my early-married life as doctors sought to unravel my immune system. It was my "norm," and I refused, even as I had as a child, to allow my body take over my mind. I would not focus on what was "wrong with me"—I would concentrate on what was "right."

The three childbirths were very difficult and followed by long weeks of trying to recuperate. As the years passed, I continued to fight bronchitis every winter, three or four rounds of antibiotics, summer colds, and flu. By age 39 I had a hysterectomy followed, at 49, by breast cancer and chemotherapy. My poor health led me to research for better health. Remarkably, now in my early 70s I am enjoying the best health I have ever experienced; I am very grateful for every day.

My family's struggles with addiction led me to research how and why alcoholism and drug addiction tend to be inherited. How could so many of my family members on both sides who were wonderful, intelligent, and talented people become addicted to alcohol, prescription, and over-the-counter drugs? What's more, our family had more than our share of suicides—on both sides of the family. What was wrong?

Was it *addictive personalities*? But the typical *addictive personality* profile did not fit.

When I read about a link between diabetes and alcoholism, I knew I was on to something as both were prevalent in my family. Being a "night owl" and avid reader, I began substituting scientific research for fiction during my late-night reading, plowing through health journals and medical research, often into the early morning hours.

Bits and pieces of research stayed in my mind and in my files, providing evidence that the body can "hijack" the mind and the mind can "hijack" the body—a silent takeover of sorts that slips in unawares so that a person is captured before they realize what has happened.

I started teaching high school students in 1964, and for more than 50 years I have served as an educator and counselor. In 1966 I began "connecting the dots" between learning, behavior, and nutrition. I was teaching high school literature when a well-respected older colleague of mine mentioned she gave extra points on test day to those who ate breakfast. I remember it like it was yesterday. I was sitting there in the teacher's lounge, eating my Pop Tart and drinking instant coffee with powered creamer. "What difference does that make?" I asked.

She replied gently, "They do a better job because they think better with a good breakfast."

From that day forward, I began to emulate her. I encouraged parents to feed their teens differently. Food stamps provided families a greater variety of foods than many had ever seen, but they also could afford more "junk food" as a result. Soda pop, candy, chips, and snack food was stuffed in lockers for between-class breaks. Busy, affluent mothers were depending more and more on "convenience foods" that took minutes to prepare. Fast food restaurants were popping up everywhere. Increasingly, my students talked about TV dinners and eating in front of the television set.

At the beginning of every school year, I gave a questionnaire on foods, leisure, and family life. It was a sociology study that enabled me to understand my students better. As the years passed, the answers changed. By 1974, most of my students were on a steady diet of processed foods; fast foods; and lots of sugary drinks, desserts, pastries, and candy. I didn't have to be a "rocket scientist" to see a correlation between what was happening with diet and the classroom. Many reported not having a single meal with the family around the dinner table all week.

The old adage "You are what you eat" often came to mind when I was counseling children who couldn't read, teens with behavior and learning problems, and adults with broken relationships. My counseling questionnaire held typical questions like "What's your favorite color?" but also questions about the body: *"Do you have digestive problems? Do you have irregularity or loose bowels?"* Often, I could go ahead and check "Yes" even before they answered because I had already figured out that most who came for counseling had digestive problems. I could even predict which emotional problems they would discuss when they answered what sort of digestive problem they had. At that time, I accepted the commonly taught concept that emotional and mental disorders *caused* digestive disorders. Now I know that these disorders may be triggered by an unhealthy *gut* and may actually precede the mental disorder. At that time, however, I had no idea the *gut* held so many of the answers—all I knew was there was a connection between the digestive tract and the brain. Something in the body was affecting the brain, and that spilled over into "attitudes."

To many parents I have said, "You think this is your child's attitude. It's not. It's his/her body. I just don't know what's wrong in their body." I am sure some of them thought I was "up a tree," but many followed my simple suggestions of changing their diet, their music, their TV viewing, and arranged more outdoor exercise and activities. Improvement tended to follow within a few weeks.

In 1978, I was introduced to Dr. Walter Murray, an Atlanta pediatrician. Our collaboration began when he asked me my opinion, as a teacher, concerning learning and behavior problems. I responded that

I thought something was wrong in their bodies that affected the mind and, as a result, their behavior. "So do I," Dr. Murray responded. He and I both suspected it wasn't just poor classroom discipline and changing educational policies.

From that point on, we would discuss various students with learning and/or behavior problems. He'd suggest zinc or certain vitamins or minerals. For some, he'd order a vitamin and mineral deficiency test, which was very expensive at the time. For some, we would create a diet with foods to potentially increase, decrease, or balance neurotransmitter (chemicals in the brain) production from amino acids.

One day when I arrived, he told me that the "cause of disease had been discovered." "Really?" I responded, thinking it must be some strange besetting bacteria. Instead, he drew me a picture on his pre-scription pad of a *free radical*, explaining how molecules with unpaired electrons cannot perform their designed functions. They damage other cells, causing a chain reaction producing disease and malfunction in the body and brain. I was intrigued to say the least.

Returning home, I told my husband, Glenn, who has had to listen to all sorts of my medical and science speculations. When I said, "They are called *free radicals*, he said, "Well, that sounds like a political party, and they are probably right!"

He often laughed about those *free radicals* as I bought book after book to study how they affected the body. These were the days before the Internet and Google. Within a few years, however, I could access online publications and medical and scientific publications that heretofore had been inaccessible to me.

It was the mid-nineties before I heard the term *leaky gut*. I was very privileged to have as my personal physicians Dr. Viktor Bouquette and Dr. Gez Agolli, who also became my personal friends. They never seemed to tire of my questions and would carefully explain how the gut could "leak" toxins and food into the cells and bloodstream, causing inflammation. This was decades before many doctors had even heard of permeable gut. All too often, those who are ahead of the crowd are labeled "quacks." However, now almost every physician who knows any-thing about health will acknowledge *leaky gut*. Together, Drs. Agolli and Bouquette helped me with some of my students with metabolic testing and supplements as we attempted to alleviate symptoms of learning and behavior problems. By then I had started my own private high school where I could combine educational practices, character development, and counseling.

For years, my close friends—Charlotte, Shere', and Vicki—have lis-tened to me verbalize my ideas about human behavior. They have heard me excuse many bad decisions that people made by saying, "Well, they probably have hypoglycemia or perhaps low thyroid or maybe low pro-duction of serotonin or they could have hit their head in an accident." I know it must have gotten pretty "roll the eyes" as my mind constantly probed the physical reasons behind broken lives. They listened to my diatribes about babies and children and adults watching TV because I was convinced it "changed the brain" due to how the light entered the eyes, on video games because I felt they caused the body to produce too much adrenaline, on too much competition in sports for children and teens as it caused too much testosterone, and on and on. Traditional answers about mental, emotional, and addiction disorders being just *bad choices* and bad experiences did not add up for me. I was convinced it had to be more.

By the time my children were in high school, or maybe earlier, the children began to pay attention when I was talking about mental and physical health. A few years ago, one of them said, "Mom, science is catching up to you." They had heard on TV or read on the Internet some finding that supported something I'd speculated on years before. It's been a long journey as I've sought to figure how the body affects the mind and behavior.

This book is not designed to be complex. It is designed for the person who wants to know *Why?* and *What can be done to change my life?* While it doesn't give an easy, quick course of action, it does include a roadmap that you may be able to follow to a new life.

I am often asked, "With no formal medical training, how did you learn all of this?" Maybe it was my "gut" telling me. I believe it was something more—I believe it was Divine help.

I was asking.

I was searching.

I still am.

PART ONE

How the Body Affects the Mind

Can the body "hijack" the mind and silently
take over the brain and mental processes leading to
emotional, mental, and addictive disorders?

Below the Surface: Emotional, Mental, and Addictive Disorders Are Not All in Your Head

I stand gazing over a vast, frozen marshland. A winter storm has dropped another layer of snow on land already frozen from months of cold and freezing weather. Only a tiny tributary of water breaks the stillness, a meandering stream that offers a settling and feeding place for sea birds.

One swoops down, sees below the surface, and snatches life away before the sea creature is even aware of the bird's presence. A fine breakfast for the bird; the end of the road, or should I say "stream," for the other. The feeding chain—where one species becomes another species' food, a necessary link in a very long chain that stretches from the smallest building blocks of nature to the largest sperm whale, from a blade of grass to the beef on our plates.

I am struck by the sheer frozen beauty of the scene before me. Somewhere out there, the marshland stops and the ocean begins. I can't see the demarcation, the line that will show itself when the dawn brightens the landscape. There is not enough light to see where one stops and the other begins.

To my left, a forest hugs the curve of the marshland, reaching out to the edge of the marsh and to the ocean's edge, where the tide finally plays out and grabs the sand, making promises of returning every day. Humanity has been unable to stem the rush and flow of tides; they do exactly what they have done since the beginning of time.

I watch dawn reveal more and more—at first, the frozen marsh; now, as the growing light scatters the dark, I can see where the ocean begins, a darker horizon visible against the morning gray. I wonder, if I had a small boat, could I row my way out of the little ribbon of flowing water, round the curves and marsh, straight out to the sea? Would my boat be strong enough to allow me to explore the water's edge, or would it flounder, dashed by waves too harsh and tempestuous for such a small craft?

A seagull breaks my thoughts, challenging another for the same sea creature. A very hostile takeover. The fight is over. The weaker lost. Maybe this bird is well known to the others; or maybe it's just to be expected—every now and then, another bird is going to swipe your breakfast. Get over it and keep on fishing if you want something to eat. By the time the two haggled, the food would probably fall right back into the water.

My eyes go back to the frozen wasteland. Beneath the surface of the ice and snow are thousands, maybe millions of microorganisms playing their role in the great scheme of life. They build together what they cannot understand and what they have no ultimate control over, a masterpiece of the universe—an elaborate ecosystem too small to be seen by the naked eye.

I study the ripples in the small stream, wondering what is below the surface, wondering what a diagram of layers of marsh plants and creatures would look like, remembering the examples from illustrations in textbooks. I cannot see what lies below the frozen marsh, but I know it must be there, not just because I've read about ecosystems in books, but because I see birds that sit upon the water using their body temperature and moving feet and wings to contribute their part, while at the same time taking their part.

The dawn has broken bright and the light shines on the snow. Another world has emerged from the gray, one of shimmering light and green trees and mounds of snow. I need to begin my day's work while the icy layers of the ecosystem continue their day's work, deep beneath the surface of a frozen marshland.

CHAPTER 1

Below the Surface:
The Body and Brain Connection

Gazing at the frozen marshland, I could only see what I could "see." The ice and snow covered everything like a white blanket hiding the ground and layers of brackish marsh. I could not see beneath the frozen wasteland to where thousands of microbes and sea creatures were living out their lives, their destinies as dictated by what they are.

Likewise, we can only see the surface of people's lives. We don't see the underlying conditions in the mind and body that often dictate the behavior, and all too often we judge that behavior by personal and cultural standards. We habitually attribute behavior to "choice," and while there is great truth in "choice" it is very difficult to ascribe "choice" to all circumstances.

The sea creatures and microbes in the frozen marsh don't make choices; they will live and die exactly as designed unless certain elements change their destiny. A chemical spill or environmental toxins or land development would affect everything about the marshland, changing the ecosystem for years—maybe even forever. Your body is the same; your microbes, molecules, and cells will do what they were designed to do unless there is a catalyst—something that changes their roles and what they do, often rendering the cells unable to carry out their task in your body or even transforming them into other cells, so strong and malignant that the slight changes can eventually lead to death of the body or the mind. How does it all begin?

Millions of years ago, the history of your bloodline began, collecting from your ancestors traits of strengths and weaknesses, your own unique identity in blood. This, in turn, was transferred in total to the sperm and egg. We call this *genetic inheritance*—the color of your eyes, the possibility of inherited diseases, and thousands of other possibilities. Oftentimes, we even allude to personality traits that seem to be inherited. "He's just like his grandfather—moody and hard to understand. You never know what he's thinking." Or, "She's like my aunt—always positive regardless of what's going on in her life."

Can we inherit green eyes and a bad temper? Is there something that makes us respond intuitively or by instinct like a sheep dog to sheep? A bird dog to hunting? The long line of your genetics plays an amazing part in developing who you are and how you think. One drop of blood or just a particle of your DNA can now tell scientists more about you than you know about yourself—the origins of your most far-distance ancestors, where they lived, and the blend of people groups that finally merged into you. There's not a lot you can do with this information because you cannot change your genetic or inherited past. You can, however, change the present, and you can change the future of your life and that of your descendants.

Let's begin with how *you* were born. Millions of sperm swam toward your mother's egg, each one racing the next one until you were conceived. When contact was made, the sperm released an enzyme allowing it to enter the egg. At that moment, the race was over. The millions of combinations of inherited genetic traits were settled. You were there and the building of you began. Your dad had contributed his side of the family, for better or for worse. While in the testes, hopefully, defective sperm was phased out and the healthiest sperm won the race. The blueprint for your life began.

Mom took over the nurturing and nourishment, and that played a major part in the formation of you. Now, if she had morning sickness, she may have missed nutrients that you needed. If she smoked, she may have passed on to you nicotine dependency. Cells in your body have cup-like "receptors" that open and close according to what they were designed to do for the body. They can be fooled by toxins, etc. that "mimic" the nutrients, etc. they were designed to receive. Interestingly, the neuro-transmitters glutamate and acetylcholine receptors in your developing brain would have accepted nicotine, not recognizing it as a mimic. Low birth rate, failure to thrive, low intelligence, ADHD and ADD, as well as other problems can be traced back to prenatal nicotine.[1]

If your grandmother or grandfather smoked, they unknowingly created a prenatal dependency for her. The first time you smoked a cigarette or used tobacco, your brain may have responded with, "Wait a minute! I remember that, and I can use it!" Quickly placing the nicotine right into the glutamate and/or acetylcholine receptors, it tried to do its job. After all, the brain's job is to benefit you. However, brain cells can accept counterfeits.[2]

Shortly after that first experience with nicotine, you would have wanted more. Your friend whose mother did not smoke may have decided after the first cigarette that she wanted no more of it. But you would have found yourself trying to get more nicotine. Perhaps you made it through without nicotine but found yourself drawn to other drugs and alcohol. The brain is a marvelous "machine," but it doesn't always know what to use and what to leave alone; it uses "cravings" to convince you to feed it. Those cravings often start in the womb.

This is also true of alcohol. You may have been born literally wanting a drink—that's right: "Mom, could I have a shot of that? Just put it in my bottle." (What's a mother to do?) If you haven't yet carried a child, make sure that you start building a body now for that child. There is no place in pregnancy for drug or alcohol or nicotine dependency. No mother wants her child born with a ball and chain for a lifetime. The American Academy of Pediatricians recently released a study saying that no alcohol usage is safe in pregnancy.[3] The body will accept alcohol, drugs, and other toxic substances into cell receptors. The body and brain will then insist on more even while the body is making fewer and fewer of the necessary neurotransmitters for stable mental health. This cycle, which may begin in the womb, is hard but not impossible to break. Any drug, even if it is a prescription antibiotic, can affect the developing baby.

Some of you may remember the Thalidomide Tragedy—babies were born with limb defects or limbless. *Thalidomide* was thought to be a harmless new class of tranquilizers that produced relaxation and sleepiness. And it helped women with morning sickness. Over 10,000 babies were born with lifetime struggles because their moms had morning sickness and had hoped to lessen it with thalidomide.[4]

Of course, your mother's diet was of extreme importance while she was "building" you. Too much of this, too little of that and you could have been born with allergies or vitamin and mineral deficiencies. As the months passed and you grew, you became a part of the household. You could hear and possibly even see in the last few months. A developing fetus opens eyes around the seventh month and will respond to a bright light. The problem is, we don't actually know the effects of artificial light and how much light can enter the womb and reach the fetus. We live in a world of electricity and man-made light, and we can measure light, but we don't really know how much light from television and other sources can penetrate the womb. Nor do we know enough about microwaves from the oven and from cell phones and Wi-Fi. What is known is enough to scare us: microwaves can penetrate the tissues of the body and the brain. Signs at convenience stores warn that microwaves are in use and may affect pacemakers by their penetration. The skin cannot stop the penetration of these waves. Likewise, the use of cell phones may be dangerous to the baby in the womb, not to mention the mother.[5] There is growing concern about how electromagnetic fields affect all of us, as we were not designed to have these harmful rays penetrating the body.

While there are many potential hazards to the developing fetus, your mom's body did the best it could to protect you—the placenta has an amazing ability to shield the baby from harm. However, the placenta could not shield you from emotional and physical duress your mom may have experienced. Domestic abuse, verbal abuse, and psychological abnormalities of the people surrounding her could have affected your development and how you viewed life from the inside out. Loud noises, conflict, and emotional pain take their toll on the baby in the womb. The baby, who hears the mother's voice in soothing and low tones, responds in the womb.[6]

The baby recognizes the mother's voice and her smell shortly after birth. Inside the womb and after birth, the baby recognizes the one who carried him or her for nine months. Therefore, an adopted baby will need a lot of soothing, love, and cuddling to form new bonding. The first understanding of what the outside world is like occurs in the womb. If that world is rocked by emotional earthquakes, the baby can be adversely affected and can form a temperament that reflects the emotional stress in the womb.

If you have struggled as long as you can remember with emotional or mental health as well as physical health, it may not be your genes. It may be the result of a difficult nine months in your mother's life. Your emotional responses may have begun in the womb when fear, anger, rage, hate, or other negative emotions and the neurotransmitters—the chemicals in your brain—produced accordingly crossed the placenta. You may have spent most of your gestation in a negative environment or in the womb of an ill mother, either physically or emotionally. If that was the case, negative responses may seem natural to you. For you, the glass may be *half-empty* most of the time.

It may be difficult to see the glass as *half-full* as you may habitually be in a "No!" position. It's just easier to say "No" to a request without even wondering if "Yes" could work. Those early days, even before you saw light, shaped much of your personality and temperament. If you were adopted or if circumstances changed after your birth, your responses to life may have become more accepting and warm. The cells in your body, however, remember fear, pain, and trauma.[7] Even now, you may have irrational fear, and your approach to life may be one of caution and suspicion. The good news is that you can change your outlook on life.

Beginning to look *below the surface* of what you feel and how you react may be just the beginning of a new life for you. Below the surface of mental and emotional disorders is an intricate pattern of cellular responses that are caused by certain enzymes, trillions of gut inhabitants, and metabolic links that shape your personality and response to stress. Just as I could not see the ecosystem of the stunning winter scene before me, mental turmoil; personality disorders; addictions; and a collapsing mind, will, and emotions can be hidden by an exterior that may be as "serene" and as covered as the frozen landscape. Just as the snow and ice transformed the scene and hid all the underlying elements of the microbes and sea creatures, you or someone you love may be struggling to emerge from a frozen life.

But it doesn't have to *stay* that way. The strong and emerging field of *epigenetics* offers hope to change your potential genetic inheritance, and a growing understanding of how metabolism affects not only the body but also the emotions is shedding light on major misunderstood diagnoses.

The birth process, your first impression of your new world, may have much to do with the development of emotional, mental, and addictive disorders. In the hours before labor, the woman's body responds to a fascinating system that cooperates, changing normal muscles, ligaments, and actual bones into a miracle of birth. Like Transformer toys that morph from a truck to a robot, the body becomes a birth machine. When all systems work and work properly, a woman is able to deliver a fully developed baby that mystifies even the most skeptical—the body meets the demands of issuing a new life into the light of day.

As the baby moves through the birth canal, some of the fluid in the birth canal is swallowed and some is absorbed through the skin. These fluids contain small amounts of the mother's *gut flora*—the good and bad bacteria and a tad of her digestive enzymes as well as bacteria from her mouth.[8] Most will have heard of probiotics and digestive enzymes that make up part of these bacteria. If you are following the latest research on emotional, mental, and addictive disorders, you are hearing about *gut flora* due to increasing evidence that the gut controls much about the brain and, consequently, the mind.[9]

Yes, inside your gut (digestive system—especially the stomach and small intestines) reside trillions of inhabitants. You have your own "ecosystem" just like the frozen landscape and layers below it. These microbes, parasites, and yet-to-be discovered inhabitants are busy producing or not producing neurotransmitters for the body and brain. As the baby passes through the birth canal, these microbes become a part of the baby's digestive system greatly affecting the production of brain chemicals called neurotransmitters—the chemicals that aid in signaling between brain neurons. These chemicals determine more about your thoughts, actions, and memories than you might guess.

If a mother has eaten a steady diet of processed foods, taken numerous courses of antibiotics, and has a poor colony of gut flora, so does baby. Her gift to her infant should be a good, strong supply of bacteria to keep the gut healthy and happy. However, if she is in short supply, so is baby. Antibiotics during pregnancy can lower gut flora and allow more bad bacteria to multiply. The baby can't "pick and choose"— what mother has is what baby gets. It may be that "inheritance" when it comes to personality and mental, emotional, and addictive disorders begins with abnormal gut flora. Grandmother passed poor gut flora to daughter, who passed it on to baby.

With Caesarian birth, the transfer of gut flora in the birth canal does not happen. Life begins with very little gut flora, and that flora is similar to what is found on the skin, instead of the birth canal. However, some midwives and doctors manually smear the baby's face and mouth with the body fluids, hoping to transfer these important microbes.[10]

As father and others begin kissing and holding baby, other beneficial and maybe not-so-beneficial microbes are transferred, colonizing the baby's gut. With baby facing a new world, the bacteria heads to its new domicile—the baby's gut. Its job is to prepare the gut to digest breast milk, a little at a time. If the baby is breast fed, the baby begins to suckle colostrum, introducing antibodies and building a tiny "ecosystem."

A baby is born with "open" spaces in the gut making it permeable, which enables nutrients from mother's milk to pass into the body rapidly with little need for digestion. This is convenient for the first few months, but eventually the gut has to be prepared for food. A child receiving mother's milk continues to receive mother's gut flora from the milk, preparing the baby gut for food in future months. Breast milk creates a mucous coating which is designed to seal the gut, enabling only the right size molecules of nutrients to pass through the walls.[11] Without breast milk, the sealing of the baby's gut is compromised. For some babies, it takes as long as six months to seal, especially those born Caesarian or by difficult birth. Normally, it takes two to four months for a baby's gut to seal, but the first twenty days are the most important.

Giving a baby processed foods and adult foods—soda pop, sweets, etc.—can kill off good gut flora and cause bacterial changes in the gut, bringing distress and pain. Mom, in an effort to comfort baby without even realizing the source of the pain, may administer a pain soother, such as acetaminophen, without realizing that the gut is not prepared for such a shock.[12]

Even with the best-sealed baby gut, certain foods and a lack of "good bacteria" can cause the gut to be too "open"—too permeable. This allows toxins to pass into the bloodstream and into the body. Toxins from formula or from breast milk containing overflow toxins from the mother—such as yeast, alcohol, high sugar consumption, pesticides, herbicides, heavy metals, and other toxins—can pass from mother to child. Infant formula containing vegetable oil, soy, sugar, corn, cow milk, and additives cannot properly be assimilated in an infant gut. Instead, toxins can enter the tissues of the body, affecting genetic expression as well as the brain and nervous system. An irritable bowel lacking beneficial bacteria and overgrown with yeast and other harmful microbes can cause an unhappy baby and developing child. Giving an infant baby food before six months of age can add to improper gut development.

From pre-birth to death, the gut will continue to colonize bacteria. By the time a child reaches adulthood, he or she will be carrying about four pounds of bacteria, enzymes, parasites, and microbes.[13] It's hard to believe that you have that many visitors in your gut, but the truth is that's how many we know about. There's probably many, many more. These friendly and unfriendly visitors reflect where you were born, who your ancestors were, and what foods you were designed to eat from your native homeland.

The *Human Microbiome Project*, a part of the *Human Genome Project*, has discovered much about how microbes govern our bodies and brains (see hmpdacc.org). For example, their research says about 100 trillion inhabitants live in the gut. Like the ecosystem of a frozen wasteland, they do their work—for us or against us—unseen by the naked eye.

Perhaps as high as 80–90 percent of your immune system is bacteria, fungi, viruses, and other microorganisms—your microflora. If the microbes get out of balance, you become physically or mentally ill.[14] An unhealthy baby gut can not only cause an unhappy baby, but also possibly set up a chain of events in the body that affects lifetime struggles with mental, emotional, and addictive disorders. For one child, it could be an autoimmune disease; for others, learning and behavior problems or even serious mental disorders like schizophrenia.[15]

An infant with high toxic levels will usually begin to display symptoms around age two, which is the age when many infants are diagnosed with Autism. In the developing child, other learning and behavior problems may be identified as parents struggle to figure out, "What's wrong with my child?" Repairing the gut can go a long way toward healing the brain due to the high production of neurotransmitters in the gut. In lab tests, rats with sterile guts and low gut flora showed high risk-taking behavior.[16] How does this translate to the human child? The ecosystem of the gut is as fragile as the brain—too much of this can mean too little of that when it comes to neurotransmitters like GABA, glutamate, serotonin, dopamine, and others.

Building a better balance of gut flora can mean a more balanced brain, one that can begin to acquire the social and academic skills that so many children and adults lack in our present society. Working 24/7, your gut should be your body's best friend and the organ you consciously feed and care for. Ignoring the gut's needs and demands is usually painful as the gut sends out its distress signals—smelly gas, rumblings and discontented sounds, and pain. However, most of the damage and malfunctioning is silent; the takeover, gradual.

Yes, there is definitely something wrong, but for so long now we've been looking in the wrong direction. Psychologists have looked at experiences with other humans as the basis for mental and emotional disorders. Addiction has been greatly misunderstood as simply the consequences of making bad choices. The "much more" behind these disorders is slowly emerging as discoveries are made about how the body truly functions and how it influences the mind.

CHAPTER 2

Your Ecosystem: Changing Your Mind by Changing Your Diet

It was only a few years ago that scientists discovered that we have a *second brain* and that it is exactly where you'd guess. Seems that *gut feeling* written about in ancient literature and felt by most of us is the *second brain* doing its job. You probably know exactly what I mean—you feel fear, *butterflies,* anxiety, etc. in your gut, along with impressions and intuitions. *My gut tells me* and other such expressions reflect that experience whether we know about the science or not. The recent discovery that we make more neurotransmitters in the gut than in the brain, however, is changing a lot about what we know about gut and brain connections.[1] In fact, we have about one hundred billion nerve cells in the digestive tract—more than we have in the spinal cord. Dr. Max Planck of the Institute for Psychological Research in Munich says it is possible that the stomach network may actually make our unconscious decisions that are later claimed by the main brain as conscious decisions of its own.[2]

Neurotransmitters are chemicals in the brain and body that relay signals between neurons—nerves. They are the driving influence in how you think, how you feel mentally and physically, and how you view life in general, and they are often described as a *chemical soup* in your brain.

Being bipolar, manic-depressive, and chemically imbalanced are all terms that mean practically the same thing—the chemicals in your brain are not working together for your best interests. While there are many neurotransmitters as well as hormones that act like neurotransmitters, we will concentrate on just a few for our purposes in *Silent Takeover*.

When you were an embryo, some of your tissue started developing your digestive system—esophagus, stomach, and your intestines. That same tissue formed your primary brain and nervous system. As you grew, a long tube formed connecting your gut and your brain, eventually becoming the *vagus* nerve that connects gut to brain and brain to gut. What you eat is directly related to the condition of your mental processes in the gut and primary brain.

In order to digest food, processes are set in motion from the first smell or sight of food. You may have experienced salivating while waiting for some food that looked or smelled delicious. What happens if the person has a poor sense of smell or can't smell? The eyes will help, but that person will need to work harder to introduce necessary gut flora in order to enhance emotional and physical health. Food has to be digested to be useful to the brain and body. Chewing the food well, even if the taste is missing due to lack of smell, as smell has much to do with taste, will get the digestive enzymes on the job of digestion. Often, when a child won't eat or appears to reject food, the child cannot smell the food. Or the food feels disgusting—too lumpy, too sticky, too slimy, too crunchy. While it may sound a bit like Dr. Seuss in one of his children's books, the reactions are not just those of a "picky" eater. The cells of the body aren't responding because the eyes, nose, and touch are not cooperating. A hypersensitive smell can be problematic as well; food may smell awful to a person even though it is a pleasant smell to others.

Digestion continues from the mouth down until one of three things occurs: you utilize the nutrients from the food; you store the residues because they cannot be used or eliminated; or, you excrete the remains. *Nature calling* is shared by all mammals and is a necessary part of mental and physical health. However, many people with emotional and mental disorders experience problems with elimination: irregularity, constipation, or irritable bowels. Like the other mammals, we were designed to have feces leave the body efficiently. In other words, we were not designed to have to use toilet paper any more than sheep, goats, or a dog. Where ancient people left their feces had a lot to do with their safety and evolution of culture. The Hebrews were told to *cover their feces*.[3] This act alone would have made for a more pleasant community.

Any good farmer will tell you that animal feces reflect their diet and what they need in their diet—large and smelly: need more hay and too much grain; green and mushy: too much spring grass; could make the animal bloat, forming so much gas that it presses against the heart and dies. My husband and I raise a few sheep and goats, a "petting zoo" for the grandchildren. When our animals are fed properly with a balanced diet, they drop small balls of feces with no smell that simply fertilizes the pasture. Many animals, however, are carnivores (meat eaters). Eating a steady diet of grains can cause their feces to have offensive odor and deposits.

The same is true for you. When you are leaving feces with a terrible odor, passing smelly gas, and using lots of toilet tissue, your gut is telling you loud and clear that you are eating the wrong foods, and you lack the proper digestive enzymes and gut flora to turn the remains of the food into a normal bowel movement. When you have a "clean wipe," meaning nothing is on the toilet tissue, you have a gut that has the proper *microbiome*. By adding a few changes, you can achieve this balance. Balanced gut flora will allow the food to pass through the process and be deposited daily with very little clean up. An infant with large, foul smelling, loose stools or hard stools is already showing signs of an imbalanced gut.

Providing the right environment for serotonin, dopamine, and other neurotransmitters to be produced is beneficial to the brain and the body. As much as 80 percent of your immune system resides in your gut.[4] We have all had the experience of a virus, bacteria, or other culprit multiplying so rapidly that it got the best of us. According to Bonnie Bassler, Princeton, NJ, these invaders can communicate with each other using a "chemical language" called "Quorum sensing." When the molecules secreted from bacteria reach a certain mass, they can recognize and overtake the other bacteria.[5]

When these are pathogens—the "bad guys"—your mind and body can suffer with long-term chronic health issues until the "good guys" are able to retake the territory. The use of antibiotics kills "good guys" and "bad guys." Your gut needs to be repopulated after antibiotic use. This is why you may have been told to take a probiotic after antibiotic use.

Over 40 years ago, a pharmacist/friend suggested that I always follow a round of antibiotics with *lactinex* granules. I trusted him and faithfully gave my children *lactinex* when they took antibiotics. I didn't understand why at the time, but I remembered that when antibiotics were first introduced, we were told to drink buttermilk with the prescription to prevent an irritated stomach. Taking care of your gut and the gut lining is one of best things you can do to start the physical path to healing of mental, emotional, and addictive disorders. Now, over thirty years later, the word *probiotics* is common and almost everyone knows they need to take probiotics for their digestive system. Many rely on pills that may contain billions of all sorts of good probiotic bacteria, but all too often the bacteria cannot live long enough to colonize the gut. High or low pH affects how the good guys live. The body prefers to take nutrients, probiotics, and enzymes from food. Unsweetened yoghurt, kefir, and fermented vegetables may be more effective. Digestive enzymes can help to create the right digestion and environment for your body to process nutrients. This simple change can make major improvements in physical and mental health.

From birth forward, your gut flora is dependent on what goes in your mouth. Years ago, when most of America was rural and most everyone had a garden and fruit trees, it was easier to feed your flora. Vegetables and fruits grew in mineral rich soil and fit nicely into the body's matrix; the body knew what to do. It used what it needed and excreted the rest. However, in the past six decades the American food supply has changed dramatically. According to *Scientific American*, you would have to eat *eight* oranges to get the same amount of Vitamin A that your grandmother got from eating one orange.[6]

Efforts to increase production and reduce labor—along with commercial herbicides, pesticides, fertilizers, hybrid seeds, and genetically modified seed—have changed the essence of fruits and vegetables. You are not eating the same fruits and vegetables of fifty to one hundred years ago. The soil is depleted of many necessary minerals, and the body cannot always recognize and process the newly developed fruits and vegetables efficiently. The practice of "laying by" a field to let the soil rest and replenish has been replaced, and commercial fertilizers are used to produce "bigger and better crops." Farmers have been "re-educated" as to how to use the latest growth enhancer, and that includes feeding antibiotics and hormones to their livestock for larger cows and chickens. Glyphosate (*Round-Up*, etc.) is routinely sprayed before planting and harvesting in spite of the many links to detrimental mental and physical disorders.[7] Many fields are now sprayed before and after harvesting with glyphosate to kill weeds and help to dry out the harvest.

Using pesticides, growth hormones, and herbicides takes a toll on the body; eating those fruits, vegetables, beef, and chicken affects your body. Chicken breasts are almost as large as turkey breasts. Does that tell you something about early puberty and the changing American girl's body? What does it tell you about male breast growth? When you eat a food that has been altered beyond what the body can recognize, your body doesn't know what to do with it. Your body considers the toxins as invaders and, consequently, sets off an autoimmune response. Preservatives, additives, flavor enhancers, fillers, and other additions to food play a major role in the breakdown of good, balanced gut flora.

When your gut becomes too permeable (leaky) with too many gaps in the lining, it's not just nutrients that escape into your blood—it's pollutants and toxins from your food. As fluids flow through the body, there are receptors[8] that will accept these toxins and mimics because they are too compromised to know the difference. Residues from processed foods and other items that affect the body, as well as chemicals in lotion, soap, etc., will be stored in your body. If in your joints, it could be cause arthritis. These toxins, if the body cannot excrete them, can be stored in your liver, kidneys, and elsewhere. However, the brain seems to be the place where many toxins hide, fooling the neurotransmitters and

blocking the release and uptake of important neurotransmitters like serotonin and dopamine, glutamate and GABA, preventing proper brain
signaling between neurons and brain hemispheres.

If you add sugar to the mix, you are feeding the enemy in your gut
and harming your metabolism to such an extent that you may already
know that your body is calling the shots on when you have sugar. Your
body may demand sugar so strongly that you are driven. Can it be that the
"bad guys" are communicating and ganging up on your body, causing a
chain reaction that results in brain fog, confusion, poor decision making,
etc. not to mention health issues like diabetes and high blood pressure?

There are certain nutrients that you must have if your "engine" is
going to work efficiently. Foods contain compounds known as amino
acids. The right balance of amino acids greatly affects mental, emotional, and addiction disorders. Your body can produce about half of
the amino acids needed for strong physical and mental health. The remaining half, called *essential* amino acids, needs to be eaten in your daily
food as amino acids are not stored in the body. Meat, seafood, and dairy
provide complete amino acids while most plants do not. Plants, such as
beans, lentils, nuts, etc. need to be combined with other plants to provide complete amino acids. For example, beans and rice or beans with
corn bread make complete amino acids.[9]

The need to balance amino acids is usually well known to vegetar-
ians. Children who won't eat meat will need to have a diet with balanced
amino acids as well. What may be ignored, however, is that the body
simply cannot make the right vitamins, especially the B vitamins that
are so important to mental health, without the right nutrients. Many
of these nutrients are found in meat. People who don't eat meat may
struggle with getting enough nutrients unless they are careful about
food combining. Promoting environmental health and being responsible for our planet is appropriate and to be admired. However, many
children and adults who struggle with mental, emotional, and addictive
disorders are not consuming enough protein for their bodies to supply
what the brain needs. The rules in food combinations as well as careful
attention to vitamin and mineral deficiencies must be followed.

I have counseled with many mothers who were so weary with food battles that they simply gave up and allowed the child to live on chicken nuggets and French fries. Others, in an attempt to be "trendy" or who may be following some political or religious belief, may be so deprived of protein and thus amino acids that their mind or a child's mind is suffering from simple starvation. Distended stomachs and thin limbs can be a sign of insufficient food intake and lack of protein. The craving for sugar is often the body begging for real food. The brain is asking for something to keep it going. This is extremely important in addictive disorders—the brain can only ask for what it knows and re-members. Therefore, if chocolate made it "feel better," the brain will ask for more chocolate. If street drugs or prescription drugs made the brain "feel better," it will demand more. Getting proper intake and a balanced diet go a long ways toward recovery of emotional, mental, and addictive disorders.

One of the best ways for a person who has never struggled with ad-diction or mental disorder to identify with those who do is to consider how you respond to extreme hunger. Most of us become confused, agi-tated, quick to anger, "snappy" in responding to others, and downright ugly. You may have experienced this and remember "grabbing" anything you could find—regardless of unhealthy contents—because you were so hungry. Imagine living at that level all the time because your brain is demanding whatever made it "feel" better. Multiply the intensity.

Imagine being a child and being dependent on someone to feed you. I have locked in my memory the experience of watching a teen mother in a tribal village in Northern Thailand, where we were visiting, feed her baby potato chips. The baby was desperately trying to eat the chips. Ignorance and lack of education can be reasons for many in our world, but for most of us ignoring science and truth about nutrition is a matter of convenience. We live fast-paced lives and want fast foods with little planning and preparation. Toxic buildup and toxic gut is passed on to a child at birth, and then improper nutrition can further the consequences. In adults, stressful lives and addiction to leisure and entertainment can be thresholds for depression, bipolar disorder, and development of schizophrenia as the body breaks down, affecting the brain and mind. When it comes to addictive disorders, it is my strong belief that gut issues and nutritional deficiencies precede the addiction, including blocked neurotransmitter receptors from toxins in food.

Emotional, mental, and addictive disorders can follow physical conditions where the "ecosystem" became impaired. Slowly, the person slipped into a downward cycle that became deeper and deeper. For the past six decades, American culture has grown more and more dependent on going to a physician, giving a list of symptoms, and getting a prescription. Trying to explain to a parent that a child or adult must be "rebuilt" from the inside out with balanced gut flora, balanced amino acids, vitamins, minerals, and pure water sounds like a mountain too high to climb.

However, many people who take medications find they don't have the desired results and they have side effects. Trying to find an answer, they find their way via Internet or other to natural health practitioners. All too often, however, the person leaves that office with a big bill and a bag full of supplements. Trying to take the supplements as directed and getting a handful of pills down a child with learning or behavior problems or mental, emotional or addictive disorder becomes too daunting. They eventually give up. If you are identifying with this, let me encourage you to try as much as possible to use natural food as your "medicine." The famous quote by Hippocrates, *Let food be thy medicine and thy medicine be thy food,* is still the best advice.

Many recognize the word *serotonin* due to the increase in prescribing antidepressants that recycle serotonin in the brain. However, it is not commonly known that the amino acids found in certain foods can be converted into serotonin and that more serotonin is made in the gut than in the brain.[10]

Can it be that by correcting the gut flora and eating a diet with complete amino acids and other nutrients, many people who suffer with these disorders can see remarkable improvement as well as perhaps full recovery? To determine how your body is absorbing nutrients and amino acids, it may be helpful to request an amino acid absorption test from a reputable lab like Great Plains Laboratory, Genova, Dunwoody Labs, or Doctor's Data.[11] Metabolic testing can unravel many unsolved problems in health.

This information can then be used to increase intake of certain foods and nutrients to provide the "building blocks" for brain repair. It can also reveal an overabundance of certain amino acids and/or neurotransmitters that are too high. The use of protein supplements in bodybuilding and diets can affect the brain because these supplements do not contain the natural ratio of amino acids in food as found in nature. Manipulating these ratios and increasing proteins by significant amounts not only challenges the kidneys but also throws off the proper balance of amino acids as designed by nature. It may be that the sudden development of emotional issues among athletes and body builders may be from the ingestion of an improper balance of amino acids over weeks and months at a time. Having serotonin and dopamine levels that are too high may be more dangerous than too low and lead to psychotic behavior.[12]

Some amino acids are more influential in affecting neurotransmitter production than others. You have probably heard of *tryptophan* due to media coverage of how this amino acid affects you following a Thanksgiving meal of turkey and high carbs. That "I feel good!" and "I need a nap!" feeling is the result. Recent research suggests, however, that because other ingested amino acids compete with tryptophan, it's more than just the turkey affecting your mood. In short, tryptophan converts to serotonin and melatonin; feeling content and happy in the daytime and sleeping well at night are both regulated by intake of tryptophan.

Another amino acid, *l-tyrosine,* is converted into dopamine, a neurotransmitter you may have heard mentioned in Parkinson's disease as well as associated with learning, behavior, and addictive disorders. Dopamine also converts into norepinephrine, another neurotransmitter involved in the "reward" center of the brain that is associated with lack of focus and learning. Your body can make l-tyrosine, but you still have to consume foods with this important amino acid. Eggs, salmon, poultry, dairy, nuts, avocados, bananas, legumes, and seeds are all good choices. However, your "finicky" eater may not eat enough foods with tyrosine for a healthy brain.

The body can make tyrosine, but a very important amino acid, *phenylalanine,* must come from food. These two amino acids greatly regulate mood, confusion, apathy, depression, focus, memory, and appetite. You may be familiar with phenylalanine due to infant testing for PKU. Babies born missing the enzyme *phenylalanine hydroxylase* cannot convert phenylalanine. If this is not treated in the first three weeks of life, damage is permanent. Those individuals must avoid a diet with phenylalanine and take tyrosine supplements. This important amino acid also affects thyroid hormones and adrenaline in addition to dopamine. Severe emotional and mental disorders, rigidity, walking disabilities, speech, and depression such as seen in Parkinson's may be associated with imbalances in tyrosine and phenylalanine. Fish (long considered "brain food"), beef, poultry, pork, dairy, eggs, soy, and various nuts and seeds are good sources of phenylalanine.

The surprise may be that the artificial sweetener, *Aspartame,* is one half phenylalanine by weight.[13] It is not a surprise that people who eat or drink products with aspartame often struggle with gut issues, mental, addiction, and other serious health issues.[14] Because phenylalanine converts to norepinephrine, necessary for signals between neurons in the brain, it is no casual matter to induce imbalances by mindless eating habits. Calories do matter, but feeding children and adults aspartame in food or beverages may be contributing to a disturbed gut, which can contribute to emotional, mental, and addictive disorders.

Careful attention to eating foods high or low in essential amino acids can be the catalyst for change in mental disorders. However, consuming a steady diet too high in certain amino acids found in protein supplements, protein bars, and processed foods can alter the mind, causing personality changes. Changing the diet and maintaining a healthy diet is not a quick solution but contributes much to a healthy mind.

Sometimes, dieters experience a serious alteration in personality, which affects their family and future because of personality changes. Diet pills and artificial diet products can affect not only the gut, but also certain neurotransmitters in the brain. Concerned partners and family members may insist on medical evaluation, which is usually followed with anti-depressives and/or sedatives. The underlying problem is not discovered nor dealt with, leaving a confused individual who no longer knows what direction in life to take. If your emotional or mental or addictive disorder started a few months after a diet that utilized diet pills, you may have set off an imbalance in your neurotransmitters.

Changing the diet to natural, unprocessed foods rich in natural amino acid ratios can do much to change the body and mind. Another simple but powerful change may occur with adding foods rich in essential fatty acids. The body can make some of its own fatty acids, but like amino acids, the healthy mental and physical benefits come from a proper balance of fatty acids. Most Americans tend to get an overabundance of omega-6 fatty acids, one of the fatty acids from processed foods. This disturbs the natural ratios found in nature and can disrupt bodily functions, including those of the brain. Both omega-6 and omega-3 have been covered extensively in the media due to evidence that adjusting the intake and correcting the ratio can make a big difference. Increasing omega-3 fatty acids in the diet provides measurable improvements in stress, anxiety, cognitive decline, and mood disorders such as depression, bipolar, and schizophrenia.[15]

Just as it may be difficult to know whether or not you or whomever you are trying to help is eating and absorbing the optimal amino acids, it may be difficult to "guess" whether or not you are eating enough of the "good" fatty acids to counteract the "bad." Metabolic testing can be a great help from a reputable lab that can help you understand what to eat and what not to eat, as well as making decisions about taking omega-3s. Even too much of a good thing can be harmful, so it's a good idea to consult an expert on how much omega-3 to take.

The body is designed to support brain function, but it has to be fed properly. Amino acids and fatty acids are just parts of the picture. Getting someone who is already struggling with life to eat certain foods and take supplements may be a battle, but it's a battle that is worth it. Learning how to increase these important foods may be as easy as adding certain oils, seeds, and nuts to the diet. Educating yourself and getting a nutritional advisor may be assets. Many who work in the natural foods stores and clinics can advise on fatty acids. Getting the body balanced in amino acids and fatty acids may bring better brain balance as well as give the person strength for the next steps on the path to recovery.

CHAPTER 3

Emergence: When Mental Illness Is Not What It Seems

One of the first indications that nutrition had something to do with mental disorders happened many years ago when a healthcare attendant was moved with compassion to provide vitamins and minerals to patients in a mental institution. Within a few months, some improved greatly and were able to be released.[1]

Perhaps the attendant had read about the *pellagra vs. schizophrenia* discovery made by Dr. Joseph Goldberger in the early 1900s. Mental institutions in America and Europe were filled with people who had the same "mental" disease. A Swiss doctor, Eugen Bleuler, coined the word *schizophrenia* in 1911, but *dementia praecox*, the same disorder, had been described since the late 1800s. Clearly, there was a mental disease taking the minds of thousands. Disordered logic, illusions, hallucinations, skin eruptions, diarrhea, and in some cases, death accompanied the mental illness.[2] Those suffering with this illness appeared to have personalities that were "split."

Dr. Goldberger was assigned by the Surgeon General to study pellagra as the epidemic of mental illness grew. It was especially prevalent in the South among the poor sharecroppers who worked in the fields following the Civil War. Dr. Goldberger, noticing that their diet consisted mainly of pork fatback, molasses, and milled corn in grits and cornmeal, suspected a nutritional deficiency could be behind the "insanity." He went so far as to inject him and his wife with fluids from pellagra victims to prove it was not a physical, contagious disease. He discovered that by adding a small amount of brewer's yeast to the diet, he could not only prevent pellagra, he could cure it. Thousands were released from hospitals, having recovered from "insanity."[3] A few years later, *nicotinic acid*, vitamin B_3, was isolated and proven to be the missing nutrient. By the 1940s, meal and flour and other foods were "enriched" with B vitamins, which had been removed from the grain through milling processes.

By 1952, Abram Hoffer, PhD, MD proved with a double blind, placebo-controlled study that B_3 could cure schizophrenia with a 90 percent cure rate.[4] Dr. Hoffer was also a pioneer in recognizing and treating another disorder, *pyroluria*, now called the *Mauve Factor*. This condition is often diagnosed as a mental disorder and can be misdiagnosed as ADD/ADHD, Autism, Asperger's, bipolar, depression, and other mental problems. It is a malfunction in the blood that prevents normal absorption of zinc, biotin, and omega-6s.[5]

You may be interested to know that it was Dr. Hoffer who introduced Bill Wilson, co-founder of Alcoholics Anonymous (AA), to the link between vitamins, minerals, and nutrition to addiction. Under the guidance of Dr. Samuel Shoemaker, an Episcopal clergyman, and the powerful Oxford Group in America, both Bill Wilson and Dr. Bob Smith were recovering alcoholics, having already chosen abstinence. However, both were struggling. Through Dr. William Silkworth of Towns Hospital in New York, Bill learned that alcoholism is a disease of mind, emotions, and body. It was Dr. Hoffer, however, who led Bill to start taking three grams of niacin daily. After two weeks, his anxiety, tension, fatigue, and craving for alcohol ceased. In the foreword to Bill Wilson's book, *Alcoholism: The Cause and The Cure*, Dr. Hoffer says that due to the success with correcting the underlying malfunction and deficiency in his body, Wilson conducted his own trial. He put 30 people on niacin who, while sober, were still suffering the mood and mind conditions that accompany alcoholism. After one month, ten were well; after two months, ten more were well; the remaining third did not show improvement until after three months.[6]

Deficiencies in niacin (B_3) can not only affect cravings for alcohol and drugs, but also niacin deficiency can cause changes in sensory perception, such as hearing voices, distortions in visual perception (seeing things), and other "mental" symptoms. Other B vitamins such as B_1, B_2, B_6, B_9, and B_{12} are necessary for emotional and mental health as a process called *methylation* is dependent on these vitamins to produce and utilize brain neurotransmitters and important functions impacting neurodegenerative diseases as well.[7]

Vitamin B_3 and B_{12} are abundant in animal liver and used to be a mainstay on American tables. People heard of this simple solution to "insanity," depression, and anemia (not enough red blood cells, which can cause depression). However, liver can be filled with environmental toxins, herbicides, pesticides, and additives to livestock food. It can no longer be considered "safe" unless it is organic.[8]

Blood and urine tests of people with emotional, mental, and addictive disorders—including depression, bipolar, OCD, schizophrenia, and drug and alcohol addiction—tend to show deficiencies in B vitamins. B_6 is often low in those with depression and behavior problems; some studies have shown that 75 percent of depressed patients were low in B_6 and 25 percent of obsessive-compulsive patients. Marked improvement in autism, agoraphobia (panic attacks, anxiety), and Alzheimer patients have occurred with simple B vitamin therapy. Other studies show supplementing B_1 and B_2 may eliminate depression; adding B_{12} can effectively improve bipolar (manic-depressive) illness.[9]

B_9, *folate*, is well known for preventing birth defects, but less is known about its importance in mental health. According to Mental Health America, studies have shown it to be as effective as psychotropic drugs in reducing depressive symptoms in people with normal and low folate levels, improving cognitive function and reducing depressive symptoms in elderly people with folate deficiency and reducing depressive and other symptoms in people with depression and alcoholism.[10]

By now, you may be wondering why emotional, mental, and additive disorders are not routinely treated with vitamins at first symptom. Oftentimes, poor absorption can hinder the efficiency of vitamin and mineral therapies. The gut is so "ill" that these important nutrients can pass through without the benefits. For example, if a person takes a proton-pump inhibitor, such as *Nexium* or *Prilosec*, the gut can be coated and little nutrition is absorbed.[11] Unfortunately, these are often prescribed for long-term use contrary to instructions from the pharmaceutical companies. Trading GERD, which can be remedied with proper food and diet, for dementia is a bad trade-off.

Finding the right dosage of vitamins can be difficult as "one dose does not fit all." Most with emotional, mental, and addictive disorders may already have eating issues and are already deficient when they start vitamin therapy. They may need high dosages not only of B vitamins, but also vitamin C. The brain requires proper vitamin intake to operate normally. In a perfect world, these vitamins could be absorbed from foods that are rich in B and C vitamins.

A compromised, commercialized food system that has stripped nutrients from food and added ingredients that the body cannot process will not only prevent vitamin and mineral absorption and utilization, but also may be contributing to increasing violence and crime.

A provocative article by Kimberly Hartke, published in 2012, questioned if the mass killings that happen all too often can be traced back to pellagra and other vitamin deficiency disease. She says that Dr. Weston A. Price as far back as 1930 found that primitive tribes that ate whole foods with diets high in animal fats had no need for prisons. In the same article, Hartke mentions that Barbara Stitt, a U.S. senator who had worked as a probation officer, reported that changing the diet of prisoners often eliminated the hostility and other behaviors that had been acted out in crime.[12] Has our broken and all-too-often-aggressive society at least partially developed because of the radical changes in how we feed our children and what we consume ourselves?

Knowledge that mineral deficiencies and overloads affect emotional, mental, and addictive disorders first came to my attention over 30 years ago when I was conferring with Dr. Walter Murray concerning my students. We were already recommending to the parents certain dietary changes and seeing results. Dr. Murray suggested adding 40 milligrams of zinc. Within a few weeks, I could see a difference—less chewing on pencils, less picking at skin, and better attention.

Why would adding this simple mineral make a difference? Zinc supports many functions in the body; in fact, over 300 enzymes require adequate zinc or they cannot do their job. Low zinc levels have been found in depression, behavior and learning problems, anorexia, dysphoria, epilepsy, as well as other disorders. The adolescent body needs larger than normal amounts of zinc due to puberty. Zinc levels drop when estrogen rises one week before the menstrual period. Importantly, adequate zinc must be present to keep copper levels at normal range. When women are pregnant, they need more copper and zinc for the developing baby. When the baby is born, zinc is supposed to lower the copper back to normal range. If this doesn't happen, the familiar *post-partum depression* sets in. How many women have gone to their physicians hating post-partum and hating themselves, not understanding their emotions and deeply concerned for their baby, only to be given an anti-depressive. Or, they've been told to "get a grip" on it. For some women, copper levels remain high for years—or the rest of their lives—and they never overcome post-partum depression.[13]

While high levels of copper can cause psychotic mental disorders, low levels of copper cause a decrease in dopamine and norepinephrine (major neurotransmitters) significantly contributing to any mental disorder. In addition, calcium, manganese, iron, phosphorus, and potassium need to be at optimum levels for optimum mental health. Poor absorption in the gut, inadequate intake of foods containing these minerals, and drinking water from copper and lead pipes can cause a cascade of malfunctions in the brain to occur. These deficiencies are not sudden; over the course of week, months, and years, the body tries to compensate. Often an emotional or physical illness will occur following a move into a different house, or a person may improve after a move to another house. The change in drinking water, chemicals in the house, and different food purchases due to moving to another house in a different area can decrease or increase mental health problems.[14] According to one study where there were high copper levels in drinking water (copper pipes), at least one family member in each family had an emotional or mental disorder.[15]

Low levels of magnesium, on the other hand, may prevent your neurotransmitters from being as effective. Researchers at MIT say magnesium can increase learning and memory.[16] Perhaps it would be prudent to consider the underlying causes of the onset of the emotional, mental, or addictive disorders in every individual before medication is prescribed. Ingesting foods and using products with metals such as aluminum, lead, mercury, and cadmium may be involved in disturbing emotional and mental health balance. Aluminum may cause nerve fibers to become "tangled."[17] Vanadium may cause sodium to become too high, preventing cells from being able to build sufficient electric charge for nerve transmission. Electric signaling initiates neurotransmitter release into receptors. Preventing signaling means preventing neurotransmitters from doing their job effectively. This affects everything in the body and brain.[18]

These metals are common in public drinking water, baking powder, aerosol, and other deodorants. Aerosol spray can go directly to the brain through the nose and store in the brain. Lead from canned foods, pipes, car gasoline and exhaust, and paint can store in the tissues of the brain and body. Lead is now recognized at the national level as being dangerous to brain and nerve development. If you purchased a house or land recently, you may have noticed the "lead report" that was required. Illusions, hallucinations, and social withdrawal can occur with high cadmium residues. Cadmium is in many processed foods as well as in plastics and food containers. Mercury is suspected in many emotional and mental disorders, including ADD/ADHD and Autism.[19]

A former student of mine who had severe learning and behavior problems was tested for heavy metals when he did not show improvement with educational methods that were effective with other students. A metabolic test for heavy metals showed extremely high lead. In spite of all my questions to the parents, we could not find the source; they felt their son was just rebellious and incorrigible. When I visited their home, I noticed an old car in the garage that the father was restoring. In a casual conversation, I learned that the child and father spent long hours in the garage cleaning car parts with gasoline, and had been doing so since the child was two years old. Gasoline, unless "lead-free," contains high lead content.

Metabolic testing for heavy metals is often effective. However, in vitamin, mineral, hormone, and enzyme testing, the "normal" may not be the range you need for emotional, mental, and addictive disorders. These conditions may require higher than suggested RDA (recommended daily allowances) as the body begins to correct deficiencies and ratios. If possible, use food, especially raw food and juicing, to get maximum nutrition into the cells. This may be a difficult battle, especially for the first three to six weeks as the person adjusts to a new way of living. It's important to ask your doctor to check your vitamin D_3 routinely as increasing your time outside and taking vitamin D_3 may greatly improve your mental health.[20]

Prescription medicines, on the other hand, may be needed short-term, but rarely is anyone "cured" by antidepressants, etc. The brain simply adjusts and makes less of the necessary neurotransmitters, causing the need for more medication until "tolerance" occurs. The words from family and doctors "I've done all I can do for you" are hard to hear by someone desperate to live, as well as to live life differently.

Many in the field of counseling began decades ago to suspect that nutritional deficiencies and emotional instabilities were linked as the quality of foods declined. As the dinner table changed, so did the home and the child and the fathers and mothers. Emotional, mental, and addictive disorders continue to increase around the world whenever the food sources are changed. Could it be as simple as changing what you eat? But changing what you eat is not simple, is it? Your body, addicted to additives, sugar, etc. will fight you, but the war can be won.

CHAPTER 4

A Gathering Storm:
Why Pills Are Not a Cure

Years ago, many families hid mental, emotional, and addictive disorders. In my family, my aunt who was considered "retarded" was taught to go to the back of the house when visitors approached. Perhaps it was for her safety, but most likely it was to hide her from public view. She was humpbacked, unattractive, could not speak clearly, and walked with a limp. However, she could love and she loved me. In return, I loved her deeply and her influence on me was immeasurable.

On my maternal side, I had a beloved uncle who had suffered a brain injury. He was a marvel. He could do amazing math addition and subtraction in his head and could strip the net at the free throw line again and again in basketball. The injury only affected one side of his brain. Our nationally famous basketball coach allowed him to teach the players how to do the same. Uncle Bill never matured mentally beyond a ten year old in many ways, but he was the world's best babysitter as he knew enough to protect us from danger but played with us like a child. He died an old man with hundreds of friends whom he had influenced in spite of his limitations. Both my aunt and my uncle, in spite of their limitations, poured so much into my life. Much of what I do now and have done for the past fifty years is because of them.

Mental illness as well as strong addictive disorders in my family con-tributed to my desire to find out what could be changed and what could be done. As the years passed and psychotic drugs did not live up to what we had hoped, I dug deeper into research. In the past few decades, focus in the medical science world has shifted to connections between the physical body and the mind.

For over a hundred years, much of psychology developed around an Austrian, Sigmund Freud. He believed experiences in the past caused emotional and mental disorders. He proposed *psychoanalysis* to help the person recall the experience and confront it. His first book, *Studies in Hysteria,*[1] was published in 1895 and was highly influential in developing the field of psychology and counseling. Trying to get to the "root" of the emotional problem and uncovering the past became the norm in counseling.

From ancient times, however, healers sought to cure mental illness with potions, exorcism, and medicinal springs. In America, mineral water springs were very popular and people traveled for miles to "take the cure." Drinking natural mineral water and absorbing it through the skin did indeed help many people regain their mental and physical health. One such spring, located near Atlanta, Georgia, is called "Lithia Springs" due to the lithium in the water.

In 1949, John Cade, another Austrian, published his findings that lithium could successfully treat acute mania.[2] Lithium became a common treatment and is still used for bipolar in some cases. However, it was over twenty years later—1970—that the FDA approved lithium for use in America. It took another 28 years before the science behind lithium was explained—lithium stabilizes glutamate, the brain's foundational neuro-transmitter, by improving sodium transport. Too much glutamate equals mania, hyperactivity, and erratic, unstable brain activity; too little gluta-mate results in depression, lethargy, lack of focus, and lack of purpose.[3]

Lithium is also found naturally in soil and systemically is taken up into plants. Meat and dairy contain lithium.[4] One has to wonder why we don't know more about the use of increasing or decreasing lithium naturally through the diet. Finding the right balance can be challenging. Even with the drug *lithium*, it is difficult to find the right dosage as food and water can affect the levels of lithium in the body due to absorption. The possibilities of finding the right balance of lithium from food and water is dependent, once again, on the absorption of the gut and the mineral being available in the soil where animals graze and plants are planted.

With so much emphasis on "psychological" issues behind emotional, mental, and addictive disorders, research on the underlying causes and metabolic similarities in people were often ignored. This is still true decades later. It was not until 1921 that another Austrian, Otto Loewi, discovered the connection between the *vagus* nerve (in the gut) and the heart. He said it came to him in a dream. By using two frog hearts in separate containers, Loewi showed that a chemical released by the vagus nerve in the frog's gut made the beating of both hearts happen. The chemical was named a *neurotransmitter* because it transmitted across nerve gaps (synapses). In later years, the same chemical was named *acetylcholine*.[5] We know now that this neurotransmitter affects learning and behavior as well as the development of Alzheimer's.

In 1950, the first pill for anti-depression was developed, initiating the explosion of mind-altering pills available today. With one of every ten Americans on some sort of antidepressants, the market continues to expand. *Prozac* was developed in 1987; annual sales are now over $1 billion. *Zoloft* followed in 1991 and *Paxil* in 1992.[6] I recently counted 45 different antidepressants available in America.[7]

It only takes watching one advertisement of these pills on television to note the side effects, which include potential suicide and homicide. Because the use of prescribed drugs is not always admissible in court, it is difficult to legally tie some of the unthinkable tragedies happening in the world today to the use of these popular pills. However, even a cursory glance at the psychiatric drugs taken by mass murderers is evidence of a growing concern over the use of these medications. It is reported that the dosage of *Zoloft* that James Holmes had been prescribed (who committed the Batman theater killing in Colorado) had recently been tripled.[8]

Dr. David Healy, a British psychiatrist and founder of RxISK.org, says psychiatric medications were involved in 90 percent of school shootings.[9] The disturbing increase in suicides among teenagers[10] and military personnel may follow the disturbing increase in prescriptions for psychiatric drugs among these two groups.[11]

For grieving families with no answers as to why their family member committed suicide or an inconceivable homicide, these statistics offer little solace. Symptoms of a physical disorder can be identical to those of an emotional or mental disorder. For example, hypoglycemia (low blood sugar) can have the same symptoms as clinical depression[12] including agitation, depression, anger, rage, anxiety, panic attacks, and an increase in suicide risk.[13]

Desperate parents often mistake clinical depression or other emotional or mental disorders for hypoglycemia. In my own experience working with teenagers, it was common for me to ask the pediatrician for a blood sugar test if the student was on an antidepressant. All too often, the doctor would find blood sugar "in the basement." Rapid growth, puberty, poor eating habits, too little quality protein, inadequate vitamin and mineral intake, and lack of sleep may be some of the major reasons behind much teenage depression. With a growing epidemic in emotional, mental, and addictive disorders, we must recognize that a malfunctioning mind accompanies a malfunctioning body.

A dysfunctional thyroid gland can also cause similar symptoms of emotional or mental illness. Hyperthyroidism (overactive) can cause anxiety, emotional instability, irritability, and depression. Underactive thyroid production (hypothyroidism) can show symptoms of depression, paranoia, psychosis, slow mental processes, memory loss, and loss of initiative and interest in life or former interests.[14]

Often, it is difficult to get a true thyroid function test due to outdated standards as well as lab tests that give only partial results. One of the simple ways to test for low thyroid is a simple temperature test. Putting a thermometer under the armpit before getting out of bed and keeping a detailed account for 30 days is a fairly reliable test for both hypothyroidism and hyper. An early morning temperature of under 97.8 degrees most likely indicates a low functioning thyroid, while a temperature of over 98.2 may indicate a hyperthyroid condition.[15] Taking this report to your doctor may enable a better diagnosis of a thyroid condition.

The American Thyroid Association estimates that 20 million Americans have some form of thyroid disease. Out of those 20 million, 60 percent are unaware of their condition.[16] Could the high incidence of depression be tied to the thyroid gland? Will prescribing a psychotropic drug correct a thyroid disorder? Or is it possible that millions of young and old Americans are struggling with a common disease that can and should be treated?

Treating the thyroid, as well as treating iodine deficiency, does not carry the same list of side effects as that of mind-altering drugs.

Interesting and alarming is the fact that salad greens and vegetables grown in Southern California are grown in fields irrigated by the Colorado River, which has been contaminated with rocket and missile fuel since World War II. Rocket fuel (perchlorate) is a known to damage the thyroid.[17] The EWG (Environmental Working Group) estimates that over 2.8 million women of childbearing age in the United States are eating perchlorate-contaminated lettuce each day during the winter months. About 1.6 million of these women are getting a dose of perchlorate that is greater than the EPA's proposed reference dose.[18]

Dr. Barbara Schildkrout, Harvard psychiatrist, says that over one hundred medical conditions can masquerade as psychological conditions.[19] How does this add up in your personal experience? The South leads the nation in most prescriptions for mental and emotional disorders as well as prescriptions more likely to be filled.[20] Does this reflect a cultural curiosity or culturally accepted medical practice? Prescribing a psychiatric drug when there is an underlying undiagnosed and untreated medical condition is not the same as a "Band-Aid." Instead, there should be a moral responsibility that reaches beyond just the individual and family. We can no longer afford to wantonly and casually prescribe psychotropic drugs as if they were M&M's, disregarding the potential side effects. These are mind-altering drugs and their job is to alter your behavior, often leaving you emotionless and out of touch with the people you love most. Could this in any way explain the "remorseless" response of offenders as well as those who unexpectedly kill family members as well as random homicides?

Can it really be possible that emotional, mental, and addictive disorders can start with abnormal gut flora, progressively deepen due to inadequate and faulty diets—causing an imbalance in brain chemicals (neurotransmitters)—and then cascade into self-medication or psychiatric drugs, harmful habits, potentially dangerous behavior, and deepening destruction in a person's life? When it comes to unraveling emotional, mental, and addictive disorders, there are no easy answers. However, a number of researchers, scientists, and medical professionals continue to look for answers. Finding them, they often have a battle to get the information to the public due to lobbying, marketing, and a "head in the sand" approach by many.

I guess all of us would love it if a pill could cure emotional, mental, and addictive disorders, but that pill does not exist. Instead, we have to find physical and underlying conditions in cellular metabolism as a starting place. This is no easy task, but it is possible. Malfunction in the body affects the brain, the production of neurotransmitters in the body and brain, neuron conductivity, and brain hemisphere activity. It is no casual matter to overlook the body when searching for answers for the mind. Biochemical imbalances in the brain can cause a person to take offense and consider himself or herself misunderstood and treated unjustly. In time, their way of viewing the world becomes skewed, and all too easily psychological disorders can develop.

PART TWO

How the Mind Affects the Body

What role do our daily decisions play

in the Silent Takeover of the body?

On the Surface: Daily Decisions Affect Emotional, Mental, and Addictive Disorders

I stand gazing over a blue ocean that reaches the horizon, drawing a barely visible line against the blue of the sky. Waves crash against the rocks, transforming from sea blue to sea green when the water catches the light. "A perfect day," I whisper to myself as I let my eyes follow a rippling current that looks like a map in the sea to the horizon, where the blue of the sky blends with the blue of the sea.

A pelican's shrill call interrupts. I watch the strategic dive into the water. The bird emerges with a fish still wiggling. Wrong place, wrong time for the fish. Right time, right place for the bird. Nature has her own laws and systems.

I take a deep breath, smelling the rawness of shellfish and sea life. I want to hold on to this utter contentment that fills my mind and emotions. Yes, "A picture is worth a thousand words," and I long to keep this picture for those dark, winter days. Winter has her own peculiar beauty, but the sea on a summer day reaches deep into my soul.

The moments pass until I wonder what's beyond the point where the coastline juts inland. The sand is warm and fine, a soft massage as I walk barefoot ahead. The white of the sand against the blue ocean—a feast for the soul.

Ahead, a little boy is packing sand into a red pail, working diligently to mound the moist sand into whatever he envisions. I stay on my path but move aside a few feet to give mother and child their own space. He looks up at me, and possibly recognizing a "grandmother type," says, "Will you build a sand castle with me?"

My first thoughts are about myself: do I want to stop my precious walk on the beach to build a sand castle with a child I don't know? His eyes are the color of the water. I slow my pace, deciding that there's probably nothing more important right now than building a sand castle with this little boy. I sit down, looking at his mother to see if she objects. She is amused. His little mound of sand doesn't show much promise. I say to him, "Sure. I'll build a castle with you, and I know how to build magical castles with turrets and tunnels!" He fixes his eyes on my face as if to wonder if I really mean it.

We dig a moat around his mound as I explain we will need a lot of water to build a magic castle. By now, his mother is watching. With her hand, she is holding her place in the novel she is reading. The beach umbrella has created a cozy nook and a low beach chair makes a nice reading spot. I dribble a handful of water and sand creating a sand castle turret on top of his mound. He is impressed, "How do you do that?" I smile, knowing that he will learn as he attempts to mix just the right sand and water mix.

His mother, quiet until now, says, "My aunt built a castle like that for me when I was a little girl. I had forgotten about it." Putting her book aside, she settles beside us on the sand. We build together for a few minutes, helping him create his dream. They are smiling at each other, and he laughs when the ripples of the water come too far and snatches a part of his castle. "We'll build it back!" he declares triumphantly and sets himself to do it. I rise, conscious that they no longer need a third partner.

I say to her, hoping she will hear me, "There's nothing more important for you to do today than build a sand castle with your child." I long for her to understand how rapidly the years will pass and how moments like these can remain in the memory for a lifetime. She looks intently at me. I wonder if she will remember my grandmother words and apply them to her life or if the fiction she is reading will prevent a greater story from happening. I say goodbye explaining to him that I need to walk toward the curve where the sea slips out of sight. I need to see where it goes. I promise to stop by on the return walk and that I will expect to see the biggest castle on the beach. He grins and turns back to his castle, rebuilding what fell back into the sea.

The sea and the sky, the happiness of a child with his mother, and the warm sand hugging my toes as I walk further along the beach. I put my sunglasses back on shielding my eyes from the brightness of the sun as it climbs higher in the sky, changing the color of the sea. Just beyond the point, there may be an islet that may charm me into the water I love, and I will swim a while before I walk back to check on a castle by the sea.

CHAPTER 5

On the Surface: How the Mind Changes the Body

We can't all live on a beach in a sunny climate, staring at the sea and walking barefoot on the sand. But we can find ways to restore the mind by making conscious decisions to do what we can to make our neurotransmitters more efficient. As I walked on the beach, there was a "cocktail" of neurotransmitters being produced and firing inside my brain. They were finding docks for completing their job of making me feel "happy and peaceful"—that powerful concoction the mind loves. Had I been able to actually measure my neurotransmitters, we might have seen a great increase in *serotonin* as sunshine connected with parts of my retina reaching the hypothalamus. The sunshine and the vitamin D it supplies are a "dynamic duo" in correcting serotonin imbalance. The blue light all around me and the blue colors of the sky and sea would have not only increased my production of serotonin, but also would have sent calming messages through my cells as they "remembered" association with the beach. "Ah, this is good."

The color blue, even on a painted wall, brings about measureable effects in the body as the pulse and heartbeat respond. Blue sky and blue ocean affect the body and the mind.[1] Natural lithium from the seawater and sea air would have entered my body as I breathed the ocean air and swam in the ocean water.

As I walked toward the curve of the sea, toward an "unexplored" destination, *dopamine* could have increased due to its response to adventure, excitement, and the unknown. As I stopped to interact with the child, levels of *oxytocin* may have increased, especially when the mother and I connected on the needs of the child. That night, most likely I would have slept better because the sunshine would have reset my internal "clock" by increasing *melatonin*, enabling me to slow down my busy mind and go to sleep. Our bodies repair as we sleep, and poor sleep will eventually break down the immune system. Our cells will do what they are designed to do—if they have what they need to perform their duties. The body follows a careful timetable of organs doing their jobs completely unbeknownst to us under the anesthetic of sleep. This timetable is so exact that the time of death can be determined in forensics by the activity of the body at certain times. However, autopsies of depressed people show an "out of sync" with the normal timetable of cellular functions. Their brains show alterations at the cellular level in the "clock" of the body.[2]

Months and years later, when sitting at my desk with a stack of papers and a full calendar, if I let my mind go back to that day on the beach, my body and mind will increase in those neurotransmitters and my stress levels will lessen. In the past few decades, much has been discovered about the brain and the mind. Yet we have not begun to understand exactly how the body, brain, and mind work together in synergy, producing not just our *mind*, but also our will and emotions, our personality, and our response under stress and happiness. Production levels of neurotransmitters can be measured in blood and urine tests. However, production levels are not static; they increase and decrease according to many factors, including food, beverages, actions, and even thoughts. In fact, the body is so sensitive to the mind, will, and emotions that telling a lie can be detected on a lie detector test.

Years ago I had a "stress measurement card." If you touched a spot on the card and it turned black, you were stressed. I was a newspaper writer at the time, so the spot on the card was usually black, indicating high stress, especially as deadlines approached. If I took a few minutes and re-membered snorkeling in a blue sea with all sorts of beautiful fish, my card would turn a blue color, indicating I was no longer stressed. The subcon-scious mind responded by changing chemicals in my body, which affected my mood. Now, remembering snorkeling might not increase the chemi-cals as high as the real experience, but nevertheless it caused me to relax.

The mind is much more complex than mere chemicals in the brain. Your own thoughts and daily actions can make the difference in emo-tional, mental, and addictive disorders as many "overcomers" will tell you. They learned to think differently and, consequently, make different choices. Addiction is when the disorder has progressed beyond personal control. While a day at the beach may not cure emotional, mental, and addictive disorders, it could go a long ways toward "lifting" the mood. Understanding a little bit about how the *intrinsic*—thoughts, actions, and daily decisions—affects neurotransmitter efficiency can enable you to change your own body and offer help to your loved one.

If you look at a blue sky even when you are not at the beach, your neurotransmitters change. Sunlight increases serotonin production as well as melatonin. A gray sky, on the other hand, can cause Seasonal Affective Disorder (SAD) in many people. The signs of SAD start creeping in around October when seasons change. Sluggishness, depression, de-spondency, sleepiness, craving for sugar and carbohydrates, and subse-quent weight gain becomes the norm.[3] Now, if you hibernated all winter, that would be all right, but most of us have to keep going. A crisp, white snowfall and bright sunshine on the snow can cause serotonin and mel-atonin to increase. People in winter climates with winter sports are not usually as susceptible to SAD.[4] The Mayo Clinic suggests a light therapy box or lamp may improve or even eliminate winter depression.[5]

Taking vitamin D_3 and getting outdoors on bright winter days may help, and if you can, switching to a winter vacation in a bright, warm, sunny climate for a week could bring you out of a depression spiral. It is well established in research that low vitamin D is often present in de-pression, SAD, schizophrenia, and other psychiatric disorders in adults and adolescents.[6]

SAD, while caused by deficiencies in the body, can also be changed by making some good decisions. Sitting in front of a television, spending too much time on a computer or cell phone, and staying indoors may sound more comfy in the winter, but these activities not only can increase your SAD, but also, they can lower your immune system because electronics produce *positive ions.*

Contrary to what it sounds like, *positive* ions are actually not good for you. Positive ions occur when an atom loses an electron, a negative charge, and has more protons than electrons. Now, for most of us that's chemistry and physic expertise, and we may choose to opt out without giving this information a chance to be understood. However, it is just everyday life.

Electricity, microwaves, cell phones, computers, electric blankets, florescent lights, air conditioners, furnaces, and even your toaster produce positive ions. Clothes dryers, polyester and synthetic fabrics, carpet, dust, pollution, and strong, high winds can produce these molecules. They are so small they can pass directly into your blood stream, lungs, and respiratory system and affect your immune system.[7] Making a decision to lessen positive ions in your home can make a "happier" home with everyone feeling better; it can also mean fewer trips to the doctor's office and potentially fewer antibiotics.

It's common with the stress of urban life to escape more and more into an electronic world. Everyday life is filled with electronic living with televisions, computers, cell phones, microwaves, and other technology squeezing the mind, depleting serotonin and creating positive ions. Deciding to not retreat into these worlds will show you how addicted you are. Try going a day without checking your phone or e-mail. The more you "disconnect," the greater the dividends in your physical and mental health. Increasingly, use of these electronics, especially cell phones, is being connected to cancer and neurodegenerative disorders. The International Agency for Research on Cancer has classified cell phones a class B carcinogen.[8]

So, if there are positive ions and they are the "bad guys," are there negative ions? Are they the "good guys"? As you may have guessed, negative ions have gained an electron and they are able to "take out" the positive ions by attaching to them. Opposites attract. This weighs the positive ions down and causes them to drop to the ground or to the floor below. While you may not remember "feeling" positive ions, you will remember "feeling" negative ions. Remember my walk on the beach? That calm, peaceful feeling I was experiencing wasn't just the serotonin increase; it was all of those wonderful negative ions being created by the crashing water and nearby ocean. When you are outside, you are in negative ions. Walking in the forest, standing beside a waterfall, going outside after a rainfall, and walking in a plowed field does "something" to your soul. You feel refreshed and your mood will most often be lifted within a few minutes of outdoor air and negative ions.[9] All of those electronic hours need to be balanced by outdoor time. The use of negative ion salt lamps or other aids can help, but they cannot replace time outside. When you have to work on something electronic, listen to your body and mind. When you feel like you have to "get a breath of fresh air," follow the body's instructions and requests—go outside. Making it a habit to eat lunch outside, for example, can help you restore the negative ions you need.

I began studying positive ions in 2006 when I read that the FDA warned that computers could cause stress and depression. They called it a "positive ion danger."[10] As I explored more about positive ions, I discovered decades of research on how *negative* ions could do just the opposite. Negative ions improve physical and mental health. Studies from 1935 until the present—a span of 80 years—show improvement in depression, mood disorders, and overall health with negative ions. One study reported a 350 percent improvement in cognitive functioning[11] in mice trials. This particular study was followed up by another study reporting a 23.6 percent improvement for learning disabled and an astounding 54.8 percent for mildly mentally impaired.[12]

In 1950, Dr. Albert Kreuger, University of California, along with Dr. Felix Sulman, Hebrew University in Israel, discovered that negative ions stimulated production of serotonin, 5-HT.[13] In 1995, CBS Evening News reported that a study at Columbia University showed that high-density negative ions were as effective as antidepressants in relieving winter depression.[14] So you may be wondering, why all of the development of psychiatric drugs if doses of negative ions available free of charge outdoors can make such a difference?

Recent scientific research is uncovering more and more about the positive effects of negative ions. Due to our indoor lives dominated by electronics, there is an imbalance in exposure to positive and negative ions. Instead of children playing outside, too many children are inside using their iPad, computer, or watching television. We were created to utilize negative ions to *restore* our mind and emotions. In order to be healed of emotional, mental, and addictive disorders, one of the first steps may be to determine to disconnect from electronics and use every minute you can to be outside in nature where sunlight and fresh air filled with negative ions can begin its job of healing body and soul.

American life has shifted from rural life with outside chores—where children worked alongside their parents with livestock and farming—to the present day, where a child may have only seen a cow in a petting zoo and a tomato plant on a patio. Many children and adults are inside almost all of the time. In the past, children ran outside for "recess" and after school to play ball and play with other children. Now, "virtual" games are replacing outdoor play with friends. Check this out for yourself—ask a child if he would rather play a video game, watch TV, use the iPad or computer, or go outside and play. Most will choose electronics, as their minds prefer them to real life.

In the years ahead, there may be half empty sports arenas and stadiums as elementary school age children are not acquiring the same "rush" with real life sports. In addition, *play* is how children learn life skills as they relate to one another, learn to set goals, and learn the fun of working together toward a common purpose. They learn how to live in community relying on each other. These life skills are already showing a great decline as children become more isolated by their electronics. Many families have lost the joy of being a family because everyone has their own television set and electronics. Children come in from school where many have been using computers during the day, grab a snack, and head to their rooms where they are absorbed in an electronic world. If there is a dinnertime, they eat, and head back to their rooms. Their parents, in turn, who have set the example by being enslaved to the television and computers, follow suit. Television, computers, cell phones, etc. have replaced the family life of years ago. We can expect more emotional, mental, and addictive disorders as these children become adults, unprepared for living a real life filled with family and friends. They will know more about their favorite characters or their favorite video game than their own family members.

Sunshine, fresh air, and simply walking barefoot outside can bathe you in those healthy negative ions and help to counteract positive ions. *Grounding* or earthing may sound like something out of science fiction, but these are just words expressing reconnecting our own electricity to nature's electricity. If you think you are not an "electrical" being, try touching metal on a cold day. The shock you feel is real. Walking barefoot balances the negatives and the positives, and there's a good possibility that our lack of balance due to the electronics we use are adding to mental and addictive disorders. Mike Flynt, author of *Senior* says, *Today's scientific community continues to confirm E=MC2. We are energy beings in an energy universe.* Mike is continuing to research and provide science and information about grounding and protection from electro-magnetic fields frequencyflow.com. He recommends insoles to help with protection and to help replicate in the body what occurs when we are outside in nature.

Emotional, mental, and addiction disorders, regardless of onset, tend to worsen unless steps are taken to reverse them. When we speak of a dark mood or feeling surrounded by darkness, it is all too easy to move deeper into depression by literally turning off the lights. Finding a person sitting in a completely darken room can be a sign of deepening depression. The slide into depression can be the Ds: disappointed, disheartened, disillusioned, disrespected, despondent, defeated, and sadly, even death. Death doesn't have to be physical; it can be the death of a relationship or a plan or a dream. Another sign of deepening depression can be hours spent on video games or on the computer. What may seem harmless at the beginning can take over the life, and the person can be drawn back to the video game at every conceivable moment. At the beginning, it may be a diversion to get the mind off a painful memory; within a short time, it can become so addictive that a person will get up during the night and go back to a game. What is happening to the brain that makes video games for adults and children so addictive?

The conscious brain may be saying, "I need to quit this." On the other hand, the subconscious brain that is in charge of keeping you breathing and your heart beating may be getting what it needs the only way it can—through the *adrenaline* rush that comes from playing the game. Almost all of us are familiar with the *fight or flight* response in the body. The body perceives an emergency and that the body must "fight or flee." To prepare for either, surges of adrenaline flood the cells. People have done amazing things on high adrenaline—lifted cars off accident victims, saved people from raging rivers, and millions of other feats of courage and strength. Adrenaline is increased when another hormone, *cortisol,* rises. You probably know cortisol from hearing about how stress causes weight gain right around the middle. It also increases blood pressure, lessens pain, and raises blood sugar.

These are all great in a real emergency and the body does what it can to help us. However, the subconscious brain cannot distinguish the difference between *real* and *imaginary.* If you watch a scary movie or TV show and the suspense is building, your body responds. You may get sweaty hands and bite your fingernails; your heart starts beating faster and your blood pressure rises. You may even say to yourself, "This is ridiculous. This is just a movie!" Or your emotions may get so wrapped up in a movie that you shed real tears. How many grown adults cried in *ET?* The idea that grown people would weep over an imaginary creature from outer space may sound silly unless you were one of them. The body *responds* as the *mind* perceives.

Thus, the action in a video game is perceived as "real" to the subconscious or automatic brain. Cortisol and adrenaline, also called *epinephrine* (neurotransmitter) are released in *fight or flight* mode. The body's response to imminent danger is designed to be used only in real emergencies—a few times in a lifetime, in war or in sudden danger; it is not designed to be used again and again, many times during the day, followed by days and days and weeks and weeks of high alert in the body.

Adrenal fatigue, depression, certain medicines, and emotional wounds and hurts can cause the body to feel so lifeless that the surge in adrenaline encourages the subconscious brain to ask for more. After all, it has the job of keeping you going—heart beating, lungs breathing, brain thinking, legs moving, etc. If your subconscious brain could talk, it might say, "I can't live without some adrenaline and my reserves are too low. I don't have enough to make me want to go to work or to do anything. Get back to that video game as it gives me a shot of adrenaline so I feel like I am alive."

While one might watch a frightening movie, watching the rerun won't bring about the same effects in the body. The conscious brain "knows" what's going to happen. However, in a video game, the player gets further and further into the game by achieving success. That boost of dopamine to the reward center and the adrenaline rush together is highly addictive. All too soon, however, the brain reaches "tolerance" and the same thrill is not there. The next video game will have to be more dangerous, more intriguing, or more violent to get the same results in the body and mind. Eventually, a virtual experience is not enough. The body and mind demand the real thing. Add antidepressants such as *Prozac, Zoloft, Paxil,* and a plethora of other potential mind altering chemicals into a brain and body depleted of adrenaline. A recent study links adrenaline stimulation to glucagon, which could be considered in lay terms as the opposite of insulin. Insulin can raise blood sugar; glucagon can drop blood sugar. When these are artificially caused by surges of adrenaline, the body can develop problems with either or both. Glucagon may be involved with bipolar and depression as well as what is considered "late stage" bipolar.[15]

A very disturbing report from renowned psychologist Dr. Philip Zimbardo, Stanford University, says that young men are sacrificing relationships because they are addicted to "arousal" and that this level of arousal is found in pornography and video games. It is not a natural arousal and must be "fed" increasing amounts for the same effect. Norwegian mass murderer Breivik reported that he prepared his mind and body for the shooting of 77 people by playing *World of Warcraft* for a year and then *Call of Duty* for 16 hours a day.[16] Adrenaline addiction is a very serious malady and rarely can one just "taper" off.

One of the effects of antidepressants is to remove the emotional response of a person's actions or relationships. Antidepressants have been called the "I don't care" drugs. The end result could potentially be a person with no emotional response desperate for adrenaline or something to make them experience reality. You may have heard a person confess, "I just wanted to *feel* something." Many decide an emotionless life is not worth living. If they are addicted to violent video games or graphic violence in movies or television, they may decide to act on their desires to experience in real life what has been virtual and not reality. If they like to shoot people virtually, what would be the feeling in real life? When the line is crossed and the person is more into "virtual" life than reality, that person is capable of almost anything he or she has experienced in their virtual life. Many parents have no idea of how addictive video games are and how detrimental they are. It keeps the kid busy and occupied so the parent can do what the parent wants to do. Knowledge of how the mind works can be a powerful ally in preventing and repairing emotional, mental, and addictive disorders.

Sometimes, an eventual spiraling out of control can start with amphetamines prescribed to "calm down" a hyperactive child. For most, amphetamines will "speed" up mental and physical activities. However, in some neurotransmitter inefficiencies, these drugs work to slow down firing of neurotransmitters. Children who take amphetamines, such as *Adderall*, can develop stressed adrenal glands due to the "speed" effect on the body.[17] In addition, a frantic, overworked, overstressed parent can be all too happy to have a few minutes of quiet while the child plays with a video game. There's no warning on the box: "*Warning—this game may be addictive and may cause your child to develop an addictive need for adrenaline, which can lead to increasingly dangerous games or activities in real life.*"

Overworked, overstressed teachers with overcrowded classrooms often insist on medications for disruptive students to help teachers handle the education nightmares we face in many schools in America. Adding just one extra child to an overcrowded classroom can change the dynamic of the room. Asking teachers to teach with "both hands tied behind their backs" is unfair to students and teachers. A new system for a new time in America—one that carefully examines the underlying metabolic causes of behavior—can change the classrooms of America in record time. Continuing to use outdated and ineffective systems will continue to lower achievement.

On another note, amphetamines are sometimes present in "diet pills" and may lead to personality changes.[18] I've seen several marriages implode due to personality changes and disorders after diet pills were used for several months. You may recall that *Fen-phen*, a very popular diet pill, was associated with personality changes and psychosis.[19]

We sometimes jokingly refer to someone as an "adrenaline junkie" due to high-risk sports or behavior. However, it is no laughing matter when the need for adrenaline reaches a point where the person's life choices are being affected. That is addiction. Many marriages, homes, and futures have been destroyed by addiction to video games, violent and dark movies, and pornography. In a fascinating TED Talk, Philip Zimbardo explains how pornography creates adrenaline addiction. He says that substance addiction makes a person want *more*, pornography addiction makes a person want *different*.[20]

Often times a parent or other friend or relative will watch explicit scenes or graphic violence on a television show. Engrossed in the action, adults can overlook the little eyes also watching. "Parental guidelines" go only as far as the parents are willing to forego their own television preferences for the sake of their children. Are we so foolish as to think that children and teenagers ignore what their parents are watching? Many times in counseling sessions over the years, I've heard wives and mothers tell me they beg their husbands (or vice versa) to turn off programs that neither man nor child should watch.

Many of you have heard the old story of how a frog will jump out of a kettle of water if thrown in while the kettle is boiling. However, if placed in the kettle when the water is cold, the frog will stay in the water while it heats to boiling. The frog's reflexes do not warn that the frog is being boiled to death. If a person without any prior experience with explicit sexual or graphic violent content were to suddenly walk into a room with either on the screen, they would drop their head or look away. What does it take to shock you? Can you still be embarrassed by what you see or hear? Have you become calloused and hardened by slow degrees to where you no longer insist on high standards for yourself and your family?

Have you watched some of the PG-13 movies that your teen may be watching? A number of studies indicate that sexual content in movies and TV are related to teen sex.[21] Unless you are choosing to keep your head in the sand, you have already figured that out. A boy, a girl, a sexually explicit movie, the back seat of the car. Perhaps one of the greatest deterrents to unwise sexual decisions as well as pornography addiction could be as simple as turning off the TV and refusing to watch programs that "cross the line."

The need for adrenaline is powerful and can lure the brain into decisions that affect a lifetime. The brain latches on to explicit sexual scenes and locks each scene and each word in a sexually explicit sentence in the memory. Written text in books and magazines do the same, silently taking over the potential for healthy relationships. While most parents would quickly say they don't want their partner or their children involved in watching pornography or in outside-of-marriage sexual activity, they may not be as quick to refuse to allow it in their personal viewing and reading.

Where is the line? Could the "bad" seeds of a full pornography addiction have started when an actress revealed too much in a television program? Did that lead to wanting to see *less* and being repulsed by vulgarity or did it lead to wanting to see *more*? Many people are so afraid of being labeled "Victorian and prudish" that they will go along with the flow, harming their children, family, and themselves. Those magazine and catalogue advertisements lure the eyes and the mind. Are you brave enough to cancel and complain? Silence and complicity can turn out to be deadly for the soul, especially that of a developing child and teenager.

It's easy for a child or teen to recognize hypocrisy. "Do as I say not do as I do," will come back to haunt the parent in future years when poor choices are being made by their children. High-risk behavior, video and TV addiction, and addiction to pornography can be initiated by the person with the remote control in their hand. Most parents would not invite a drug dealer in or encourage their family to use drugs; nor would they invite other people with detrimental character in to lure their family into lurid and vile areas of life. They would bar the door and refuse entrance. It's harder to guard the door of the mind.

Just as a walk on the beach can send beneficial chemicals soaring through your mind and body, so can a television program or movie affect hormones and neurotransmitter production in your body and brain. Adrenaline, dopamine, serotonin, and other hormones and neurotransmitters increase or decrease, affecting the efficiency of their transmission and how they do their job as you watch and participate in activities. You hold the key, or should I say the *remote control* in these decisions. Getting on a path to recovery of emotional, mental, and addictive disorders can begin today by changing *how you are spending your time.* In addition to the steady dose of positive ions that cause serious physical defects in mind and body, the content of these electronic virtual experiences affects neurotransmitter production and response to daily life and people.

In past generations, the sight of a person in jeopardy or distress in public would elicit compassion and help from strangers. The sight of someone suffering or dying would so affect the observer that they would become emotional. Now, thousands of hours of watching people being murdered and die on television has hardened the subconscious mind. Accepting violence as "normal" behavior is being enacted every day in America. A compassionless generation is lacking the tenderness of the human soul, whether it is in the classroom or on the streets. Teaching bravery, honor, compassion, and self-sacrifice is almost impossible when the conscious mind and the subconscious mind have become slaves to false truths and false living.

Remember the *oxytocin* I mentioned in the reflection on the beach? Oxytocin is a very interesting hormone/neurotransmitter. You may know it as the *love chemical.* Mammals release it before birth so that the mothering effect takes place. The body releases it to prepare a mother to give birth and to feed the baby. Due to research in the last two decades, much is known about skin-to-skin contact in birth trauma. A baby is placed on the mother's skin to begin bonding as mother gives and baby receives oxytocin and vice versa. In a Caesarian birth, the father may be urged to hold the baby close to his chest, skin to skin, for the same response. Animals that are uninterested in their offspring can be made to mother with injections of oxytocin. Some autistic children improve in social skills with a sniff of oxytocin inhalant.[22]

Oxytocin is so powerful that some studies indicate it holds the reasons some people are monogamous and some are not.[23] Not surprisingly, the body attaches to the source of the oxytocin. Mother to child. In later years, it's *man* to oxytocin in the first sexual encounter. The brain not only remembers and lays down a neural pathway, the brain also may choose to hold on to that encounter and try to return to it. When a person is promiscuous, the brain begins to move toward "tolerance." It does not respond in the same way with more encounters. Many single people today roam through their youth so affected by these encounters that they struggle to find a mate. Date after date. Encounter after encounter. They have reached "tolerance," and one-night stands result in efforts to find someone who matters to them. Finally, they begin to seek alternative choices because they were designed to have a bonding experience from that first encounter. I remember listening as a twelve-year-old girl tell me she decided to "get it over with" because her friends were telling her she needed to be able to say she had sex before thirteen. What sort of wrong messages are we sending? How much will we tolerate in our homes with media authority that overrides the parent?

When a woman watches movies and television that show people falling in love, oxytocin increases in her body. Many women watch multiple movies during a week's time, often filling their nights after work with a "chick flick." Others curl up with a romantic novel with no idea that one of the reasons this is so addictive is the upsurge of oxytocin. The upsurge in oxytocin is addictive. When supplies are low, they go back for more. What does this do to a marriage or to a family? Mom may be so absorbed that family life is disrupted with forgotten appointments, nothing for dinner, and a short-tempered mom because she wants to get back to her novel or movie. In addition, it's all too easy to compare their husbands to the movie characters who are just that—movie characters. We tend to identify with people in movies. If you're not too embarrassed to admit it, you've probably walked out of a movie theater in that actor's *persona*—you were acting like the character. How does this, if it's a daily routine, affect the personal growth of the viewer?

The ups and downs of emotional and mental disorders, as well as addictions, are complex. A movie from three days ago still may be lingering in your mind, cropping up with scenes or sentences. Those lags in brain activities are from over stimulation—visual as well as physiological. Often in working with children who could not read or who could not comprehend, I would ask them to tell me everything they "saw" in their mind. Many times it was cartoons from the previous Saturday or a TV movie from the night before. That mental activity was dominating the brain, preventing the concentration necessary to read and comprehend. All too often, the parents were surprised and defensive when I would ask them to limit television and computer use to an hour a week so that I could teach their child to read and retain information. However, if your child sees you reading a cheap novel, even if it has a religious label, you stand a good chance of teaching your child that the unimportant is more important than the truly important in life.

An addiction to oxytocin is a serious addiction and very difficult to break. The more a person reads about or watches people falling in love virtually, the more the brain desensitizes and considers this important life experience as routine. What sort of mixed message are you sending to your subconscious brain? Your body will respond as the subconscious responds. Eventually, a person can become confused over *who* they really are as they seek to balance what they are watching and reading against their real life. In counseling, I have often heard people refer to various movies or books that "caused" them to see the kind of person they wanted to be with or whom they wanted to be. Quite often, their wife or husband did not measure up to the movie role.

Emotional and mental disorders such as anorexia and other eating disorders may be connected to a lack of oxytocin. Interestingly, when a person "cuts"—a term used to describe the cutting of the skin in emotional and mental disorders—a release of oxytocin occurs.[24] Could it be associated with a society out of sync with the body, where oxytocin, one of the body's most important hormone/neurotransmitters, is skewed by a steady diet of TV and movies and novels? Males receive that blast of oxytocin if the woman they are with is the woman they love.[25] If not, it is the antithesis to love and can greatly hinder lifelong relationships. Designed to be the "soul-mate" chemical that signals, "This is a good mate choice," the role of oxytocin in relationships has been sabotaged by unwise choices that are applauded by a broken society filled with broken homes and lives.

Is the lack of interaction between family members causing a deficiency in oxytocin production in the body? Could it be that consistently watching movies of love and romance is causing imbalances in both oxytocin and vasopressin (the male hormone involved in mating and affection)? Are you short-circuiting your relationships by substituting shallow movies that not only waste your time, but also your production of important neurotransmitters? Are you wasting your life on silly, romantic movies and daytime dramas, reality "love" shows, "virtual love" that gives you a false oxytocin boost but at the same time renders you less capable of knowing real love if it comes your way? Are you self-medicating emotional wounds by absorbing yourself in romantic movies and books? Will either of those truly heal a broken heart, soul, and spirit? Many times unresolved grief, disappointments in life, and unresolved conflicts are "medicated" by movies, television, and reading fiction. These issues are affecting your mind and your body. Perhaps it is time to expose the pain.

You control much about your own hormones and neurotransmitters by your daily choices and decisions. Your gut, food choices, vitamins, minerals, and enzymes play a major role in neurotransmitter and hormone production. Equally important is how you spend your time. All of your five senses are involved in good emotional and mental health. The touch of a hand, a hug, a kiss, and intimate contact increases oxytocin in women and men, causing men to cling to a woman they love.[26] This is too rare and wonderful to sabotage by consistent viewing of false love and false ideas about men and women.

Several decades ago, I began to notice that casual conversations revolved more and more around TV and movie plots and characters. Typically, when teens got together, they watched a movie. For the guys, sometimes it was a game or athletic event. Then, the ensuing conversation was about the movie or the game. I began to wonder if they knew how to have an evening of fun with conversation and activities without a movie or game. "Want to come over and watch a movie," was the norm for hanging out. We are, by design, social creatures and we like to be with people at least some of the time. But, have you tried to carry on a conversation with someone watching TV? You will note their eyes turn back to the TV even though they are trying to pay attention to you. True communication drops, and usually the speaker will either exit the room or tune in to the TV. If this is your child or partner, the message you are sending is loud and clear: TV is more important than what you have to say. In 1999, Western Reserve University looked at the viewing habits of over 2,000 children. Their findings were that those who watched the most TV were the most depressed, anxious, and angry.[27] That was 16 years ago. Do you think there is less TV watching now? How about content? Is it "better" or "worse"? Is this a path you need to be on hours and hours every day? Is this how to spend a life?

Almost every counselor who works with mental, emotional, and addictive disorders will agree that a breakdown in communication with family is common. "I can't talk to them," is frequently heard. Communication begins early in life. The soothing voice of the mother, the sounds of Daddy talking, the first words, and then childhood prattle. Babies who are left to cry and toddlers who are ignored perceive the message of "I am not listening to you." By the time the child reaches the preteen years, if a true communication of love has not been established—"I am listening to you and I enjoy listening to you and talking with you"—it's often too late. When children are punished according to the mood of the parent, you can expect the same response back from the teenager: *I will be a brat because I don't feel good (just like you were a brat-parent to me when you didn't feel good).*

Children learn attitudes by observing attitudes in their parents. If either mother or father tends to be moody and hold their family "hostage" according to the mood of the day, this will be reflected in their children. It will seem normal to them. If the family is happy only if Mom and/or Daddy are happy it represents a broken communication bridge. Becoming a mature adult, able to control moods and emotions, is not a matter of age. Sometimes self-examination is necessary if you are trying to help someone in your family. Unfortunately, generations can hold on to rage, moodiness, and poor emotional health, passing from generation to generation until someone breaks the mold. They make a decision to become emotionally healthy and to model that to their children and grandchildren.

Broken communication can be overcome, but why let it develop? Go the entire 100 percent if necessary to "cross the bridge" in order to really hear and understand the person in your life who is struggling with emotional, mental, and addictive disorders. Your daily choices dictate to a great extent your production of neurotransmitters.

Changing your mind necessitates a change in daily decisions and choices about how you spend your time. Your brain will continue to rebuild, restore, and develop throughout your lifetime. It was previously believed that brain development stopped at age eight. In later years, science said that the brain continued to develop into early adulthood. "You can't teach an old dog new tricks," became the maxim. However, in recent years, it has been discovered that the brain continues to learn and develop as long as it is involved in learning activities where action takes place with the learning. Interestingly, the only time the brain is static and "off duty" with development is when you are watching television. It really does "veg." In the elderly, television watching is linked to atrophy (shrinking) of the gray matter in the brain.[28] It is all too easy to retire and find there is not enough to do and no reason to leave the house. The recliner and remote control fill up the hours of the day and night, and life becomes a steady routine of watching television. Is it surprising that knees held in that position become painful even as the brain begins to develop *sundowners* or dementia?

Watching the screen—television or computer—is even more dangerous to an infant and developing toddler and child's brain. Over twenty years ago, when learning and behavior problems became more evident in the classroom, I began considering how the screen—as in television and computers—affected the emerging development of a child's brain. I noticed a peculiar pride in mothers and fathers when they told me that their four-month-old would "watch" television. Something in my "gut" told me this was not healthy. In June of 2003, I read that Dr. Jane Healy in *Failure to Connect* says *computer games and learning programs disrupt the normal brain development and actually prevent the brain from wiring itself properly.*[29] This is a very serious statement.

I also began hearing what I call *Teletubbies* Talk. The infant prattling sounds were sounding like the tones from the popular children's show. In addition, I began to wonder how an infant or toddler would learn how to talk properly with so many different voices and accents heard on television. The infant brain develops rapidly with neurons laying down pathways. As the infant observes though the eye, the brain begins to build pathways on how to eat with a spoon, for example. Confusing messages are relayed through television screens and computer screens. Equally alarming are the studies that indicate that an infant "fixes" on a mother's voice while in the womb. The sound of her voice is the sound the baby knows immediately after birth. There may be other voices—the father and siblings—but the most important voice is the mother's. Her voice is the guiding tone that the infant responds to and recognizes. In the cacophony of voices and sounds from an all-present television, a baby is hard-pressed to recognize his or her mother's voice.[30]

Years ago, I began to warn young mothers that I felt watching television did something to the brain, and that I felt ADHD was somehow connected to television and computer screens due to the way that light enters the brain. Then, in 1997, hundreds of Japanese children became ill with seizures and vomiting after watching a new cartoon, *Pokemon*. Doctors attributed it to the flashing red lights in the eyes of the main character.[31] Many clinical studies now report irregular brain neuron development in children under age two who watch television. Brain signaling across hemispheres as well as neurons are affected, causing "wiring" to be inefficient and potentially harmed.[32]

Now, it is commonly known that the American Academy of Pediatrics recommends that children under age two not watch television, videos, or computers due to evidence of language delays and links to ADHD.[33] A recent report indicates that there is increased aggression in three year olds who watched TV directly or indirectly—the TV is on in the house.[34] Increasingly, research is leading to not just academic deficiencies and behavior issues being linked to infants and children watching television and using computer and iPad screens, but also to structural changes in the brain that can affect function for a lifetime.[35]

How can making the choice to turn off the television, computer, and other electronics change emotional, mental, and addictive disorders? What the mind perceives and how the cells respond determines neurotransmitter production and efficiency. Preventing these disorders in developing children and teenagers is a revolving door—exit, or just keep going around and around. There is really not a "safe" limit even though this sounds unrealistic. I am often asked, "How long should I allow my baby (or child) to watch television?" No one can answer that question; it's like asking how long should your child be exposed to toxins or danger. I am not sure there is a "safe" time limit. The way the light enters the brain affects brain development; the rapid moving screen, especially HDTV, affects the brain processes; and the content determines to a great extent how your child views life and humanity.

There is a quote by eighteenth-century English poet and artist William Blake that says, *We become what we behold.* If we behold vulgarity, violence, antisocial behavior, pornography, and unhealthy nudity, murders, and gratuitous sex, etc. we can expect our children and grandchildren and future generations to degrade even further into lower standards of living. Your choices affect every cell in your body and the production and efficiency of your neurotransmitters and, to a great extent, those of your children and members of your household. We truly are in a battle for the mind and the soul.

CHAPTER 6

Beginning Today: You Control More Than You Think You Do

As I reflect on more than fifty years of listening and counseling, there is one cause that seems to overwhelm and derail many people; in fact, it's one you have encountered regardless of your mental health. *Willpower.* The battle to make ourselves do what needs to be done is often lost to the powerful pull of procrastination, discouragement, and apathy. Being defeated time and again causes the mind to think, *It won't work for me. It may work for other people, but not for me. Why even try?*

Then, of course, the lure of escape begins. "I don't want to think about this right now; what can I do to get my mind off of this?" If this continues long enough, all too often, a person gives in or gives up. They simply, like a fish on a line, let themselves be drawn deeper and deeper into whatever emotional, mental, or addictive disorder is threatening their lives. Others may begin to consider suicide. Suicide can be by slow degrees. I've spoken to people who have strong "death wishes." They don't want to hurt their families anymore. Instead, they begin to consider how they can die naturally. They begin to intentionally crash their health or mull over how to stage an "accidental" death.

Taking the first step toward emotional, mental, and addictive re-covery and positive good health begins with understanding what is mal-functioning in the body. Often, psychiatrists and medical doctors will give a patient a questionnaire about symptoms in an effort to prescribe the best antidepressant, etc. This is not a perfect science, and it's some-times difficult to know which is the best drug for the patient. This is common procedure due to medical training and America's propensity to want "instant cures." "Doc, can you give me a pill to change my life? This one is not worth living."

In the 1960s, pills offered great hope. Now, five decades later, we have reasons to suspect pills designed to help the brain function better could make matters worse. Side effects may be more dangerous than the disorder, in some cases. Indeed, one of the disturbing side effects that recently came to light is that antipsychotic drugs may actually shrink the brain.[1] For those of you who have been taking prescribed pills for emo-tional, mental, and addictive disorders, it is imperative that you don't stop taking those medications without medical supervision. Stopping "cold turkey" can result in seizures and death. Instead, if you want to explore malfunctions in the body and brain, which may be behind the malfunctions in the emotions and mind, you may want to find deficien-cies and overloads. This is best done by finding a doctor who will order metabolic testing from reputable labs, and a doctor who knows how to read the results.

Dr. William Walsh, who has documented this sort of testing for over 30,000 patients identifying their underlying problems, says he sees an 80 to 90 percent cure rate in depressive disorders and 70 percent in schizophrenia. His work is based on Dr. Abram Hoffer's work mentioned earlier and Dr. Charles Pfeiffer. Dr. Walsh is training physicians from several nations in nutrient treatments for psychiatric disorders. His goal is train thousands of these doctors in restoring normal function to the body and brain.[2]

Taking the first step toward recovery may seem impossible due to your finances. Unfortunately, most insurance companies will only cover partial lab testing. It may be difficult for you to ask your doctor to order these tests, but you deserve real answers to the malfunction in your body. That step forward may also be hindered by the familiar procrastination or fear that you cannot be helped. Knowledge of how the body affects the mind, however, can be the key to unlocking doors for you.

Even taking a baby step in the right direction can make a difference. The larger step is a jump—a jump across a chasm of ignorance, doubt, fear, supposition, and manipulation by forces of greed that enslave millions to pharmaceuticals. There are medical conditions that need to be treated by medicine, and we are grateful for medical knowledge and medicine when that is the best course of action. However, when a system is failing and you are falling with it, it is time to exercise your will. There is no substitute for your *will* in your own recovery.

It may be too difficult to change the entire direction of your life in one day, unless that decision is to find out the overloads and deficiencies in your own body and brain. Surprisingly, your own efforts to self-medicate by taking multivitamins and supplements may be derailing your success. For example, if you already have a copper overload, taking a multivitamin with copper can make you worse. If you are already too high in folic acid, taking folic acid makes you worse. If you are too high in certain amino acids, you add to the overload. The overload of amino acids in protein shakes may be detrimental and can raise serotonin and dopamine and other neurotransmitters too high. Be wary of any food that is not in its natural composition as found in nature.

Exercising your will to "get to the bottom" of your disorder—or that of someone you love—must be followed by compliance. That means you must use your will to stay on the protocol for months instead of expecting full recovery in a few days. It takes a long time to rebuild many cells. For example, it takes a year for many brain cells to rebuild. A steady course of improvement—better than you were—depends on you doing what you can do to get well. If you are in the bottom of a well and someone throws you a rope, take it.

Another aspect of the *will*, your most important ally or enemy in recovery, is substituting healthy alternatives for activities that pull you down. Leaving your old group of friends behind is one of the most difficult. After all, they have been there for you, encouraging you to do what they are doing, handing you another drink or drugs—providing a ball and chain along with their friendship. The need for "family" is a very real and important human need. Breaking away may be the hardest and most important step you make. Finding and establishing healthy relationships in another group may be what you need to increase your own willpower.

Like the sheep in our pasture at home, we tend to like being with the herd at least some of the time. An ill sheep separates from the flock. If we can't help that sheep, it will eventually turn its face away from the herd and die. Sheep don't fight to live. When they are not ill, our sheep stay on the same path through the pasture, day after day, season after season, following each other. That path is filled with urine and feces; it's often muddy and slushy, giving them painful foot-rot; it's not the shortest distance to their destination; and it's easy for a predator to track them. However, they walk right behind each other on the same path.

When you watch this day after day, you just can't help but wonder why one of the sheep doesn't "get it" and start a new path through the fresh, clean grass. Regardless of our efforts to explain to them that it's a bad choice to stay on that same path, they just keep walking. Now, there's a difference in a sheep and you. You can divide your friends into two groups: 1) those who are heading in the right direction in life and 2) those who aren't. If you want to get well, you must not think about their loss right now; you must think about yourself. Maybe you can help them later, but many addicts who gain a measure of freedom want to go back to help their friends. Before long, they are back on the same path. Cutting off toxic relationships is as important as cutting off toxic chemicals in your recovery.

Finding the will to recover may lie in a decision to change your mind about yourself. Not everyone is born bright and beautiful with an athletic body to rich parents. Maybe you feel you drew the short straw, and everyone else in your family got the best physical and mental attributes. Maybe you have a disability; maybe you have been dogged by extreme poverty. How can you find the will to try or to try again? What if you don't have a reservoir of happy memories? What if you are alone in your efforts, facing disbelief from family and rejection?

Have you ever taken someone else's word for something? As simple as it sounds, deciding to take someone else's research, knowledge, and experience as truth for your own life may put your foot on the first step toward recovery, even if that means a brand new path for you. If you are struggling with an emotional, mental, or addictive disorder, you may not be able to see where the path leads any more than I could see beyond the horizon when I was walking on the beach. As you know, the horizon is not a stationary point. It will just keep moving ahead of you. How do you know that happiness, contentment, fulfillment, and freedom from addiction is not possible for you? Take the word of people who now walk in freedom and contentment—it begins with a first step. The Chinese proverb, *A journey of a thousand miles begins with a single step*, emphasizes the importance of that first step.

In addition to the power of your personal will, as weak as you feel that may be, making initial steps to change your choices of how you spend your time and what you eat can begin to make significant changes in your mind and personality. Simple acts like living with fewer electrical lights and more natural lighting can begin to reset your serotonin and melatonin levels. Sitting under an electric light at night, using your iPad, computer, TV, or cell phone interrupts your production of melatonin, confusing your body as to daylight and dark. This is due to *blue light*, which is beneficial in the daytime to improve serotonin and melatonin production. Red light, on the other hand, is the natural color that tells the body to get ready for sleep. In the evening, the body needs to gear down so that the sleep process can begin. In nature, we have blue light in the daytime, and as evening draws near, the setting of the sun causes red light to be more plentiful. Physical health and mental health are dependent on sleep.

Some of you will remember Macbeth's soliloquy in Shakespeare's drama of the Scottish lord who murdered King Duncan and usurped the throne. In it, Macbeth, now torn by anguish, longs to sleep but sleep evades him:

Sleep that knits up the ravell'd sleave of care,
The death of each day's life, sore labour's bath,
Balm of hurt minds, great nature's second course,
Chief nourisher in life's feast (Act II, scene ii, line 34).

Shakespeare says it so well—sleep does give us a reprieve when
we are burdened. It ends the day, regardless of how the day played
out; it refreshes the body and heals sore, aching muscles; it soothes
mental pain; it is the nourishment that allows us to keep our bodies
alive. If you don't sleep, you will eventually die, as the body cannot remain alive without the cleansing and rebuilding of cells that sleep produces. Short-changing your sleep is extremely damaging to the mind
as well as the body. The importance of sleep and the effects of sleep
deprivation are often overlooked in emotional, mental, and addictive
disorders. Sometimes the slippery path of addiction begins with an
over-the-counter sleep aid, increases with prescription sleep medicine,
and evolves into full-blown addiction as the body spirals deeper into
physiological and psychological distress. It is common now to hear that
children are being given sleep medications because they cannot fall
asleep and/or stay asleep.

When I was a child growing up in the South, I used to love summer
evenings. Without television and air conditioning, most of us headed
to the porch. The crickets and night insects were chirping, and we'd
watch fireflies light up the sky. The red glow of sunset had signaled the
end of the day's work and electricity was to be "saved." On our porch,
you could smell gardenias and tea olive blossoms. If the soft summer
breeze was just right, you could smell the magnolias. Gentle evenings
with the old folks rocking in their rockers with simple conversations
about the day's work and what needed to be done the next day helped
me as a child to learn the importance of finishing tasks and how my role
contributed to the family. Some evenings we would shell peas and but-
terbeans, turning baskets of them into small piles of the shelled beans
and peas by the evening's close. I loved getting to run to the pasture
and throw the hulls to the cows or pigs. Eventually, the adults would
head off to bed. I dreaded the words "time to go to bed" as I longed to
hold on to the day.

In our busy lives today filled with the glare of electric lights and few fireflies due to pesticides, we have to make time to sleep. Insomnia can be caused by physical disorders like hypo or hyperthyroidism, irregular hormones in males and females, pain, chronic disease, and mental activity that includes too much processing and worrying, as well as anxiety. When a person is not producing enough melatonin, the "sleep" hormone, their sleep will be affected and will worsen as melatonin production remains low. Getting enough sunshine and light, preparing for sleep in the evening by turning off all electronics an hour before bedtime, removing all electronics from bedroom (including cell phone), and eating a tryptophan-enriched snack before bedtime may be enough to cure insomnia.

For many of us, the day doesn't seem long enough to finish tasks. Busy mothers working as well as managing a household often report often having only five or six hours of time to sleep. Many people work night shifts and second jobs. Most of us need "downtime," and all too often that "downtime" is in front of a computer. Life and its demands can be the reason that many are sleep deprived and are living less than their best due to loss of sleep. Maybe it's FaceTime, or Twitter, or eBay, etc. The combination of electronics, blue light, surfing the TV or web, and mindless activity is not a good "bedtime snack." Instead, it works the opposite way. It's a good plan to turn off your electronics at least an hour before bedtime in order for your mind to start "downloading" the effects of the day.

Even if it's educational, you are not retaining what you are watching. The brain is designed to be involved in learning. For those of you over 25, remember when we used to draw a map and give landmarks when we were giving directions? Then, the next time we drove the route, even without our directions, we could usually find the destination, unless it was complex with lots of different streets. Even then, most of us could figure it out. What about now with your GPS? Have you noticed you don't remember how to "get there" and have to reset your GPS to the address? That's because you are not laying down neural pathways as you did when your brain had to concentrate on a drawn map and landmarks. This carries over into *all* electronic learning. Unless the brain is actively involved and is laying down neural pathways, it doesn't consider that information important.[3] Try this out for yourself. There is no substitute for hands-on learning.

With that in mind, the major reason for lack of sleep is simply not going to bed during the time the body is designed to sleep. As twilight falls, the day darkens, and night descends, bodies of humans and animals receive natural signals to rest and sleep. When those signals are ignored, the "second wind" sets in. Then, it's often close to daylight when the body finally demands rest. While this is convenient in emergencies and urgent events in life, daily postponing sleep and staying up late can induce depression.

While working with teenagers, it was easy to know whose parents insisted on a reasonable bedtime. They were more alert, more pleasant, learned quicker, and retained information. When I would question a drowsy student, it was usually the same answers—up late watching TV, on the Internet, talking on the phone, and video games. Sometimes it was because the teen was working trying to pay for a car and insurance at age sixteen. Schoolwork suffered, as well as family relationships as the car was another reason to argue. Our American culture has been built around "gimme" and "I want." A conversation with the parent usually resulted in, "He wanted his own TV; that was his birthday present; he's sixteen and should be big enough to go to bed when he's sleepy," etc. Those parents who consistently chose *what's best for you* gained more respect from their children. However, getting even a great parent to understand the connection between good sleep and good mental health was often difficult. Often, I found the parent also struggled with sleep issues—sleep apnea, insomnia, and sleep deprivation. At their wits' end, they had simply given up. A report from Columbia University says teens with a bedtime of after midnight were 24 percent more likely to have depression; 20 percent were more likely to think about suicide. Those with less than five hours of sleep a night were at a 48 percent greater risk of suicidal thoughts.[4]

Even a few weeks of sleep deprivation can cause or mimic emotional and mental disorders. Depression, anxiety, obsessive-compulsive, manic-depression, anger, rage, and suicide can follow sleep deprivation. In fact, it is almost impossible to diagnose the difference—unless the ill person recognizes that sleep is the problem and makes steps to change his or her life. If a person starts using sleeping pills, a rebound can occur where the person cannot sleep without a pill. Due to the gravity of sleep deprivation, an entire family may need to adapt and change in order to help the person heal.

A TV, even in the next room on low, may be enough to keep another person awake. Due to the way the body is designed, even a tiny nightlight may be enough to keep a sleep-challenged person from falling asleep or from staying asleep. A completely pitch black, dark room with no light is best for restful sleep.[5] A partner's snoring can also bring about sleep deprivation leading to many physical diseases as well as depression and anxiety. If you are fighting an emotional, mental, or addictive disorder, use your will to make yourself go to bed. Use your will to establish new patterns for going to bed and getting up. The will is hard to tame, but the dividends from regular, eight-hours-per-night sleep may be all it takes to get you on the road to recovery.

The CDC (Center for Disease Control) estimates that 50- to 70 million people in America have some form of sleep disorder.[6] There is no way to estimate how many traffic accidents and disasters have occurred that may have been linked to sleep deprivation and how it affects job performance. A quick Internet search will yield surprising results on major disasters that occurred when workers were sleep deprived. According to Dr. Matthew Walker, Director of the Sleep and Neuroimaging Laboratory, University of California, Berkeley, sleep disruption is present in most psychiatric disorders. His studies show that brain activity in the sleep-deprived makes a major shift, causing 60 percent more hyperactivity in the emotional centers of the brain. He says that normal people will show psychiatric disturbances with sleep disturbances and that it's difficult to separate sleep deprivation and a psychiatric disease.[7] In addition, the Mayo Clinic says the quantity of sleep is linked to weight gain. Too little or too much sleep may be causing weight gain.[8] Proper sleep hygiene benefits body and soul.

A steady diet of electronic overload, positive ions, poor gut flora, lack of proper amino acids, and sleep deprivation is a recipe that can truly "drive you out of your mind." Can we expect children to navigate this course if adults can't? Getting a good night's sleep involves making hard decisions with your will to change your life. It may mean a different job and, for some people, even moving to a different area where outdoor time is more inviting, or acquiring the knowledge of recent inventions in light therapy, negative ion therapy, and dietary supplements to balance out what's lacking in the body and what nature intended. An example is the use of melatonin, the "sleep" hormone that is often referred as effective for *jet lag*. Jet lag occurs when you cross time zones and your internal body has to catch up with your external body. You may be in Okinawa, but your internal clock thinks you are in Orlando if that is where you live. Taking a small dose of melatonin enables that "clock" to reset—to help the body return to a natural circadian rhythm. Because it is a naturally occurring hormone, it is generally considered to be safe (GRAS) for those who can't sleep.[9] Because it is not habit forming, it may be effective in enabling someone who takes sleep medications to wean themselves. Of course, the best way to reset the internal clock in normal, everyday activities is to get outside in the sunlight and add exercise, walking, gardening, etc. Even a few minutes a day can make a significant difference as you are determining to change your sleeping habits.

While you are sleeping, your brain gets to work cleaning out toxins and wastes. Recent discoveries indicate that the brain relaxes cells while you are asleep, creating space for cerebral spinal fluid to move into typically closed spaces to clean out toxins.[10] Without sufficient sleep, this does not occur and those toxins build up. We are exposed to chemicals, pollution, pesticides, herbicides, heavy metals, and medications daily. Residue settles in cell receptors interrupting proper brain activity including neurotransmitter production and efficiency.

Another major ally in your fight to exercise your will is the production of some amazing enzymes that not only work while you are sleeping, but also while you are awake. These enzymes work to clean out the toxins that may be causing malfunctions in your brain that affect your body. In fact, when these enzymes are effectively being produced, your cravings for sugar, alcohol, nicotine, and other addictive substances, including carbohydrates, may decrease. Normalizing glutamate and dopamine production decrease cravings for addictive substances.[11]

Your body naturally produces *anti-oxidant enzymes*—superheroes in the fight against *oxidative stress*, which may be the major cause of physical and mental disease and aging. These enzymes cross the blood-brain barrier, converting toxins, causing residues and toxins to become a part of cerebral spinal fluid so that these harmful residues can be emptied out of the body. Three of these enzymes, *superoxide dismutase, catalase,* and *glutathione,* are so important that low production can not only lead to diseases like Alzheimer's, dementia, MS, ALS (Lou Gehrig disease), and hundreds of physical disorders, but low production is also linked to psychiatric disorders as well as addictions. Dr. Martha Herbert, leading Harvard physician in ADD/ADHD and Autism, says she is convinced that low glutathione is the link to these disorders.[12] This is a powerful statement considering her position of influence among medical doctors and researchers in this field.

Every cell in the body makes glutathione, and all cells have to have it. It affects muscle recovery, the liver, the kidneys, and all functions in the body. However, the brain uses the most glutathione. You can't live without it. If you are not producing enough glutathione and other anti-oxidant enzymes, your body and brain will show it. The body will build high levels of *oxidative stress*—the accumulation of free radicals, which are molecules with unpaired electrons.

The free radical molecule reacts with other molecules causing a chain reaction that can lead to cellular damage. When the cell is overwhelmed with free radical damage, the end result can be disease and malfunction. Your body's defense system—antioxidant enzymes—are donors of electrons. They "lend" the free radical an electron without becoming depleted. In other words, they eliminate free radicals by stabilizing them. Oxidative stress is linked to psychiatric disorders as well as addiction and may turn out to be the major cause of psychiatric and addictive disorders.[13] There are over one hundred and fifty thousand clinical studies on pubmed.gov concerning *oxidative stress.* Pubmed.gov is internationally recognized and used by medical scientists and researchers as an online medical library for peer reviewed science.

Due to the importance of glutathione in the body, injections, IVs, and oral supplements have been used to try to increase glutathione. However, these are not sustainable as the body recognizes glutathione and digests it. Neither NAC (N-Acetyl-Cysteine) nor *cysteine,* the precursor, can produce adequate glutathione when used as supplements. Due to the changes in foods, it is almost impossible to give your body enough building blocks to make adequate antioxidant enzymes, including this most important antioxidant enzyme, glutathione, whose job it is to clean out toxins in the cells, especially those in the brain. A toxic brain unable to clean out toxins will store toxins.

Recent research is pointing to the use of acetaminophen as a cause, maybe the major cause, of low glutathione production. Taking acetaminophen slows down and stops the production of glutathione for hours.[14] For many people, taking a couple of acetaminophen tablets is an everyday occurrence. Most people know that acetaminophen should not be used with alcohol due to potential liver toxicity and death; however, they assume it's fine to use it in cold and fever preparations and give to infants and children. Preventing the body from producing glutathione is extremely dangerous and contributes to an inflamed, diseased brain that no longer functions properly. In a rapidly developing brain between birth and age three, acetaminophen can cause serious damage. Some scientists are labeling it as one of, if not the cause of autism due to the reduction in glutathione production. Dr. William Shaw, Ph.D. has published a very thorough study called *Increased Acetaminophen Use Appears to be Major Cause of the Epidemics of Autism, ADHD, and Asthma.*[15]

Interestingly, when a person overdoses on acetaminophen or there is significant liver toxicity from acetaminophen, the standard medical procedure in the emergency room is to flood the body with IVs of NAC in order to try to produce enough glutathione to clean out the acetaminophen from the cells in the body and brain. For the past decade, glutathione has grabbed the attention of many research scientists as more is discovered about how glutathione affects the body and brain. We will explore the role of glutathione in addictions in a following chapter. Suffice it to say that you will hear more about glutathione from medical professionals as research expands almost daily concerning the link to many mental and physical diseases. Presently, low glutathione is linked to cancer and neurological, immune, cardiovascular, thyroid, pancreatic, and inflammatory conditions, including macular degeneration. Your best ally against declining health in the biochemical arsenal is probably glutathione, especially with the brain.

When you are awake, very little cerebral spinal fluid flows into the brain. It is during sleep that the antioxidant enzymes move toxins into the CSF in the brain so those toxins can leave the body and recycle the CSF. Swedish scientists report that missing just one night's sleep increases the amount of certain substances that are present in damaged brains.[16] A baby can be born with low production of antioxidant enzymes. A child's natural production of antioxidant enzymes may have been slowed or hindered. Additionally, there are other factors such as a diet too low in antioxidant fruits and vegetables and aging.

As we age, we decrease in production of these powerhouse enzymes, which may explain the decline in mental function and changes in personalities. A chain reaction is slowly set in place—less glutathione, less ability to convert harmful toxins into fluids that are able to leave the body. Because much of this conversion occurs during sleep, when you add up poor sleeping and low glutathione, you can get a silent takeover of the brain which will not only lead to emotional and mental disorders but also physical disease. Getting consistent sleep and producing enough glutathione may be the prescriptions you need to correct many mental and physical disorders.

Using your own willpower may be the most difficult part of your recovery or that of your loved one. We often consider the power of the mind to heal, but much of this is due to willpower. When the emotions are torn and bruised, making the choice to go to bed is not as attractive as other activities, especially if those activities involve addictions. Often we consider only drugs and alcohol as addictions; however, choices become habitual.

For example, start stopping for donuts and coffee at a certain place each morning. Within a day or two, even as you get near the location, your body and mind will suggest, "Want to stop for donuts and coffee?" Even though you know (and you do) that sugar-laden pastries are bad for the body and the brain, it may be almost impossible to resist that donut, especially if it's nice and warm. Even if you decide to just get coffee, the smell may draw you in and you find yourself saying, "Add a raspberry jam donut to that order."

A simple illustration, but your body and its demands are not always in your best health interests. No, in fact, an inflamed brain that hasn't rested will be carrying toxic neurochemicals and waste that the brain desperately needs to detoxify. On "empty" and needing to concentrate to do your job, your brain will ask you for something to make you feel better. That's when your knowledge and willpower need to join together to defend you against your own poor decisions. Make a good choice for protein and something healthy.

Controlling the will in changing your emotional, mental, and addictive disorders may not have worked for you before. You tried and failed, again and again. Due to the delicate balance of the brain's "chemical soup," you may not have had the cooperation of your body as you tried to "change your mind." The body and soul (mind, will, and emotions) work in tandem; if one is imbalanced, the other will be. The road to recovery involves changing the will, which affects your emotions and mental processes, which affect the cells in your body, which affect the mind, will, and emotions. Your decisions affect your cells; your cells affect your decisions. Until both are corrected, you may bounce up and down without long-term sustained improvement until you become confused and hopeless. Your lifelong habits, which enabled toxins to gain a stronghold in your body, thus affecting the brain, may be holding you hostage. Your own willpower has to be activated to win this victory.

Finding your way out of emotional, mental, and addictive disorders involves every day of your life. You may not have initiated the path that led to where you are. It may have begun before you were born, generations ago. However, *you* now determine where that path will lead. It can lead into darker and darker places, or you can begin another path, one that takes you away from the darkness. Would simple choices be worth it if six months from now you are *better*? If a year from now, you are medicine-free and addiction-free and you have a new life? If it takes a year for some brain cells to be rebuilt, the best time to start rebuilding those cells is today.

CHAPTER 7

Finding Solutions:
Developing a Healthy Mind

Just as certain conditions in your body affect your brain chemistry, your daily choices as to how you spend your time affect your brain chemistry. Your brain chemistry in return affects your body and your health in general. It's difficult to separate one from the other. You may feel like a dog chasing its tail, going nowhere and making no progress. Depression and other psychiatric disorders make you feel bad; you just don't feel good enough to change your life. Addiction is obsessive by its very definition; you are driven with an uncontrollable urgency to get more of the addictive substance or activity. Your mind and body—already inflamed, malfunctioning, and ill—spiral deeper and deeper. Due to the undeserved shame of emotional, mental, and addictive disorders, a person may only accept help when the body is ill.

While the underlying cause of the illness may be a collapse of the soul—the mind, will, and emotions—the symptoms of disease are real because the mind affects the cells in the body just as the body affects the brain, which to a great extent determines how you perceive life and relate to the people around you. A sick body can make a sick mind; a sick mind can make a body sick. It's often difficult for a physician to know the difference. Lab tests are helpful, but those tests must be designed to look for underlying conditions that are not routinely tested.

In fact, when it comes to common diseases like heart, blood pressure, cancer, diabetes, and neurodegenerative disease, your physician may tell you that you need to reduce the "stress" in your life. Stress is both mental and *oxidative*—it is in your cells. Mental stress tends to build more oxidative stress; oxidative stress increases your mental stress. This is a two way street that can lead to a "dead end."

The Center for Disease Controls says that 85 percent of diseases most likely have an emotional link.[1] That may be surprising to hear, but if you consider what happens to your body when you are emotionally upset, it all adds up. Your heart starts pounding, your blood pressure increases, your adrenaline surges, your cortisol rises. Just as your subconscious brain cannot discern between real and virtual in a TV drama, sports, or video game, the emotion center of the brain can respond in much the same way.

Due to the emotional intensity of the circumstances, you may have the impulse of *fight or flight*. All systems are on alert. That can include the emotional response to sorrow, emotional wounding, fear, trauma, physical injury, and many other emotions. The sudden burst of cortisol and adrenaline can be very beneficial in helping you become creative in a dangerous situation or even in job related stress where you need to perform or produce with excellence. However, keeping these hormones high due to emotional stress—whether real or imaginary—affects not only your hormones, but also your blood sugar levels. There are a number of studies that link emotional duress to the development of type II diabetes.[2] Interestingly, type II diabetes rates are three times higher in patients with bipolar disorder.[3] In August of 2015, a very important study linking bipolar to metabolic disorders was published, which may open the door to additional research on links between metabolic and mental disorders.[4]

More commonly known is the link between emotions and the heart. "She died of a broken heart," is actually possible. Sorrow, especially tragedy and senseless loss of life or suicides in a family, can lead to serious health problems in the future, including cancer.[5]

Where the heart is concerned, it is well known that anger, rage, shouting, and grief affect the levels of C-reactive protein, an inflammation marker for the heart. More important than cholesterol, high C-reactive protein (CRP) indicates that heart functions need attention. Recycling stressful memories and battling stressful decisions can raise this marker; trauma experienced in childhood can increase the likelihood of heart problems in the future.[6] Anger takes such a toll that up to *two hours after an angry outburst, people had nearly a five-fold increase in heart attack risk, and a three-fold risk increase for stroke.*[7]

Surprisingly, stress hormones are also heightened and on constant alert when people are lonely and remain in isolation and solitude. If this is not corrected, the immune system begins to break down. Many of us have seen this—there is a loss of mate or child, a divorce, or even an "empty nest" and a formerly healthy person develops a chronic health problem.[8] Rejection and loneliness are evil twins in breaking down health.

Negative emotions such as aggression, hatred, prejudice, anxiety, hopelessness, and insecurity not only hurt the people around you; these emotions hurt your health. If you are suffering from any sort of heart problem, it's imperative to change your emotional response to adversity. Just plain old being grumpy, hard-to-please, stubborn, and resistant to change not only hurts the people around you, it can damage your heart. Deciding to change how you respond may actually save your life and reduce the stress in the family that has to deal with you.

Psychological trauma changes brain structure, affecting the part of the brain associated with emotions and survival.[9] In recent years, there have been thousands of people, male and female, who have developed eating disorders. While we may remember reading in literature or hearing someone speak of someone who "just pined away," we may not associate that with present-day eating disorders. Yet they represent the same grief and trauma processes in the body. The body could not withstand the level of grief or trauma. It's not enough to say to someone who has experienced deep grief, trauma, or offense to their body and/ or soul, "Just get over it." We cannot measure how another person feels, or even what we would do or how our bodies would respond in the same circumstances. What one person can handle may break another person's mind and body. We are not carbon copies of each other; emotional pain in another person may not be the same measure as emotional pain in another.

When a person experiences trauma or maintains high stress levels for a period of time, the origination of most diseases, *inflammation,* increases and continues to increase. Until a few years ago, the high stress connection to development of illness was not understood from a scientific viewpoint. It was evident, yet it was not understood in cellular biology. Several years ago, Carnegie Mellon University reported that the body loses its ability to regulate inflammation when cortisol is chronically elevated. Cortisol's job is to handle sudden stress. Prolonged stress—such as is common in our hectic lifestyles, jobs, and family life—renders cortisol less effective in counteracting stress. The immune system becomes insensitive, causing the person to be more susceptible to infection, illness, and the development of chronic health problems.[10] In short, the body breaks down under constant stress.

Inflammation is now considered the cause of most diseases. In 2004, *Time* magazine's cover highlighted the link of inflammation to disease. Now, a decade later, research continues to uncover the links between high adrenaline, cortisol, inflammation, oxidative stress, and disease.[11] For many years stress has been considered as one of the causes for autoimmune disorders. In an effort to meet some high demand, the body launches a full attack on "invaders." When the attack on the body, mind, will, and emotions lessens and maybe even ceases, the body forgets who the enemy is; it continues to attack and attack the person's body. Stress can trigger and then retrigger autoimmune attacks.[12]

Just as the memory of my walk on the beach can raise my neurotransmitters and bring about calming influences in my brain, so ruminating and obsessively thinking about what has happened in your life that shouldn't have happened, or what could happen, can derail your health. *Regret* is a powerful emotion, causing all sorts of chemical changes in your body, and is considered a significant cause of depression.[13] Sadly, regret hinders us from recovering from stressful events, making us our own "worst enemy" in moving forward with life.

Finding motivation to change how you think is not an easy task. Yet the results can be life-changing as stress chemicals and inflammation are lowered. It is not uncommon, when the cause of a chronic disease isn't found, that a person will receive a prescription for an antidepressant. This is a not an "easy way out" for the doctor; instead, it is an attempt to lower the body's physical response by easing emotional stress.

In children, the task of diagnosis is even more challenging. A physician may grapple with whether a condition is genetic, environmental, traumatic, psychological, or physiological. With autism and other neurological malfunctions in the body, it may be all of the above, made more difficult by a child's inability to describe the symptoms. Many desperate parents go from doctor to doctor, hoping the next one will be able to "fix" their child. Complex questions in health and how the emotions affect health don't have easy answers; the answers may be more complex than the questions.

The good news is that by changing your emotional response, you can improve your health and the health of those around you. The constancy of a family being held "hostage" by another family member's outbursts of anger, hostility, aggression, or bouts of depression, mania, or threats of suicide can be changed. The problem is that change demands the cooperation of the person who may consciously or subconsciously practice acute or passive aggression against the loved ones.

Families tend to protect their family members. Children have been known to lie about abuse in order to protect their father, mother, or other family member because they are afraid of worse treatment or because they love the person. Maybe their mother has an angry outburst followed by waves of physical hugging and kissing the child. *Maybe that's all the physical love the child experiences.* Sadly, sometimes a child will misbehave intentionally in order to get the parent's attention. They will act out and receive the punishment because they know they will later be loved and hugged by the parent.

Remember the body's need for oxytocin? This need can be so great that the child or adult will tolerate abuse in exchange for the mother's hugs and love after the abuse. In fact, manipulation of a child's emotions by holding back or using love as a reward is a cause of emotional instability in later years. As an adult trying to be a spouse or parent, the childhood treatment has become a part of the personality. Many families "walk on eggshells" in order to keep someone from disrupting a day or evening. Is this a way to raise a child? Is it a way to "love" your family? Is it a path to health and wellness for you?

If you have been depressed for a few years, or for as long as you can remember, it's important for you to solve that depression whether it is from gut and the ensuing neurotransmitter inefficiency or from events and circumstances in your life. There are therapies and counseling that can help, as well as simply being outside and among people, but these alone are rarely adequate to heal long-term depression. Nor are they effective if you have an underlying and undiagnosed malfunction in the body, such as a thyroid disorder, blood sugar issue, or low glutathione production.

Recent research says that depression actually shrinks the hippocampus and the amygdala in the brain. The good news is that it can be reversed as the hippocampus can regenerate neural connections rapidly.[14] The hippocampus is responsible for memory consolidation and affects our ability to suppress and resist unwanted thoughts and memories. It also affects weight gain.[15] The partnership of depression and weight gain has shackled millions of people as they try to lose weight but are driven to overconsumption of carbohydrates as the body tries to produce enough serotonin for the body and brain.

With the breakthrough in understanding that the body and brain operate together and the body determines to such a great extent how the brain functions, it is predictable that a lot of what we know about mental and addictive disorders will be completely revolutionized in the next decade. We cannot separate the mind from the body as the functions of each are dependent on the other.

With that in mind, let's consider how other emotions may affect the body. The following symptoms are from a list of how worry and anxiety affect the body: difficulty swallowing, dry mouth, dizziness, rapid heartbeat, headaches, muscle aches and tension, dizziness, nausea, shortness of breath, excessive sweating, and tremors.[16] These are physical symptoms of a condition in the *mind* that responds to a real or supposed threat. Whereas the bank is not likely to hunt you down and beat you up, your mind, frantic over paying your mortgage, responds with *fight or flight*.

Post-Traumatic Stress Disorder is considered an emotional or mental disorder. However, clinical studies show that there is a physical breakdown in the body as well due to high oxidative stress in the body and brain.[17] It is impossible to separate the physical symptoms as if the person had a separate health problem. Proper metabolic balancing heals not only the mind, but also the body.

Most of us could easily associate high blood pressure with anger or resentfulness, holding a grudge, or hatred, but these conditions in the mind can actually cause the cholesterol[18] and triglyceride levels to increase.[19] It may be that the reason your medicine is "not working" is due to unsettled emotional issues. Harvard University links chronic respiratory, gastric problems, and heart problems to anxiety.[20] Rheumatic arthritis has been linked to depression. It is not known whether the pain produces the depression or vice versa.

What about jealousy? Studies show a link to a greater risk for Alzheimer's.[21] Vindictiveness? Resentfulness? There is even a new disorder named PTED which stands for *Post Traumatic Embitterment Disorder.* This disorder tends to follow an event so negative to the person's emotions that they can no longer function normally. Not surprisingly, it can affect the body in much the same way as PTSD.[22]

People react differently to stress and emotional pain; for one person, it can be heart disease. For another, cancer. Yale University published a study in 2014 indicating that stress could be the cause of cancer as certain "pathways" in the body were affected.[23] You may have noticed how someone who goes through a death of a loved one, a divorce, or some emotional trauma develops cancer within a few years. The mind is not healed; thus, the body suffers. Even the pH (balance of acidity and alkalinity in the stomach) is affected by the emotions. Fear, anger, and any sort of emotional upheaval, even happy ones, can affect the respiratory system, changing breathing patterns. This affects the pH of the fluids in the body, which affects every organ, causing the pH to become acidic.[24] An acid environment is associated with bacterial growth and many diseases, including cancer. Liver, kidney, pancreas, the skin, and the gall bladder are all affected by the emotions. Women with gall bladder conditions were found to have higher stress, depression, aggression, and emotional instability according to a research study in Germany.[25] It is important to understand that not all gallstones, kidney stones, and other health problems are caused by unsettled emotional distress. These are presented to show the intricate balance in the person, mind, and body. The search for emotional and mental health involves health for the body as well as for the soul.

There are many unknown reasons why the body reacts to our emotional health, but because cells remember pain there is a good possibility that painful memories affect pathways in the body. In addiction, families tend to teach "problem-solving" techniques to their children. One family may scream and rage when things don't go right, while another family may ignore extreme emotional wounding as if it never happened. Repeating these actions year after year sets up a platform for chronic health problems. Wound upon wound, anxiety followed by anxiety, insult after insult, misunderstandings, passivity, intentional sabotaging of family events, cursing and condemnation, and a long list of other emotional responses go deep into the cellular structure of the body. It's not just the heart that is broken by emotional wounding, it is the promise of hope. After so much, the body and soul lose hope that tomorrow will be any different from today. Unfortunately, there are times when, in order for the body to emotionally heal, the person has to place distance between the source of the wounds and themselves. When safety, especially safety for children, is at risk, distance may be the only choice.

If you have been on a self-destructive path for as long as you can remember and you know you are destroying your health and the health of those around you, the good news is you can change the way you think and the way you live. Small steps can make a huge difference in your health as you learn to shift from "overdrive" to "drive." When you are on "drive," you hold the wheel and you determine the speed. Of course, there can be an accident due to another car or other unpredictable occurrence. Maybe you have a blowout or a flat tire; maybe a deer dashes in front of you. Likewise, there will be events in life that are unexpected. Most likely, you have already experienced more of these than you want to remember. That may be the key to gaining good health. If you can shift away from *wanting to remember* hurts, wrongs, and offenses to preventing your mind from living there, you have a great chance to find your way to wholeness in emotional and mental health.

Often addiction begins by trying to block painful memories. The door to escape worked once, and for a few hours it didn't hurt so badly. Regrets, bad choices, criminal activity, sheer foolishness, and pain caused to others were forgotten. However, it came back like a flood once the effects of the drug or alcohol wore off. In my experience in counseling, rebounding pain and regret continue to drive the addiction. What may have started as a dare, lack of self-identity, curiosity, or attempt to be "one of the crowd" and be accepted opened a door to addiction. Then the physical effects in the body took over. The person lost control of their soul. Addiction affects body and soul and spirit. Feeling unworthy to live, self-hatred, abusive thinking, and remorse drag the body into diseases. It's not uncommon for addicts to develop heart disease, blood pressure, diabetes, and neurological problems within a few years of acquiring a habit. Their efforts to climb back up to a new life involve not just learning to use emotions for positive gains in health, but also to overcome serious craving demands from the cells of the body. However, it can be done. Many programs that help with addictions start with teaching the emotions and the mind to think differently. Positive versus negative thinking can bring about positive rewards in your health.

PART THREE

Putting the Puzzle Together

Above the Surface: Things Are Not Always What They Seem

I stand gazing over a lush, green pasture dotted here and there with cedar and locust trees. A stream of water crosses the land and a bridge connects two small pastures just beyond the fence. A smattering of about 30 sheep and goats, with lots of lambs and young goats, paints a picture that could be an English countryside. The green against a clear blue sky is tantalizing, and I step with bare feet onto the grass and watch as the sheep begin their slow journey to the next pasture.

For some reason, the grass must taste better just beyond the bridge, or at least it must look better because the sheep follow their narrow path to the second pasture daily. There they eat their fill and then rest and ruminate under the trees.

Visiting friends often ask if we eat the sheep. "No," we respond, "they are just pasture ornaments; a petting zoo for the grandchildren." We do eat lamb, but we buy it from a friend of ours who is a proper sheep farmer. He delivers it frozen in packages to our door. Anonymous lamb; I like it better that way. Just another part of the food chain.

No, we don't eat our sheep or our goats. Ours are the friendly sort that may just walk up and want a back scratch or ear rub, or they may want to see how your clothes taste. Yesterday, my husband had to rescue a kid that had gotten himself into a tight spot and couldn't get out. Who knows why he had decided to explore where he did. Goats are curious; sheep are not.

After dusk when all was quiet, my husband was in the pasture looking for him when he heard a very faint little whimper. The little goat was begging for help but was very weak. He was almost completely hidden in a hole under the bridge. Will he get himself back into the same circumstances, I wonder? Did he learn anything from his near-death experience? All he knew to do when he heard my husband's voice nearby was bleat for help. It saved his life. He's safe now and back to "kidding around" with the other little lambs and goats.

The sheep know us. My husband can arrive at 3 a.m. after a long trip and call them. They will run pell-mell to the fence because they know his voice. I have to call them by name to get them to come. Then, they look up from their grazing as if to say, "Wonder what she wants? Is anybody sick?" I am the nursemaid and oftentimes the midwife. If we don't plan carefully, we have newly-born lambs in mid-January with seventeen inches of snow. The midwifery is tough then— plodding through snow and ice with a freezing lamb that will have to be warmed if it is to live, followed by weeks in the shed, having to feed them regardless of weather.

This morning, however, the beautiful green of the pasture meets a clear blue sky just over the treetops. It's a warm early summer day. We were late getting a ram this year, and I am glad. My eyes gaze over the flock where they are contently grazing in the second pasture. I notice that one has separated from the flock. Never a good sign when it comes to sheep. I watch her intently. I see a small, black figure on the ground beside her. It's not moving. I grab my shoes and head in her direction. She watches me come closer and closer until I can see the little lamb. It's far too small. The ewe, a "teenage mother," is experiencing her first birth. She's frantic as I pick up the tiny creature. It looks to be several weeks early.

I head back to the shed. I know she will follow me because I have her lamb. Baaing and bleating, she insists I give the lamb back to her. I tell her, "He has to have some help or he won't live." I speak comforting words, but she won't be comforted. Her voice gets louder and louder until the others began to baa and our sheep dog begins to bark. "It's all right," I tell them. The sound of my voice settles them and they go back to eating.

Grabbing a baby bottle and package of colostrum, I quickly mix a few ounces. "Here, Little One," I say, putting the nipple of the bottle into his tiny mouth. He's so weak and fragile. Yet he pulls on the bottle and struggles to swallow. He wants to live. His little eyes search my face. "Are you my mother?"

"I'm not your mother," I tell him.

As soon as the bottle is finished, I place him beside her in the pen. They will have to stay here for a few days until he is better or until he doesn't make it. She is licking him, trying to push him to her bag. I am always entranced as I watch the instinct of the lamb and mother. They know what to do without being shown. The lambs may struggle to find the bag that holds mother's milk, but hunger drives them until at last they are able to find their mother's milk. The mother nudges with her head to push them in the right direction. Their tails wag rapidly when they find the milk.

But this little guy is too little to reach the bag. He is too small and she is too tall. And she has no bag. Probably the pre-mature birth. Maybe it will come in a day or two, if he makes it. She nudges him from time to time to make him get up.

Day after day I feed him, expecting every morning to find that he slipped away and died during the night. He knows my voice. Neither are afraid of my touch. Their close quarters in the shed, a pan of grain, and a bucket of water for her has built trust. The fear in her eyes is gone. She seems to understand that I am here to help. She will know me now. And I will know her. She won't be just one of the sheep from here forward.

The little lamb jumps up when he hears my voice and rushes to get his bottle. He can drink more every day and tries to follow me when I leave the shed. When I call from the porch, he answers with his tiny bleating voice. If the lamb lives and grows strong, even years from now he will know my voice.

His weakness has allowed him special access to the shepherd. I hold him close and talk to him about living and growing strong. We watch the other lambs frolicking happily with their mothers to care for them. "Little guy," I tell him, "I don't know why you came too early, why you are so small, and why your mother can't feed you. I'm sorry that she wants to leave you and go back to the herd, but she doesn't understand your possibilities! I'll help you all I can."

The mother has given up and has jumped the fence to rejoin the herd. The milk never came, and she resisted our efforts to help her. Within a week or two, she had lost interest in her lamb. Sometimes the mothers desert a frail lamb. They seem to know the lamb is not going to live, and they refuse to feed them. Usually the mother is right, and in spite of all our efforts, they die.

I know he doesn't understand anything but the touch of my hand as I stroke his back, trying to make up for the lack of love and caring from his mother. If he lives, the next few months will be hard. He got a bad start in life. Yet with lots of care and love, he may make it. But he will be different from the other little lambs born this season. We can't keep all of them, so some of them will be sold. But this one is imprinted on our hearts. All he will have to think about in the years ahead is, "Which pasture is really greener?"

CHAPTER 8

Finding the Way Out: Understanding Addictions

I've learned a lot from our sheep and goats. Neither my husband nor I had any experience with being "shepherds" in spite of our name. When we bought our house, the former owner needed to board a few sheep until they were settled in the new place. When he called to say he had decided to sell them, I found myself disappointed that we would be losing them. Watching them graze had brought a restful peace to my soul.

"This is their home," I said to my husband. "Maybe we should offer to buy the sheep." I had become very fond of a little white lamb that had been born on "my watch." He called the owner and they agreed. And so, we became shepherds. We soon found out that every grandchild wanted to add to the flock so we went from five sheep to twenty sheep and goats in a few months. We look at ourselves every now and then, with both of us past seventy years old now, and ask, "What are we doing!"

Yet, a decade later, we are both better people for learning to tend sheep. I'm not surprised Moses, Jacob, Joseph, David, and perhaps even Jesus as a boy tended sheep. Jesus speaks so much about sheep that it is obvious He knew them well. Tending sheep is like a leadership training course. I understand so much more about why a fisherman like Peter would have to make a strong choice out of a lot of love to agree to feed the lambs. There's a lot more to John 21:15–17 than meets the eye. Even when the little goat was rescued and his life saved, will he get himself back into a dangerous place again?

Like the sheep of the pasture, we have to have certain things to keep us not only well, but content. The peace of contentment is rare and to be treasured highly. Fears and concerns for tomorrow wrack us and cause restless nights. Our bodies and our minds are overloaded with stress. Our mind, will, and emotions are often raw and on edge. In short, we are not living life the way we want to live life. Financial pressures, debt, anxiety about our families, fear of losing a job, and other doubts press on us. Where is peace when we need it!

Just as our minds change when our neurotransmitters change, which changes when our gut changes, our second brain responds to that stress and to whatever measure of peace we can find. In attempt to find solace, many turn to alcohol and drugs. After all, it looks so tempting in the movies. I speak to people who tell me they get through the day because they know that when they get home, they can get a drink. The thought keeps them going. Others tell me that as soon as they walk in a restaurant, they start thinking about what drink they are going to order. I often wonder when the *social drink* became the daily drink; the daily, addiction. Almost every movie and television drama shows actors with a glass of wine or other drink in hand. The subtle suggestion of how imperative this is to a social setting is not ignored by the young mind. The message is strong—drinking alcohol is to be expected and is a typical part of everyday life and special occasions. I remember when almost every actor had a cigarette. Until tobacco got on the other side of politics, the subliminal message of "smoking is so cool" was sent in movie after movie to naïve minds.

But what makes the difference? Why can one young person experiment with wine coolers and not become an addict and others can't? Why can one person have a one-time experience with drugs while another becomes instantly addicted? Do some people have more moral character and can always take the high road and others fail miserably? Our society condemningly sends the message, *If you lose the battle to handle your "liquor," it's your fault, you weakling.*

I've yet to counsel a single addict who planned to become an addict or an alcoholic. The teens I've worked with have told me they began with sips from their parents' drinks, wine coolers, or beer. There were parallels with all of them—they liked the way it made them feel. If a little made them feel good, what would a lot be like? Natural curiosity was a part of it, for some. For others, it was feeling the best they had ever felt until drunkenness took over. As awful as that was, they went back for more.

When it comes to addiction, it's hard to know which came first. Like the old "chicken and egg" question, were there physical, emotional, and mental issues that led to addiction, or did addiction lead to the other issues? I was a college student when I figured out that my dad came home at the end of the day defeated and depressed. He would make a *toddy*—whiskey, water, and sugar—and in a little while he was my funny, dear daddy. However, his business went sour, and ensuing debt as well as aging increased his load. I noticed he kept alcohol in the glove compartment of the car; the bottle that stayed in the pantry was being replaced every few days. My mother and I finally talked about it. We were both noticing that he was drinking heavily. While neither of us had ever seen him "drunk" or even tipsy, it was evident to us he was drinking more often. The stress of life was too much, and alcohol eased it for a few hours.

At the time, I was studying psychology and recognized the classic symptoms of depression. I remember wondering if he drank because he was depressed or if the alcohol made him depressed. Now I know that both questions are answered with "Yes." Before I graduated from college, he was admitted to the state hospital for treatment of alcoholism. I had to drive him there and sign the papers. I was young and emotionally unprepared to handle such a load. The memory of leaving him there as they locked the door still makes me cry. We were both brave, each assuring the other that this would be just a few weeks and he would soon be well.

It didn't play out that way. Dad sank deeper and deeper into depression. On one visit, the doctor told me he had been diagnosed as manic-depressive. On another visit, they said he had tried to commit suicide. On the next visit, the doctor said they were giving him shock treatments. I had no idea what the doctor meant and no idea of how those treatments would affect him. It changed his brain, leaving him with little emotion and more depression. When he finally returned home two years later, he was a different man. We rarely saw or heard his sharp wit anymore. Ambition was gone; pride in appearance was gone; purpose was gone; hope was gone. He died at 69, dreams unfulfilled. Love from children and grandchildren was about all he had left. My mother had died a few years before.

As I reflected through the years, wondering what else could have been done, I put "depression" versus "drinking" on the balance scale many times. Finally, the depression outweighed the drinking. My father was depressed and probably had been most of his life. His desires for his family were always much greater than his income. Added to that was a near-death injury as a child and tuberculosis when a young man. Alcohol was "medicine" at his family's home and an accepted Southern custom. The men drank together at family and friend gatherings. He was always the sober one, still maintaining his gentlemanly demeanor. We children laughed at the others who couldn't walk straight or talk straight. Some of them were surprised to hear Dad was in treatment for alcoholism. "I never saw him take more than a drink or two," they'd say. That was just it. He was in control until his mid-fifties. The solace of alcohol becomes "best friend" to many who suffer with defeat, depression, and death of vision or purpose.

Often, people who become addicted to drugs or alcohol are said to have an "addictive personality." That would seem to indicate some deficiency in their *psyche*, the Greek word for mind, soul, and spirit. How did that personality develop, then? Did they "choose" it, or was it inherited? Is addiction a flaw in the personality? Is it simply a moral failure? Was it inherited, and if so, how and why?

I have spoken to many people over the years and listened as they cried bitter tears over the hurt to their families, self-hatred, and lack of worthiness. Their desolate words always break my heart. Often they would tell me, "I guess I inherited an addictive personality." That makes them hate themselves even more, especially if their siblings had it all together.

My research led me to believe that it was inherited, because addiction plagued our family. As I tried to put together the jigsaw puzzle that kept my mind working day and night, I narrowed down a few things. I was one of the youngest of the cousins, and some of my older cousins had children my age. I knew my older cousins already struggled with addiction—alcohol, prescription drugs, over-the-counter painkillers, even Nyquil, if that was all they could get. As I sought to figure out the "chicken or the egg," I came to the conclusion that it was depression that had been inherited. The alcohol and drugs were self-medications. My research in the last decade has convinced me that addiction is a "brain disease" just as diabetes is a disease of the pancreas; heart disease is a disease of the heart muscle. Do we shun people with diabetes or heart disease? While we know the mind affects both of these disorders, we still recognize them as physical diseases.

In recent years, I've stepped away from active teaching and counseling to *circling data*, as my friend calls it, referring to research and more research. However, I have found more and more evidence that my hunches were correct—there are metabolic malfunctions that precede addiction. Instead of an "addictive personality," there may have been an "addictive body" that demanded more after that first exposure to alcohol or drugs. The brain and body grabbed the substance, allowing it into cells, and used it.

Nicotine is a good example. There are numerous nicotine receptors in the body and brain. In fact, the more nicotine you use, the more nicotine receptors you develop. The shape of the nicotine molecule is close to the shape of numerous other receptors in the brain and in the body, so the nicotine can trick the receptor, which opens up and lets it in. It is a "mimic." Remember how certain toxins, etc. can mimic hormones and neurotransmitters? Cell receptors are designed to open when they recognize molecules that fit their particular "shape." When chemicals, toxins, or nutrients are the same shapes or close enough, the receptor opens, accepts, and allows entrance into the "lock and key" system of the cell. Drugs, alcohol, and many other chemicals fit that "lock and key." The most common receptors that nicotine fools are the acetylcholine receptors. You may recall that acetylcholine was the first neurotransmitter discovered and is one of the foundational neurotransmitters. It affects muscles, learning, memory, reward response, sleep, and helps to keep us alert and able to concentrate. Once nicotine is inside, it prevents the normal production and efficiency for acetylcholine; the less acetylcholine produced, the greater the need for nicotine. The craving increases.

It gets worse as nicotine affects all of the brain, but glutamate takes a big hit. Glutamate is a foundational neurotransmitter; if you have glutamate inefficiency, your GABA and other neurotransmitters are affected. GABA puts on the "brakes" in the brain, causing calmness and relaxation, keeping the brain that may be irregularly high or erratic on glutamate from spiraling out of control. When nicotine blocks the glutamate receptors, glutamate is diminished. As the glutamate inefficiency increases, the brain craves more and more nicotine because it can't get the real thing, glutamate, which it prefers. Nicotine gives the brain a glutamate boost, which the brain wants, but then, within minutes, the glutamate decreases and drops below normal levels. This up and down creates a severe longing to get more nicotine to try to stabilize the glutamate. GABA, dopamine, serotonin, and other neurotransmitters are also adversely affected.[1]

When nicotine is used, there is also a dopamine boost, which is very satisfying to the reward center of the brain.[2] Dopamine is a very powerful neurotransmitter. You may have heard of it due to Parkinson's disease, which is associated with too little and irregular dopamine production. When it became possible to treat Parkinson's with a dopamine medication that increased dopamine activity in the brain, some unusual side effects began to emerge. Compulsive shopping, gambling, hypersexuality, and other "personality disorders" emerged among those taking the medication.[3]

Now, when your saintly old mother begins shoplifting, your 80-year-old father begins watching pornography and hitting on old ladies in the nursing home, it's time to look into "What is happening to my parent!" Turns out, dopamine has an amazing effect on what we call "wrong," and the old folks were experiencing compulsive behaviors due to the effect of dopamine in the brain. Internet gambling is now at record highs, as is pornography. While we are treating the "sin" or "crime," we need to also treat the brain and body. Is "addictive personality" a dopamine irregularity? Just as low dopamine efficiency can lead to Parkinson's and many diseases, high and irregular dopamine release can cause compulsive behaviors due to the effect of dopamine on the control centers of the brain. While too low dopamine can be critical, so can a level that is too high and inconsistent. When an old lady from the nursing home who rode the van to Wal-Mart to do a little shopping is stopped for shoplifting, she is being honest when she says, "I don't know why I took it." Her dopamine medication may be at fault. Unacceptable behavior is not always caused by poor decisions.

Cocaine also affects dopamine, serotonin, and norepinephrine. The customary delivery is "snorting" it. The effect is almost instantaneous because of the amazing delivery system the nose provides for the brain and body. As more cocaine is used, new receptors are increased, just as with nicotine. Severe depression and cravings occur when the person tries to quit; highs and lows become more erratic as neurons struggle to normalize. As cocaine begins killing brain cells, the user becomes less and less motivated and develops "stunted" emotions. The tendency is to increase cocaine to get back to the pleasure high. The new "normal" feels awful not just in body, but also in the mind, will, and emotions. It is already well known that cocaine can trigger cardiovascular deaths, but what is not known at present is whether or not the damage to dopamine neurons is reversible or permanent.[4]

Heroin, morphine, codeine, Vicodin, OxyContin, Percocet, Dilaudid, Duragesic, and other drugs are very addictive as they affect natural opioid receptors in our body. Opioid receptors are found on our nerve cells and affect pain, hunger, and thirst as well as mood control, immune response, and other systems in the body. You probably know the word "endorphins" and how our natural opioids help the body with pain and produce a natural euphoria. A runner experiences "runner's high" when endorphins are doing their job. At first, you just don't think you can take another step; then, you get a "second wind." Thank your endorphins.

Inducing opioid highs through drugs, however, is very damaging to the body and brain as tolerance sets in demanding more and more. Because these are prescription drugs, many people not only break the law to get the drugs, but they wreck their family and future. Getting "hooked" on prescription drugs following surgery or a painful injury is a very real problem and should not be taken lightly. Quite often, the person is too ashamed to ask for the help they need for recovery. The very doctor who prescribed these addictive drugs in the first place may continue to pre-scribe, regardless of how addicted his patient is becoming. These doctors discredit their profession. Accidental overdosing can occur due to ex-treme euphoria and pleasurable feelings. The potential for cardiac arrest is very real and taking just a "little more" can be deadly.[5]

One of the most addictive is OxyContin. Marketed as "safe," mil-lions were addicted before the news got out that it is anything but safe. It was only a matter of time before OxyContin hit the streets. It is now considered one of the most wanted street drugs. According to the docu-mentary, *OxyContin: Time Bomb*, Canadians are spending more than ten billion dollars a year on pain pills. And Americans are estimated to be consuming 80 percent of the world's pain medication. In the U.S., nar-cotic overdoses surpass deaths from murder and accidents.[6]

Addicts snort, chew, or inject for extreme highs. Even those who have been on OxyContin for short periods of time and have legitimate prescriptions, can face serious withdrawals, including anxiety, insomnia, intestinal pain and problems, flu-like symptoms like aching and chills, elevated blood pressure and heart rate, tremors, seizures and convul-sions.[7] The non-suspecting patient, anxious for pain relief, does not re-alize they are entering a cave that may not have a lighted "exit" sign. Once inside the dark cave, only someone who knows the way out may be able to help them find their way back to a life without drugs. Methadone is sometimes used to help with drug rehabilitation, but it is also addictive.

The addiction of marijuana works in a similar way to nicotine and opioids—cannabinoid receptors are almost everywhere in the brain and the brain cannot discern the difference. Marijuana hijacks receptors, affecting dopamine in a similar way as nicotine. However, marijuana not only causes euphoria and relaxation, it affects mood, memory, pain, emotions, appetite, and amplifies visual and auditory input. As marijuana use is continued, the body craves more in an attempt to stabilize and normalize neurotransmitter efficiency as dopamine increases and other neurotransmitters are reduced. GABA, so important to brain balance and glutamate efficiency, is hindered. In a short time, impaired learning, memory loss, and attention deficit can occur. When the young developing brain uses marijuana, permanent memory loss and poor brain function can occur, including lower IQs and verbal processing. It also interferes with the brain's ability to process sensory information—touch, sight, sound, and time can be affected.[8]

The longer the use, the greater increase in harmful effects on the brain. Many develop a lack of ability to concentrate and carry out plans. Appearance and behavior take a nose dive.[9] Sadly, some parents look the other way, because "everyone does it." They expect their child to be exempt from the consequences and may only step in when their child is arrested. Now, with marijuana being legalized and penalties for selling and possession lessened, we can expect increased use. Laws don't change the brain; using marijuana, however, whether short term or long term, can change the brain. All too commonly, it can become the doorway to harder drugs with more intensive highs.

In the 1960s, I taught English Literature in a high school in a small city. I had the top academic students for several periods, followed by classes for lower achievers. In my eleventh grade class, I had two young men with exceptional IQs, writing abilities, keen insight into poetry and literature. They were handsome, came from good families, polite, attentive. In short, they were a joy to teach. I loved watching their young minds come up with interesting ideas as to what the author was saying. As the school year passed, they met some strangers who came to our college city who convinced them that they needed to try, *just once*, something most of us had never heard of—*marijuana*.

They convinced them it was safe and was just a "plant." I began noticing changes in them. Slowly, they began to drop behind, and they seemed to no longer care about their schoolwork, appearance, or even their future. I met with their parents and we tried to convince them to stop using marijuana, as it was obvious the "plant" was affecting them adversely. Eventually, the boys set out on their own to the West Coast. It was months before the parents heard from them. It was devastating to the parents as well as to me, because I love my students deeply. Finally, they were found and returned home. But the damage had been done.

It was the same in the following years with other students. In my experience, marijuana is detrimental and should be unlawful. Those who sell any drugs should be held accountable. The hands of many of our law officers have been tied; they know that if they arrest the drug supplier, it's doubtful they will be convicted and sentenced. Many small towns now have serious drug problems, and the citizens feel powerless to stop it. There are effective drug tests available, and if someone shows symptoms it's better to find out before it morphs into a more serious issue or a phone call no parent ever wants to get.

There are other drugs—such as *ecstasy* and many, many others—that are popular, and people are often convinced to try them "just once." Ecstasy affects dopamine and other neurotransmitters, but the serotonin receptors are the major hit. The user can lose all sense of propriety, self-control, and a loss of inhibition due to effects on GABA and upsurge of serotonin.[10] Mistakes of a lifetime have happened when young people have taken ecstasy, lured into false promises and lies by those who only want to exploit them. This is not a time when parents can afford to be so involved in their own lives that they are blind to what's happening to their children.

Due to the popularity of antidepressants and tranquilizers, many respectable and esteemed people become drug addicts without realizing they are addicted. Maybe they had a rough experience, loss, or just felt jumpy and nervous. Naïvely, they began taking tranquilizers, sleeping pills, or antidepressants. They realize they are addicted when they try to stop taking the pills. The withdrawal is so awful that they go back to their physician, who may increase the dose. I've spoken to adults who told me, "The doctor said I'll have to take these for the rest of my life because my nerves are so bad." Nerves or addiction? Could there be another path?

Whether it is addiction by prescription, culture, or street drugs, addiction crosses all segments of our society. Were some people just "unlucky" and they became addicted while others used their prescription, threw it out, kept their alcohol under control, and stayed away from street drugs? Or was there an underlying physiological malfunction to begin with? Many counselors will readily agree that there was probably a psychological problem, but they may not know that physiological problems may be the launch pad for addiction. I spoke recently with a psychiatrist who said there was mention in his textbook as to malfunctions in the body that affect the mind, but too little was known. I asked how long ago he had gone to school. We laughed. Unless he was searching for research on how malfunctions in the body can lead to addiction, he would not know the emerging research. Increasingly, research is leading to more understanding about deficiencies that exist *before* addiction.

If you read the first few chapters, you read that your mother and father and grandparents and who-knows-how-far-back affected your genes. Where they lived, what they ate, and especially what mom ate and drank during pregnancy affected your potential for dependency. In 2011, Dr. Fred Stieff, M.D. published a book called *Brain in Balance.* Dr. Von Stieff has an impressive list of accomplishments and has detoxed over 20,000 patients. Finding his book was a gold mine, because he explains genetics and the neurochemistry behind addiction and sobriety. With experience and knowledge to back him, Dr. Von Stieff says that he believes that *imbalance in neurotransmitters* precede the urge to experiment with drugs and alcohol as well as the addiction that can follow.[11]

According to Dr. Von Stieff, alcohol affects six of the neurotransmitters that affect how we experience life. He says it is referred to as *the mother of all drugs* as pharmaceutical companies have yet to develop a drug as encompassing. Now, that is a sobering thought. Most raise one or two, maybe three neurotransmitters as mentioned above, but not six. In his words, "Alcohol moves the brain's neurochemicals like no other drug on the planet. Alcohol raises serotonin, GABA, endocannabinoid, glutamate, and at high dose, increases the release of opiates. It also has a significant end-result effect on dopamine...this makes alcohol a powerful anti-depressant (not to mention highly addictive) and an even more powerful depressant once it wears off, causing neurotransmitters to plummet."[12]

Dr. Von Stieff says that alcohol's effect on neurotransmitters is enhanced by nicotine. When a person uses both alcohol and nicotine, all *eight* neurotransmitter systems are affected. That's why it's so difficult to "kick" alcohol and nicotine at the same time. He says that it takes the brain 28 days of withdrawal from drugs, nicotine, and alcohol to regain the base level of neurotransmitters—that with which you were born.

He continues to say that if you are struggling with emotional, mental, or addictive disorders, you may have been born with a base level of neurotransmitters that was not optimal, and that maybe you were a "sitting duck" for either or all of these addictions. If you were low in glutamate, that first drink or cigarette would have met a longing that was already there—a physical longing, an "itch" that had never been scratched.

Dr. Nora Volkow, Director at the U.S. National Institute on Drug Abuse, says some do have a genetic predisposition to addiction, but because basic brain functions are involved, *everyone will become an addict if sufficiently exposed to drugs or alcohol.*[13]

When the subject of addiction comes up, most of us would turn a cold shoulder to something that is proven to cause all sorts of emotional, mental, and addictive disorders, as well as serious physical illness. If we read on the label, "may cause fatigue, irritability, dizziness, insomnia, excessive sweating (especially at night), poor concentration and forgetfulness, excessive thirst, depression and crying spells, digestive disturbances, blurred vision, aggressive behavior, anxiety, and depression" we would probably refuse to purchase the item, and we certainly would not give it to infants and children! Yet babies are introduced to it in baby food every day and begin to acquire a taste for it that can take a lifetime to shake. Found in almost all processed foods, it is linked to a 58 percent increase in depression.[14]

If you have already guessed *sugar*, you are correct. So many of our cultural activities are centered on sugar intake—birthday parties, holiday and social events, and day-to-day activities. No one is used to hearing a quiet whisper, "Yes, they had to go to rehab for sugar addiction." Nor are we usually concerned about the consequences of sugar except to our waistline. The pull and addiction of "sweet" is so strong that any sugar substitute that tastes like *sugar* will bring millions of dollars to the company that develops it. Never mind the health consequences that arise years later, as we have seen in aspartame.

It may surprise you to know that sugar works in the same way that cocaine and heroin work in the brain. That bowl of ice cream lights up the same region of the brain as heroin.[15] The habit of eating sugar and eating as much as you want may be as hard if not harder to kick than cocaine or heroin. Our bodies were not designed for sugar and high fructose corn syrup in its present composition. Honey, maple syrup, cane, pineapple, beets, carrots, etc. have a natural sweetness that our bodies are designed to handle. It's hard, for example, to overindulge in eating honey; your satiation (satisfied feeling) signals, "That's enough honey." It's not the same with refined sugar, high fructose corn syrup, and food items that contain refined sugar.

I remember walking through the cane patch when I was very young. My uncle would peel sugar cane for me, and I would chew the tiny pieces with the juice running down my chin. Eventually my jaw would become tired and I'd have to stop—a natural "stop" to overindulgence. I loved it and looked forward to when the cane juice would be ready to drink, after the stalks had been fed into a grinder that extracted the juice from the stalk. That juice would be boiled down into "cane syrup" and was a mainstay of Southern diets. A lot has changed since those years. The sugar industry is big time and sugar is cheap. After high fructose corn syrup was developed, an even cheaper "sweet" emerged. Food processors began putting it in almost everything, because we would come back for more, because it is addictive in refined and concentrated amounts. There's even dextrose in your salt unless you are buying natural salt.

As a nation, we are hooked on sugar. Even when we are paying attention to how much sugar we are using, we often don't realize how much "silent" sugar we are eating. A study published in 2007 indicates that intense sweetness can surpass the "cocaine reward" in the brain. That's right; using the same pathways, intense sweetness—sugar, high fructose corn syrup, saccharine, aspartame, etc.—affect the dopamine neurotransmitters offering a "reward" for ingesting.[16] Silently, a slow but steady need to eat more "sweets" develops beginning a cascade of problems. And because stress signals a need for serotonin, the body begs for more carbohydrates to help produce serotonin.

There are numerous studies on how sugar affects mental disorders. Several years ago, there was a British study that involved over 17,500 people that linked daily candy and sweets to violence in adulthood. Sociologists were divided over the findings, suggesting parenting, more difficult children, and other answers that might come to mind. However, it's more likely that sugar and additives change the brain.[17] A study from 1985 indicated that reducing sugar affected emotions and produced a more stable and less stressed person after two weeks.[18] Perhaps the most compelling evidence concerning the link between sugar and antisocial behavior was a study conducted by the Los Angeles Probation Department Diet-Behavior Program in 1983. They found a 44 percent reduction in antisocial behavior following a reduction of sugar in the diet.[19]

You may know people who tried to get off nicotine, hard drugs, and alcohol who found themselves desperately hungry for sugar. It's a very similar addiction in the brain and in ensuing brain chemistry. The sight, smell, or mention of a sweet treat can cause the need to eat sugar to become almost irresistible. In fact, a picture of something sweet and delicious can cause your dopamine neurotransmitters to respond.

However, *tolerance* the same as seen in drug and alcohol addiction is also present in sugar addiction. The more you eat, the less satisfied you are. The search is on to experience the same brain arousal experienced in the past—a scoop of ice cream becomes a need to eat a double scoop. Before long, some people admit to scarfing an entire gallon of ice cream. It is not a question of "They just need to control their eating." They are as addicted to sugar as someone else may be to heroin. Try giving it up entirely and you may understand the strength of the addiction. Somehow, a stalk of celery just doesn't measure up to key lime pie, and your brain and body know it.

Eating sugar and high fructose corn syrup cause inflammation in the body. Inflammation affects brain and body. Both cause irregular blood sugar levels with sharp "highs" and "lows." When your blood sugar suddenly drops, say thirty minutes to several hours after a sugar treat, your brain begins to pump out glutamate that can cause agitation, depression, anxiety, panic attacks, and anger.[20] I often talk to mothers about this. They understand that high sugar treats cause their child to act out and go on a "sugar high," but they say, "He likes it." Perhaps realizing they are potentially setting their child up for a lifetime addiction to a harmful substance may be enough for them to find a healthy substitute.

To double the effect of irregular and inefficient glutamate, dopamine, and serotonin output, add some grain to the recipe. Dr. William Davis' book, *Wheat Belly*, took the mask off the industry that has adulterated wheat and grains, creating products the body cannot utilize properly. These grains look like the real thing, but they are not. Due to hybridization and creation of pest- and drought-resistant grains, the present-day wheat and grains are not recognized by the body's matrix for food. It may taste wonderful, but when the body can't use it or excrete it, it stores these unrecognized elements. Toxins can store in the joints, the liver, etc. but especially in the brain and in the fat tissues of the body.[21] When there's not enough fat to store the toxins, the brain may be sending out a message, "Make me some more fat. I have to store these inflammatory toxins somewhere." Obesity may actually be a type of inflammation caused by addiction to grains and sugar.

Over forty years ago, some of us who were trying to unravel learning and behavior problems began suggesting to parents that they remove wheat, corn, dairy, sugar, additives, and food dyes from their child's diet. However, it was Dr. William Davis' book that caused the general public to take notice. Dr. Davis takes a very complex system and explains it. He says that wheat-derived exorphins bind to the opiate receptors of the brain. That's right—the same receptors utilized by OxyContin, morphine, codeine, and heroin. For some people, the effects are powerful; their addiction to wheat products, especially those that combine sugar and trans fats, drives them to binge eating followed by purging and other eating disorders. If they experienced emotional trauma in childhood, especially if that trauma was placated by comfort food that contained wheat and sugar—cake, donuts, cookies, etc.—the body *and* the mind may be as addicted as a person on hard drugs. On brain scans, their brains respond in a similar fashion. Wheat and sugar addictions are real addictions. It is a wise parent who learns to reward their children in other ways than with a cookie.

Genetically modified organism—GMO, which indicates a plant has been genetically modified—has been common in grain production for quite a while. Scientific research and clinical evidence shows that this tampering and manipulation of natural genetics in grains contribute to health problems[22] and disturbed digestive tracts that are hindered in production of serotonin, dopamine, and other neurotransmitters.[23] GMOs may also be contributing to the epidemic of obesity and obesity-driven health disorders due to inflammation overloads in the body.[24] In recent years, *gluten-free* has become trendy. Buying all sorts of alternatives may not be the answer, however, as some of the additives may be harmful as well. Your body has to recognize what you are eating and putting on your skin or smelling in order to use it. Wheat and grains and sugar build inflammation not only in your body, but also cause inflammation in the brain, which dominoes into other imbalances that lead to emotional, mental, and addictive disorders.

Breaking the addictive habit of eating sugar and wheat, a delicious combination that causes us to feel full, satisfied, and happy, is a hard task. Yet your particular emotional, mental, and addictive disorder may have in part been seeded by these foods. It grew into a "want more" by your own particular set of genes and lifestyle. If you feel driven to sit down in front of the TV with a bowl of ice cream and some cookies every night, you are taking your "hit" of addictive substances. Trust me, the TV advertisements are not on your side. Their job is to get you to eat more, not less of addictive food products.

There is an amino acid derivative called *n-acetyl cysteine—NAC*—a shortened version of a much longer word. It is used to detoxify acetaminophen overdose as well as other problems. You read about it in Chapter Six. It's well respected in the medical field, as most doctors know it can detox the liver, kidney, lungs, and cells. Recent research is saying that NAC is also effective in treating emotional, mental, and addictive disorders. In a double-blind study using NAC, the need for marijuana, nicotine, cocaine, and gambling was lessened. Psychiatric disorders, obsessive-compulsive disorder, trichotillomania (hair-twisting and pulling), schizophrenia, and bipolar showed significant improvement.[25]

NAC's job in the body is to increase production of our good friend *glutathione*. Yes, this is the same superhero antioxidant enzyme that Dr. Martha Herbert says may be the link to ADD/ADHD and Autism. You can't live without it as the muscles and organs have to have it. Glutathione is necessary for glutamate efficiency and can "cleanse" the glutamate receptors as well as other neurotransmitter receptors, enabling those neurotransmitters to regain more efficient functions and closer-to-desired production. Without glutamate "efficiency" (not too high, not too low), the other neurotransmitters are in trouble. Without enough glutathione, the whole body and brain are in trouble.

Neurotransmitters in the "chemical soup" of the brain communicate. Much of that communication and efficiency is dependent on glutamate. Your supply of glutamate affects your cravings as the body "longs" for the right amount of glutamate. With the right amount of glutamate, cravings for drugs, alcohol, and other detrimental additives decrease, as well as cravings for sugar, wheat, and carbohydrates. It seems your body, designed to be satisfied with proper amounts of glutamate, prefers glutamate. Glutathione helps maintain the basal glutamate concentration. This cycle is fragile, but the balance holds great hope for addiction, as well as emotional and mental disorders.

So, what are we waiting for! It's not as simple as just running out to the store and buying some NAC or glutathione so your glutamate receptors can start operating better. Efforts to "put" glutathione in the body have fallen short. Oral glutathione, injections, and IVs face the same challenge—the body recognizes glutathione and digests it rapidly. In spite of all the association to diseases and psychiatric disorders, glutathione has been difficult to increase.

In addition, you may be one of the estimated 50 percent of Americans who lack the gene (GSTM1) that allows for sufficient glutathione production.[26] Adding to that, your natural production of glutathione decreases with aging. Third, the less glutathione in your body, the greater the oxidative stress you build. To see the damage of oxidative stress, do some research on your own on pubmed.gov. You can read about hundreds of disorders. Research *oxidative stress* and *addiction*, oxidative stress, or any of the emotional and mental disorders—bipolar, schizophrenia, OCD, and others—and you will see the connection.

So can you naturally increase glutathione production? A good source for increasing glutathione production is whey from milk. If that milk has been heated and pasteurized, however, the glutathione potential is lost. Fruits and vegetables can make glutathione, but most of the fruits and vegetables we eat are now hybrids and may have lost much of their nutritional value and may be systemic with pesticides and herbicides. It's enough to make you want to order some heirloom seeds, throw out all your pesticides and herbicides, try to find some dirt that is not polluted with pesticides and herbicides, and plant your own organic garden! While you are at it, you might as well raise some cows and chickens for raw milk and healthy eggs. However, you would have to eat more fruits and vegetables than you probably want as you may have to eat *ten* servings to obtain the nutrition of one serving from fifty years ago.[27] Exercise will also boost your production of glutathione. But it is difficult to increase your levels high enough to counteract years of abusing drugs, alcohol, prescription medicines, heavy metals, and who-knows-what that may be residues in your cells.

While I am not one to promote taking a handful of supplements, the most efficient way to increase your body's production of its own glutathione may be with a nutraceutical supplement. Pubmed.gov has a number of clinical trials published on such a product, *Protandim.*[28] In one of the in vitro clinical trials, this supplement, a synergistic blend of five plants, was able to increase the body's *own* production of glutathione by almost 300 percent with just one pill per day.[29] It works in the body by activating the body's "watch dog," the Nrf^2 pathway. When activated, this pathway facilitates signaling between cells, affecting every cell in the body.[30] The "watch dog" sends a signal that the body needs additional glutathione, super-oxide dismutase, catalase, and other antioxidant enzymes to counteract oxidative stress.[31] These enzymes, especially glutathione, get busy cleansing and regulating proper cell function in the body and brain.

The hope for those with addictions is that, by changing the underlying metabolism that may be the cause of addiction in many people, the addict can grow strong enough to completely overcome the addiction. However, the body and the mind do not heal overnight. It takes four months for red blood cells to renew while other blood cells renew in a few days. The bones take three months; the skin, one month; the liver, six weeks; the stomach lining, five days. The miraculous news is that the body can rebuild![32] For hundreds of years, it was thought that the brain could not rebuild. Now we know that parts of the brain can rebuild and add newly formed neurons throughout your lifetime.[33]

If Dr. Von Stieff is correct that it takes twenty-eight days to return to the base level neurotransmitter production you had at birth, then the next eleven months must be spent in correcting the body and building a new life away from toxic friends, toxic chemicals, and toxic living. If you were born with abnormal or irregular base levels of optimum neurotransmitters, your cells were already searching for foods to fill that lack. Even as the little lamb guzzled his first bottle without any knowledge of what was in it, his body was designed to recognize it. Trying to fill the gaps in nutrition and imbalances is paramount to your recovery and your freedom. It can be done. A brain and a body that is satisfied is not craving. This is not a short, easy path, but it does get easier every day. At least, that is what I am hearing from those who have taken the path to full recovery by implementing changes for body, soul, and spirit.

Addiction to drugs and alcohol, Internet addiction, and video gaming are emerging as "addictive disorders." Clinical trials are showing that nerve wiring in the brains of teens is disrupted and white matter—the part of the brain involved in emotions, decision-making, and self-control—is affected. This is the same region that is affected by alcohol, cocaine, marijuana, and meth. These scientists suspect that the myelin—the coating on nerve fibers—may be damaged.[34] A report from BBC News says that one in eight adults in America show signs of being addicted to the Internet.[35] Just as disturbing are reports that the brains of video and computer "gamers" show significant differences in the structure of the brain. Dr. Luke Clark, University of Cambridge, says that it's plausible that even playing video games for a half of a day a week may structurally change the brain. Gaming becomes compulsive and addictive.[36]

One of the most important elements to complete freedom is for the addict to understand that he or she may have been predisposed to addiction—not because of a personality flaw, but because of a metabolic function in the body that is affecting their neurotransmitters. This can be corrected. Psychological addiction is easier to conquer when physical cravings lessen or become completely *gone*.

CHAPTER 9

Tough Questions:
How Chemicals Change Your Life

When I was a little girl, I quickly learned the primary colors. I had a small box of crayons, a real treasure to me. When I started first grade, however, I discovered that my little box of red, blue, yellow, green, orange, purple, brown, and black did not compare to the choices I had in the big school box of chunky crayons. By third grade, we had the smaller crayons and almost fifty choices of colors! There were many different shades of red and blue, orange and green. My coloring book began to show all sorts of combinations of colors—magenta, violet, azure, hunter, and sienna. Now, over sixty years later, I live in Kansas City where we have a Crayola Café and a Crayola Store that can fascinate a child (or adult) for hours. The basic eight colors have expanded into 120 colors that include two shades of black.

Life is a lot like a box of crayons and a coloring book. Content with our little box of information, we think we have all we need to know until someone comes along with another box of information and we are forced to decide what to do about it. When it comes to *endocrine disruptors,* often called "gender benders," it's all too easy to begin talking about right and wrong, morality, and personal opinions. Most of us would prefer sticking our heads in the sand and minding our own business. However, there's too much science and information available to ignore what chemicals are doing to our environment, to fish, sea life, animals, and to humans. The changes are profound. Almost every family is facing critical decisions concerning children and relatives. In the midst of it all, there are people who may not identify with their own body parts. The brain and the body seem to be on different tracks.

Just as there are physical reasons why neurotransmitters in the brain can accept mimics into cell receptors for dopamine, serotonin, etc., our hormone receptors can accept "disruptors" and "mimics." While these are not the hormones designed by our bodies, the body cannot recognize the difference. For example, DDT, an insecticide, can fit right into an estrogen receptor and set the body on a path to breast cancer. You may recall that in Chapter Four there was information about how the thyroid gland is affected by *perchlorate*—rocket fuel that is present in the Colorado River, which irrigates the produce farms in California.

Over thirty-five years ago, English fishermen began reporting they were catching fish with unusual sexual anatomy in both males and females. As the numbers of these reports increased and involved increasingly large areas, scientists began to investigate the causes behind the effects. Fresh water fish and shrimp were becoming feminized. The first place to look, of course, was in the water. Scientists began to examine runoff water and what was being emptied into the water as many industrial companies use rivers and streams for their waste products. In addition, many of these changes were noted downstream of water treatment plants. They found high, potent estrogenic components in the sewage waste. Residues of industrial chemicals, phthalates, pesticides, herbicides, and bisphenol A were found in samples of these waters where the shrimp and fish lived.[1]

Now, over 35 years later, the problem is widespread in Europe, the U.S., and in Japan. Aquatic animals found in urban wastewater not only show increased feminization, but also decreased levels of serotonin.[2] With rivers, lakes, and streams polluted with toxic chemicals and endocrine disruptors, we are facing challenges that affect not only us, but also our future generations. Animals, fish, reptiles, and birds show the effects when gender-bending chemicals are released into water and their environments.

In 2008, *ChemTrust*, a United Kingdom trust set up in 2007 to monitor and inform the public concerning toxic chemicals that affect male and female hormones in the body, published a sobering report. That report, *Effects of Pollutants on the Reproductive Health of Male Vertebrate Wildlife—Males Under Threat*, says that males in all species are being more feminized.[3] This report should be read by everyone as it shows the worldwide threat we face.

If vertebrates and mammals in wildlife are being affected, can we ignore the potential effect in human beings? The question was raised many years ago as to whether these chemicals, if capable of changing so much about fish, shrimp, birds, etc., would affect humans. And, if capable of affecting humans, what would those changes be?

Who would have thought that makeup, for example, might be a cause for breast cancer? Many in medical and science research will readily say that too much estrogen can cause breast cancer. Studies from several decades ago linked breast cancer to hormone replacement therapy. But what about other sources of estrogen, such as the chemicals called *parabens*. The *Journal of Applied Toxicology* in March of 2012 reported that 99 percent of samples from forty women in a breast cancer study were found to have parabens in breast tissue.[4] The use of parabens is widespread in cosmetics, including shampoos, foundation, makeup, and many personal care products. This is not too surprising as parabens are effective in preventing growth of bacteria and fungus. They are preservatives and prevent spoilage. In the moist atmosphere of a bathroom, bacteria and fungus can multiply rapidly. Parabens to the rescue. The industry argued that the amount was too low to affect humans.

However, when laboratory tested, the paraben residues were found to be *one million times higher* than the estrogen levels normally found in breast tissue.[5] Too much estrogen is recognized as the culprit in breast cancer, but maybe the question should be, where is that estrogen coming from?

And what are the results, in addition to breast cancer, from these extraordinary levels of estrogen? *Previous research has shown that women absorb an estimated five pounds of chemicals a year from their daily makeup routine alone.*[6] Men and children use personal care products—deodorants, shaving products, fragrances, shampoos, soap, and lotions—as well as women.

The endocrine system in your body controls approximately fifty different hormones, including male and female hormones. Men and women have both male and female hormones and hormone receptors. The amounts of the secretions of those glands determine physical appearance and functions. For example, the beard usually shows up following puberty. Those receptors, both estrogen and testosterone receptors, can be fooled by "mimics" just as the thyroid or neurotransmitters can be. They don't always recognize counterfeits, like parabens, which can "fit" into those receptors. Excess estrogen in women may bring about many health issues in addition to cancer, as well as physical changes in the body, including enlarging of breasts. What can these levels of estrogen do to males? What are the effects of high levels of estrogen on a developing baby? A million times increase in estrogen exposure to a baby? It's enough to make you stop and think!

Paraben preservatives are also used extensively in processed foods to extend shelf life. Our food, beverages, skin products, and what we breathe may be contributing more than we know to gender. The New York State Department of Health and the Department of Environmental Health Sciences and State University of New York at Albany released a study on parabens in food that revealed alarming results. The researchers tested juices, soft drinks, alcoholic beverages, infant formula, milk, yogurt, cheese, bakery items, meats, and seafood. They tested for five different types of parabens widely used in food processing. There were measurable concentrations as high as 90 percent in the 247 samples. Pancake syrup had the highest with the next highest level in red wine, followed by grain foods (98 percent), fish and seafood (91 percent), dairy (87 percent) and 85 percent of the fruit samples. When they separated the foods into food groups, they found that infants had the highest concentration, followed by toddlers, children, teenagers, and adults.[7]

Parabens also include preservatives that end in *benzoate*. Putting parabens on your scalp or skin and ingesting parabens in processed foods means you may be overloading those estrogen receptors whether you are male or female. In puberty, when estrogen levels naturally rise, females begin to look "womanly." Breasts grow, the waist becomes defined, and hips tend to broaden. What could be the consequences in infants, toddlers, children, and teenagers when parabens increase estrogen exposure by extraordinary amounts?

Other endocrine disruptors to be concerned about are *polybrominated diphenyl ethers* (PBDEs) which are present in many household products such as hairdryers, car upholstery and carpet, mattresses and bedding, airplane interiors, blenders, microwaves, coffee makers, furniture, carpet, and clothing, especially children's clothing. If there is a pair of children's pajamas in the house, read the label. If it says, "flame-resistant," you may be interested to know that the same chemicals that make those pajamas less likely to catch on fire may be affecting the hormones in the child's body. If the tag reads "not flame resistant," the pajamas will most likely be "snug" with no loose sleeves and legs. However, household dust may be more invasive than pajamas. PBDEs in carpet and bedding are very accessible to infants, toddlers crawling on the floor, and children in general who are closer to the source than a taller adult.

Effects in the body can include the following: low immune system activity, increased risk of certain cancers, increase in cognitive defects such as learning and behavior, thyroid disruption, and fertility and reproductive issues.[8] A German study on rats exposed to PBDEs indicated potential harmful effects in the offspring of female rats. The following is a direct quote:

> In PBDE-exposed male offspring, pronounced decreases in
> circulating sex steroids (estradiol, testosterone) were seen
> both at weaning and in adulthood. Anogenital distance, an
> androgen-dependent marker of sexual development, was also
> reduced in the male offspring. The males further displayed
> a dose-dependent increased preference for sweets, which is a

sexually dimorphic behavior in rodents—this finding indicates feminization in the males. A slight acceleration in onset of puberty was noted in the low-dose group.[9]

In case you are thinking, "Yea, but that's rats—not people." Scientists use mice and rats for experiments because they closely resemble human genetics and have biological and behavior commonalities.

When discussing this with young parents, I am often asked, "Why didn't someone tell us?" That's a tough question without an easy answer. Parents will have to take the lead in becoming informed as to how chemicals affect their children. Often, television is the only educator in a home, and television is funded by advertising. In addition, chemical industries have strong lobbies in the political structure of our country.

Another group of chemicals that may change more than you want changed in your body are called *phthalates*. These chemicals make plastic soft and pliable and are used extensively in cosmetic and fragrance products and in medical equipment and tubing. Even false fingernails and shower curtains may have phthalates present. Disturbingly, many baby toys, including pacifiers, are made from plastics that contain phthalates.

Phthalates are *xenoestrogens* and perform like estrogen once inside the body in spite of not being "mimics." These chemicals are linked to hormone changes in males and females, lower and less mobile sperm, birth defects in the male reproductive system, hypospadias, breast cancer, obesity, diabetes, thyroid disorders, and *death-inducing signaling* in testicular cells. That means these cells die earlier than normal.[10] Your manliness can die off sooner in life even as estrogen tends to rise in later life.[11]

Doctors, who saw increasing numbers of birth defects in male infants, began to sound the alarm bell. Instead of "seldom-seen" birth defects in male babies, they were seeing more and more. Concerned medical scientists began conducting studies that led to the implication of plastics, especially the soft, pliable kind used in medical tubes and household items including PVC flooring, tubing, etc. They found these plastics were potentially causative in asthma, allergies, and in disrupting the endocrine system by affecting male and female traits in the body.[12] In 2002, the FDA cautioned against exposing male babies to DEHP, the chemical that makes PVC soft and pliable. In 2008, Congress outlawed the use of six phthalates in industry; however, others are still allowed. The greatest danger seems to be to babies in the womb, with high exposure to phthalates followed by infants and toddlers who chew on toys and play with their rubber ducks in their bath. Our most vulnerable group is affected the most.[13]

While some of these chemicals may be new to you, you have probably heard of *bisphenol A,* which we commonly call *BPA.* There have been many studies and many reports on this chemical found in baby bottles, plastic food containers, water bottles, linings of metal food and infant formula cans, receipt paper from credit card purchases, and many other sources. Lab animals exposed to low levels show elevated diabetes, neurological disorders, early puberty, breast and prostate cancers, decreased sperm counts, and reproductive problems. In 2010, the FDA issued a report saying there was a *level of concern* regarding the brain and behavior of babies in the womb as well as infants and young children.

In 2011, a study led by the University of California reported that 99 percent of the 268 pregnant women tested had BPA present in their bodies. The report stressed the danger to developing babies.[14] In 2012, it was banned from use in baby bottles. The announcements from the FDA hit the media fan and almost everyone heard that those lovely, clear plastic bottles of water were dangerous, even though they didn't know why. Number 7, encased in a triangle on the water bottle, became important, but most were confused: "Do I want number 7 or do I *not* want number 7?" Many people changed to glass and stainless steel immediately, even though these are not as convenient.

In a remarkably short time, stores began pulling all their BPA items off the shelf and replacing them with the exciting new *BPA Free* label. We breathed a sigh of relief. Scientists had been warning of the dangers for years, but industries refuted the data with reports of their own. Yes, that is like having the fox guard the hen house. However, our relief was short-lived as reports started emerging saying the *BPA Free* products may be just as hazardous—potentially even more so.

There are at least two similar-in-function chemicals—*bisphenol S* and *bisphenol F*—that are not regulated. Plastic industries quickly replaced BPA with these chemicals. Some scientists, however, began bringing up a good point—if BPA causes harmful effects and these two chemicals are similar in composition, isn't it reasonable that they could do the same thing? In fact, that was exactly what the first study, released in January of 2015, reported. BPS significantly reduced testosterone secretion. At the low dose used, BPA did not show the decrease. That's correct. The replacement showed potentially more harm at the low dose than BPA. The study urges that the human health risk in these replacements be recognized.[15] This is a very important study. It makes you wonder if any plastics are truly safe from endocrine disruptors.

Unfortunately, the list continues. Your nonstick cookware may contain *perfluorinated* chemicals (PFCs) or PFOAs that may affect male and female hormones.[16] Lead, arsenic, and even the fluoride in your toothpaste may be adding to the chemical assault we are all under. Dr. Linda Birnbaum, Director of the National Institute of Environmental Health Sciences, says that less than 20 percent of the 80,000 chemicals used in our food and products have been tested at all. Most of them were *grandfathered* in 1976.[17] You are not going to be able to weed them all out, and your body already has some of these stored in your fat tissues and organs, including the brain.

Since the 1930s, researchers said that high doses of fluoride could immobilize sperm. By the 1970s and '80s, scientists were saying that even modest amounts—as much as a child or adult might swallow with application of fluoride gel, could cause damage.[18] However, it's not just toothpaste that contains fluoride; it's drinking water. And, once again, it's the children who are affected the most. A 2014 clinical trial on pubmed. gov indicates that long-term low exposure is enough to affect male hormones and male anatomy.[19] Other studies indicate harmful effects in females, including declining production of female hormones and damage to the uterine and ovarian structures.[20] In addition to fluoride added to water and toothpaste, naturally occurring fluoride in water can add to the overload.

According to the CDC, in 2012 over 11 million people were getting fluoride at or above the optimal level.[21] The U.S. Department of Health and Human Services dropped the optimal levels of fluoride this past year, but because fluoride accumulates in the body, this lower level may not offer much real protection. The "allowable limits" for fluoride were set in 1962, over fifty years ago.[22] Males and females have been using fluoride products and drinking fluoridated water for decades. Millions of women have carried babies who were even more susceptible to fluoride effects than the mother due to size and weight. The question you may be thinking is, "Why, then, did the government put fluoride in drinking water and recommended it to be in toothpaste?" There is a lot of controversy behind this question; however, the important thing for you is to become educated on how fluoride and other chemicals in your food and products you use could be affecting your body and the bodies of your children and family members by disrupting the normal production of hormones in the body.

Many foods contain endocrine disruptors and may even be helpful when needed in aging, but overuse can cause the same effects as chemicals. In 1983, I asked a doctor if he knew of any plants, herbs, etc. that could increase hormones in the body. He had recently come to America from another country; many countries have not relied as heavily on medicines as we have. He responded that he knew of two—grass and peanut butter. He explained that when there is sufficient grass, usually in the spring, grazing animals tend to conceive.

It seems the signal from eating grass is to increase hormones for conception because there is the promise of enough grass to feed the mother and the offspring. The beauty of the concept touched me. He said that estrogen can be found in various grasses and that peanut butter had testosterone. I was fascinated and began searching for more information as well as twirling around in my brain—*how many other foods affect hormones?* It would simply "make sense" that nature had provisions for hormone problems that would affect aging men and women. That was thirty years ago. Now, with herb shops so prevalent, the task is which of the hundreds of herbs and plants are safest and most effective. Hundreds of foods are now classified as *estrogenic* or *non-estrogenic*.

There are several foods, however, that are strong endocrine disruptors and gender benders. Soy is the first on the list. If you are one to read ingredients, start looking for products that don't contain soy. You may find yourself shocked. Soybean oil, soy protein, and soy isolates appear even in unexpected foods. Soy is an inexpensive protein, so many companies add it to increase the protein content. For over fifty years, however, scientists have been warning that soy is strongly estrogenic. It was probably the mid '90s when I read that one cup of soymilk could contain phytoestrogens equivalent to a 1.25 milligram birth control pill. In 1992, the Swiss government issued a warning that infants on soy formula may be getting as much estrogen as three to five birth control pills a day.[23]

A study from 2013 links soy formulas to toxins and endocrine disruptors such as *phylates, nitrites,* and *topoisomerase* in addition to estrogenic *daidzen* and *genistein.* According to the study, the presence of high amounts of manganese, a metal with proven toxicity in high dosage, is even more alarming. Soy formulas typically contain as much as 100 times the amount found in breast milk, a disturbing 200 times increase. Manganese can be deposited in the brain; the infant brain is especially vulnerable. High levels of manganese can lead to neurological disorders. Dr. Francis Crinella, clinical professor of pediatrics at University of California, Irvine, says his studies on children with hyperactivity showed higher levels of manganese than children without hyperactivity. He says the only source for these levels of manganese is soy-based formulas. In 2009, the National Institute of Health voted that risks of soy-based formulas were "minimal" and turned down a motion to label warning of potential risks.[24] Studies on thiamine deficient soy formula showed a significant difference in language development in babies fed soy formula and those fed other formulas.[25]

Whereas soy may offer some benefits to menopausal women and possibly older men with prostate issues, soy in a baby bottle may give a baby—boy or girl—as much as 22,000 times more than the same amount of soy in an adult.[26] One of the researchers, Dr. K.D. Setchell, is Director of Clinical Mass Spectrometry of Cincinnati Children's Hospital in Ohio. He is a highly respected international medical science researcher. He published these findings 18 years ago. If the baby bottle is plastic, you may need to add the estrogenic effects of the phthalates to that number.

A pediatrician often prescribes soy formula when there are allergies to cow milk. However, there are other solutions available. Many pediatricians do not know about the endocrine disrupting potential in soy. We are living is a world of processed foods and where food is getting more expensive. People who have to rely on food stamps and low-income families often have to buy the cheapest food available in order to feed their families. With the research supporting that soy can also contribute to cancer, we may be trading inexpensive food for greater expense later in life. In fact, while baby is drinking the soy formula, read the ingredients of what their toddler brother or sister is eating. Most likely, you are going to find soy in practically everything. Do your own test of the products in your pantry or at the grocery store.

A study published in 2005 says that infant mice exposed to *genistein*, which is found in soy, resulted in concurrent and persistent demasculinization in male mice.[27] *Daidzein*, also found in soy, appears to affect behavior as well. Maternal exposure to *daidzein* has a masculinization effect on memory and social behavior in female mice.[28] Exposure of male rats to soy's *genistein* and *daidzein* has also shown to affect testes function as well testosterone in adulthood.[29] A study published in 2014 says soy can impact fertility, sexual development, and behavior, producing feminizing effects on humans.[30]

With so many studies indicating biological changes in children and adults due to soy consumption, can we continue keeping our heads in the sand and our opinions to ourselves? It is high alert time. If you can change hormones in the body and responses in the brain by intensive ingestion of certain foods, and soy is well known to do that, can we expect the body to ignore endocrine disruptors? What are we doing to our children? What are we doing to the next generation? With hundreds of products including soy or soybean oil in their ingredients, we have an endocrine disrupting nightmare on our hands. Dieters use soy protein and soy protein bars to lower calories and increase protein. Muscle builders use soy protein. Only organic, fermented soy products may be safe for those concerned about endocrine disruptors. Start reading the labels of what you are eating and drinking.

There are many other foods, called *phytoestrogens*, that can positively and negatively affect male and female development.[31] However, most of them are seasonal. In the past, these fruits and vegetables would have been available for two to three months as they have a *growing season*. I remember in my childhood checking out the plums as soon as they had a pink sign on them. Plum season was followed by blackberry season followed by peaches, cantaloupe, and watermelon. Spring and summer vegetables were plentiful. Canning, preserving, and later freezing fruits and vegetables were a part of our everyday life.

Now, we eat seasonal fruits and vegetables all year long. Could it be that just as the grass in spring may initiate hormone changes in grazing animals, could seasonal fruits and vegetables effect similar changes? Could it be that those are the optimal amounts and that "more" is not necessarily better for us? Typically, fall fruits and vegetables are full of the vitamins and minerals needed for respiratory health during the coming winter months. Pumpkins, winter squash, fall apples, etc. are chock full of vitamin A and D. If phytoestrogens are designed to initiate hormonal changes "in the spring" perhaps we need more research on seasonal eating.[32]

Another cause for alarm is early puberty in girls as young as nine or ten. This was not as common years ago, except in some countries south of the equator where it was thought to be associated with the extra sunshine. However, there's enough research to support that *bovine-growth hormones* in milk, dairy products, and beef may be contributing to early puberty in girls, as well as in boys. It's worth noting that the U.N. Food Safety Agency that represents 101 nations banned rBGH milk and dairy. Canada also bans its use.[33]

Another very common additive is MSG, *monosodium glutamate,* a common ingredient in Chinese and Asian foods. It has been linked to behavior problems in children, headaches and other health issues, and reduced fertility.[34]

There are many pesticides, herbicides, and fungicides on the endocrine disruptor list. You may be familiar with health reports on DDT, but you may not recognize names like *methoxychlor,* which is similar to DDT (*dichlorodiphenyltrichloroethane*). Some of you will remember when DDT was "fogged" in the air to kill mosquitoes. And, unfortunately, many of us can remember spraying it liberally on our legs and feet. DDT was banned in 1972 in the U.S. Methoxychlor was banned in 2003 due to toxicity and effect on genetics. It was widely used for the last sixty years. No one knows how long it will take for the soil to recuperate and no longer contain residues. It has been found to affect not only the person who comes in contact with it, but also up to four future generations. That means that a grandmother from 1948 could have been exposed to methoxychlor on the farm where she lived. Her great-grandchildren could still be affected by her exposure.[35] This is called *transgenerational epigenetic inheritance.*

Vinclozolin, a fungicide that has been in use for many years, is still legal but restricted. It is often used on golf courses and on grape crops. Both methoxychlor and vinclozolin are sometimes mixed with other products. If the word "Caution" is on the label, read it and decide if the product is worth using. Most of us blindly ignore the small print, and as we age we can't read it without our glasses anyway. Men, it's not just your manhood at risk, it's the manhood of your future generations. Vinclozolin can affect embryonic testicular development in the womb and at puberty. It actually alters testes development and may contribute to less developed male anatomy.[36] *Legally Poisoned* by Carl F. Cranor explores the transgenerational epigenetic inheritance of vinclozolin and other toxic chemicals.

Atrazine, an herbicide that is applied annually to many crops of corn and other crops to reduce weeds and increase crop yields, has been linked to hormonal changes in amphibians—frogs in particular. Over 80 million pounds of *Atrazine* are used every year in America. Studies at the University of California found that this chemical emasculated frogs, turning one of every ten into a female.[37] Now, let me be the first to say that frogs are not human beings, but are we wise to ignore these findings, as so many studies support the dangers of endocrine disruptors? Additional research links *Atrazine* to hormone changes in fish, birds, reptiles, rats, and human cell lines, including possible links to human birth defects and low birth rate.[38]

These nasty chemicals find their way out of the fields and into our water supply and potentially into the plants we eat. Remember that for many years it was known that perchlorate (rocket fuel) could affect plants grown in ground irrigated by contaminated water, but a few years ago, it was discovered that it is systemic in animals, also. You eat it; it goes right into your cells.

Another herbicide to watch is *glyphosate*, the main ingredient in *Roundup*. As worrisome as glyphosate is, the other ingredients in this toxic cocktail may be even more dangerous, some scientists are saying.[39] Due to the systemic effect of *Roundup*, you are not only being exposed if you use it, you are exposed when you eat crops grown *Roundup-ready*— crops that have been sprayed before planting, during growth season, and at harvesting in order to "dry" crops and get them to market faster. The results are systemic; the plants carry the herbicide right into your body. There, they affect the bacteria in your gut, setting the stage for neuro-transmitter inefficiency and imbalances. There, the *shikimate* pathway found in beneficial gut microbes is affected. This pathway is responsible for the synthesis of amino acids that we have to have.[40] (See Chapter One.) If that were not enough, these chemicals can go into your blood stream and "store" in your body.[41] There is very strong science research linking these chemicals to ADD/ADHD and Autism as well as depression and other emotional and mental disorders. Dr. Stephanie Seneff, researcher at MIT, says there is direct correlation between the chemicals in *Roundup* and the rise of autism. In fact, she says that one half of U.S. children will be autistic by 2025 at the current rate of increase![42]

Glyphosate is a known endocrine disruptor. It has been banned in many countries, but its producer insists it is safe. You can read the "wars" on the Internet on both sides—industry and science. It may be another decade before the scientific community is able to wield enough public support to insist on transparency when it comes to *Roundup*. French research says it not only lowers testosterone, it kills testosterone. In addition, it throws the production of sperm and testosterone out of balance.[43] There are strong indications that prostate and breast cancer, non-Hodgkins lymphoma, and children's brain cancer may be linked to *Roundup*. Scientists have been studying the link to lymphoma for over two decades.[44] One of the most disturbing reports comes from the Agency for Toxic Substances and Disease Registry, a branch of the U.S. Department of Health and Human Services. According to their report, if either parent (mother or father) was exposed to *Roundup* during two years before the child's birth, the chances of the child developing brain cancer doubled.[45]

Is the government doing anything about these pesticides and herbicides that are potentially carcinogenic and endocrine disruptors? Yes, we have agencies and they are investigating the reports. However, it's hard to turn a large ship, and the chemical industries have strong lobbies in local, state, and national government. However, no one is keeping you from emptying your garage of these harmful chemicals. Make certain to take them to a hazardous waste facility as pouring them out exposes you and the land to these toxins.

Lead, mercury, cadmium, arsenic, and zinc are also considered endocrine disruptors. We breathe them, eat them on and in our foods, and put them on our bodies. Even rice, a food staple for many of us, is now so contaminated with arsenic that it's worth knowing more about how to protect your cells.[46] It's almost impossible to escape these toxins. Once again, infants, toddlers, and children are at the most risk as their bodies don't eliminate toxins as well and they are smaller. A small dose affects them more than an adult. Your body's production of glutathione can help you and your children lessen the amounts stored in the tissues of the body. Refer back to Chapter Eight for information on glutathione and how to potentially increase your body's production of this most important antioxidant enzyme.

If you are angry or discouraged by reading the effects of endocrine disruptors, I want to remind you that ignorance of these dangers will not solve the problems we face as a society. It's better to know and become proactive in doing everything you can to prevent and protect your families. It is good to know that the government is taking steps to inform the public and regulate endocrine disruptors. The EPA announced in June 2015 that they were implementing a plan to screen chemicals for their ability to disrupt the endocrine system.[47] This is coming after six decades (sixty years) of warnings from scientists. None of us know how long it will take to get from an announcement to actual change in the food supply and industries.

In the meantime, what about the damage to infants, children, young adults, and all of us in general? Would we see a difference in the emotions and minds of people who reduce their consumption and contact with these chemicals? Can our bodies and brains rebuild?

The good news is that much can be done to lessen stored toxins and give the cells of the body opportunity to heal damaged DNA and replace damaged cells with healthy cells. Vigilance and education are your best weapons in this battle. We are in a war. These terrorists tear at the very framework of our being, separating body and mind, soul and spirit. This war is far from being over. It is daily combat and you can begin by cleaning out your pantries and garages, changing your food choices, trying to eat as organic as possible, planting your own gardens with heirloom seeds, and buying meat without hormones, antibiotics, and other harmful chemicals. Understanding the battle is important; understanding people is imperative. Our society is victimized by chemicals that we cannot handle. It's up to us to educate, inform, and speak with our pocketbooks. There are no easy answers and no quick fixes.

PART FOUR

Redesigning Body, Soul, and Spirit

Beneath, On, and Above the Surface

*I stand, gazing over tops of trees that stand like sentinels. Dawn is just
beginning to look over their shoulders with soft rays of light. They are dark
against the early morning glow. Within moments, the rays will turn pink and
purple or perhaps shades of red. The colors of the sunrise are new every morning.
No repeat performances. I watch carefully as the glow begins and spreads across
the sky. Such beauty awaits me every day even when the sky is heavy with clouds.*

*I love to start the day like this—watching a masterpiece being painted with
colors that reach into my very cells, transforming them by the rush of colors and
brilliance and beauty. The sunlight shows itself in brilliant prisms of color—red,
orange, yellow, green, blue, indigo and violet, and maybe others I cannot see.
All of these colors, designed to restore my soul and body. This morning, a pink
cloud, fluffy like cotton candy, is edging its way across the horizon. A silver edge
outlines it.*

*Overhead the birds are singing. They were awake and singing when I opened the
door. I listen as they greet the morning. Miss Olive Lawton, born in 1900 and
missionary to China and Taiwan for almost 80 years before forced retirement,
told me the birds are singing, "Come up Higher! Come up Higher!" Her words
remind me of where I need to live. Their songs enchant me this morning, as they
are especially chipper and musical.*

*Are the birds intentionally putting on an impromptu concert with other birds
who happen to be in the trees at the time? I wonder. The tones reach deep into
my soul and body. The very cells of my body hear these tones, not just my ears.
Neurotransmitters respond to sound, and our bodies were especially designed
for these sounds of nature. From the trees in my yard, I listen to an orchestra of
sounds and cadence. We don't know all the mysteries behind their singing and
all the ways it affects the cells in our bodies.*

*The sunrise and the birds singing. Prescription for happy neurotransmitters!
I lean against the door absorbing the goodness of the morning. My roses are
in bloom; the daylilies are starting their one day of life, showing off in orange,
yellow, purple, and pinks. I reach for my garden scissors and begin making a*

161

selection of roses—a soft yellow, a Tiffany pink, a few whites, and an orange Gypsy. I deeply inhale the fragrance of the flowers in my hand. I know that the fragrance will make its journey deep into my body and into my brain where, once again, neurons will respond. The colors of the sunrise; the sound of the birds; the beauty of the flowers; the fragrance. All of it created to restore our minds and rebuild our bodies.

The sun has tipped the trees and is too bright for my eyes. I take one more deep breath and reluctantly leave the beauty of the morning. I place my little bouquet of roses in a vase and set them on a table beside me. Their fragrances blend. My Bible is on the table and I reach for it, turning to where I stopped reading yesterday. My world would be too scattered without this morning time. I need the words to reach deeply into the places in my spirit where I am carrying worries and concerns, and where gratitude for my answered prayers resides. A trysting place where I can rest my soul.

CHAPTER 10

Getting Back to the Design:
How Prayer Changes Your
Body and Soul

Years ago, while I was regaining my life after a battle with breast cancer, my husband and I took a trip to the Caribbean. He had a speaking assignment, and I needed time to stare at the ocean, snorkel in the crystal water, and re-gather broken dreams and expectations. We stayed a few extra days and took a day trip to some nearby islands to snorkel, swim, and relax. We flew in a small plane low over the islands with a few other tourists to our first stop where we would board the ship for the excursion. With an hour or so to wait, we tourists walked around, shopped, or lazily sat in the sun waiting for the ship. Naturally curious, I began to explore. I noticed a large pool encircled with a stone wall separating the pool from the ocean on one side and a restaurant on the other side. The wall was about twelve inches wide.

The pool was a "shark pool," and the restaurant threw chum—fish parts, etc.—into the water at certain times every day so the guests could watch the feeding frenzy. I was intrigued, having never been so close to sharks that were not behind glass. As I walked around the stone wall,

163

observing the sharks, I noticed two small children at the opposite end of the pool. They were sitting on the wall, dangling their legs in the ocean. The little boy held a fishing pole that was about twice his height.

I was concerned. What if the children fell in? Would the sharks grab their little arms and legs before any of us could get to them? I began a slow walk on top of the stone wall in their direction. Just about the time I was close enough to speak to them, they jumped into the ocean and quite nimbly walked to the beach on the other side. They knew where the sand bars were and were probably more afraid of the strange looking lady walking toward them on the wall than of the sharks in the water!

I turned and headed back, walking on the narrow stone wall that separated me from the shark pool and the ocean. The sharks were all occupied with activity on the other side, where the other tourists were standing. Suddenly, my feet hit a broken part of the wall that was covered in algae and as slick as glass. There was nothing to stop me. I fell into the shark pool. Now, these were probably not "man eaters" but they were a good six- to eight-foot-long sharks, and they were accustomed to heading to large splashes in the water.

Within a nanosecond, a steady voice inside said, 1) *Don't turn around.* 2) *Don't panic.* 3) *Concentrate on getting out.* That was just it. Weak from chemotherapy and neck deep in water, how was I going to get back up on that wall? As I reached for the wall, I grasped only slick algae with nothing to hold to hoist myself back up. With a supernatural jump, I raised myself up out of the water, reached over the wall and grabbed enough of the wall to pull myself out, just as the sharks neared me. I was prone on the sea wall, with the sharks so close I could feel them swishing in the water. Inches away, I could have touched them with my hands. I was wearing loose bell-bottom slacks and one of the trouser legs trailed in the water. With my hands shaking badly, I lifted it out of the water. I knew I could not rise from where I lay.

Within moments, I heard a voice, "Ma'am, would you like a hand?" Would I like a hand! It was the young Irish man, a fireman, who was on honeymoon with his wife. We had chatted on the flight over. I could not speak, but I was able to lift my hand just a little. He had me in a fireman's hold almost immediately. Lifting me up, he carried me like a baby back to where my astonished husband stood. The young fireman and his wife had seen me fall. While he ran to me, she ran to my husband. In her lovely accent she had said to my husband, "Sir, your wife has fallen into the shark pool."

We all laughed about it later, after I stopped shaking. But in the midst of getting too upfront and personal with a number of sharks, I couldn't predict what was ahead. A cancer battle followed by falling in a shark pool! Both were too close for comfort. And that may be where you are right now—in a battle for your life or facing foes that could destroy you.

Having lived through both, I can tell you that neither time did I know what the outcome was going to be. I had to just keep concentrating on getting through the cancer and getting out of the shark pool. If you have made a decision to concentrate on overcoming emotional, mental, and addictive disorders, or you are going to help a loved one, there are some steps with which to begin. The first is in your own mind.

Psalms 119:59 says, "I have considered my ways and have turned my steps to your statutes."

You can change your body and you can change your mind. If you have been reading the endnotes, you see the path of medical science that has been laid out for you. Acting upon what you have read will be a daily process as well as urgent until you are out of the "shark pool." Then, as your recovery progresses, you will become more surefooted on the path. You will be able to say with the psalmist, "You have made a wide path for my feet to keep them from slipping" (Ps. 18:36 NLT). The stone wall on which I was walking did not offer enough protection from the sharks, nor was it wide enough for me to walk surefooted. It was an "accident waiting to happen."

There is a saying from years ago that still holds truth: *If you don't know where you are going, any road will get you there.* That may be true of where you are. Not knowing where you are going may sound simplistic, but the biggest question in life is exactly that: "Where are you going?" Does life promise more than years of misery followed by nothing?

Let me be clear here—I am talking about Heaven or Hell. If you don't believe in Hell, it may be more convenient for you. But what if you are mistaken? What if, at the end of life, you realize you were on the wrong road after all? What if it's true that there is a Heaven and a Hell? What if there is a Creator God, who is Good? And the antithesis of that Goodness is an evil spirit who is opposed to God? What if it really is true that God is for you and the devil is against you?

That simplicity may offend you or cause you to slam the book shut with "Oh, no. One of those Christians!" Identifying with Christianity can cost you friends and family, position and prestige. But it's a fair trade if it means attaining a different life, one that is no longer founded on shaky ground.

If it is true that there is an *evil force* that opposes God, then could it be that he is also opposing you? Surely, he is no match for God. However, perhaps he is a match for us if we don't know who we are in Christ. Even then, he can give us a run for our lives. That may be exactly what has been going on in your life. Could it be that he is really, after all, battling us because we are the *apple of God's eye*? What if he is cunning enough to try to *get at God* by *getting at us*? Christ defeated Satan at Calvary and overcame death at the resurrection. So why would the devil be trying to battle against God? He's not after God; he is after humanity.

The devil is an ancient foe who knows our frame, our makeup, our bodies, and how we function. He knew our ancestors. Who's to know if maybe he observes us or sends some of his emissaries to take a good, hard look at us? After all, he knew our ancestors from generations ago, and he spotted a "weakness" then. He's had lots of time to learn.

Ephesians 2:2 calls this evil force the "prince of the power of the air" (NASB). We continue to learn the "power" the air holds as smartphones and computers can connect us visually almost anywhere in the world.

The air holds possibilities that we haven't discovered; ancient people did not know that the air could hold up planes and space ships. Former generations could not envision sending a message in less than a second to the other side of the world in an e-mail. Bible translators simply called the potential all around us the "power of the air." There is a power in the air that we cannot see, nor can we feel it, but we know it's there. Our huge communication towers may be fairly close to the *Tower of Babel*, if the truth were known (see Gen. 11:1–8). If you believe in e-mail, FaceTime, and instant messaging, surely you believe in *prayer*. (Actually, prayer is faster and more effective, unless it is opposed as Daniel's prayer was in Daniel 10. But we have a different delivery system than Daniel did—we pray in the Name of Jesus!)

That is why, as Christians, we pray in the Name of Jesus. It's not superstition to suggest that the "power of the air" may carry more than we know. Making sure there is no mistaken identity, we address our prayers in the Name Above All Names, *Jesus*. Our Holy Scriptures do not suggest *if* when it comes to prayer. Instead, it is *when* you pray. You may recall that the disciples, after being with Jesus for a while, asked Him to teach them to pray (see Luke 11:1). They had watched Him heal, open eyes of the blind, teach with wisdom and depth beyond anything they had ever heard. They *felt* His authority over the heavens, the sea, and the earth. Yet what they asked Him to do was *teach them to pray*. Could it be that they recognized that prayer had something to do with His abiding in the Father? Something to do with how He lived and walked among them? *Could prayer still hold a potential for healing emotional, mental, and addictive disorders even two thousand years after the disciples asked that question?*

From a physical and scientific standpoint, what does prayer do for us? An unusual thing is happening—science is validating prayer. All too often, it seems like religion and science are on opposite sides, even though they don't need to be. Dr. Martin Luther King said is so well:

> There may be a conflict between soft minded religionists
> and tough minded scientists...but not between science and
> religion. Science investigates; religion interprets. Science gives
> man knowledge which is power; religion gives man wisdom

which is control. Science deals mainly with facts; religion deals mainly with values. The two are not rivals. They are complementary. Science keeps religion from sinking into the valley of crippling irrationalism and paralyzing obscurantism. Religion prevents science from falling into the marsh of obsolete materialism and moral nihilism.[1]

Francis Collins, one of the most respected geneticists in the world and director of the *Human Genome Project*, is a committed believer in Jesus. When he wrote his best-selling book, *The Language of God: A Scientist Presents Evidence for Belief*, he said he did so because "most people are seeking a possible harmony between these worldviews (science and faith), and it seems rather sad that we hear so little about this possibility.[2]

In the last decade, more than 6,000 studies concerning prayer and health have been published. Many of these indicate that good health may be tied to religion and religious practices, such as prayer.[3] Many medical and research scientists are searching out the mystifying reasons that people of faith and prayer have certain *changes* in their cellular metabolism. There are physical and measurable changes in our brains and our neurotransmitters when we pray.

Using a SPECT image, scientists are able to watch particular lobes in the brain respond to prayer. It's not the same response that they see in Eastern meditation, which activates another part of the brain.[4] The frontal lobe is activated when we pray just as it is when we are talking to a person. The limbic system, associated with anger, guilt, anxiety, depression, resentment, and fear, deactivates as we pray.[5]

Another measurable effect of prayer on the brain is an increase in production of neurotransmitters such as dopamine, serotonin, and others.[6] The balance between these chemicals is very delicate. Increasing dopamine, the *pleasure and reward chemical,* or serotonin, *the "all's right in the world"* chemical, as well as balancing them, can produce powerful changes in people. Getting a burst of these throughout the day will not only change your brain, it can also change your day. Something as inexpensive as prayer, as readily available and accessible, that has only good side effects, and can help with neurotransmitter production and efficiency sounds almost too good to be true.

If science can prove that prayer actually *changes* the cells in the body; if it precipitates neurotransmitter production and efficiency; if it can realign the mind, will, and emotions, would it be asking too much for us to ask the Lord to *teach us to pray*? If scientific research could prove that prayer "does something" to the cells of the body and soul, would you be willing to give prayer a second look?

Prayer. Almost every religion believes in and practices prayer. Buddhists have prayer wheels that contain written truths that they trust will aid in the pursuit of compassion and wisdom. Devout Hindus memorize many prayers and repeat them during the day. Islam teaches mandatory prayer five times a day. Regardless of what you believe about prayer, it's plausible to realize that carrying a prayer wheel, repeating memorized prayers throughout the day, and practicing mandatory prayer five times a day may keep the mind on task and attentive to the dictates of the religion. It seems that in all religions prayer is linked to devotion and devotion is linked to power in the religion. The power of prayer is acknowledged even if it is not understood.

I'm asking for a second look, because some of you may be saying, "I prayed. It didn't work. I still have (fill in the blank)." If, however, you are willing to give prayer another chance in your life, it might be good to rethink some of our preconceived notions about prayer. Many of us, when we pray, consider it our job to coach God on what to do, as if He didn't know what to do. Telling the All Wise Creator of the Universe what to do is like an ant telling an elephant what to do. Well, maybe an ant isn't small enough; for sure, an elephant isn't large enough. But hopefully you get the picture. Is prayer telling an All Wise God what to do for you? If the truth be known, many of us got ourselves into the "fixes" we are in without God's help. Right now, some of you may be thinking, "Well, He should have prevented it!"

I would not have fallen into the shark pool had I not been walking on the wall. My unwise decision put me in a perilous situation. I believe the Lord helped me to get out of it, but I don't believe it was dictated that I fall into the shark pool. Nor do I believe He puts us in "shark pools" just to teach us a lesson. Would you do that to your children? He can use my shark pool experience in my life, and He certainly has. I am much wiser and I stay away from sharks; I don't even look at them in the aquarium or on television. Some memories are too painful, if you know what I mean.

If we are not wise enough, then, to instruct God on how to mind His business and our business, what is the purpose of prayer and should we pray? A simple theology of prayer might be helpful in order for us to know how we count in the universe. We counted enough for God to give His only Son as a sacrifice for our sins. There's actually a lot of history behind that statement as it relates to covenants and the power of blood in science and in culture. And, as inconceivable as it seems, when Christ conquered the devil and death on the cross, He won the earth back for us. In John 12:31, Christ makes it clear: "Now judgment is upon this world; now the ruler of this world will be cast out" (NASB).

Quite simply, Adam was given the world, but he turned the authority over to Satan who was able to enter our atmosphere here on earth because Adam and Eve did what he suggested. Their disobedience was an open invitation. That still holds true for our lives. It's the *Garden of Eden* every day when we consciously decide to follow the dictates of what may *look* good but not *be* good. Adam and Eve doubted what God had told them, disbelieved His truth, and *ate* the forbidden fruit. The Tree of the Knowledge of Good and Evil was not the only tree; it was the "testing" tree. Just as God would not force Adam and Eve to obey, He doesn't force us to obey. He desires obedience because of love, trust, and wisdom. He gives us *free will*—we can choose Him or refuse Him in our everyday lives.

Jesus won back the authority over the earth by defeating Satan's plan for Him on Calvary. Contrary to Adam, He was obedient unto death. Refusing to take the strategic plan into His own hands and refusing to break "Trinity Unity," Christ realigned the future of the earth. He won it back! What had been foretold by scripture and prophets, unfolded in history. A comic shift in authority. The promises of ages had come true. Christ, perfect in life, conquered not only temptation, He overcame death as well. The spiritual battle between Christ and Satan was finished at the cross, but the consequences of what happened to the earth in the Garden of Eden remain. Women still have pain in childbirth; roses still have thorns; lions will still eat lambs. We live in a broken world where darkness tries to overcome light.

Coming down from the cross would have allowed the devil authority over Him, the Only Begotten of the Father. The devil had already invited Jesus to be in cahoots with him. He actually promised Jesus that He could rule over all the kingdoms of the world if Jesus would bow down and worship him (see Matt. 4:1–11). A shortcut, without the pain of death and suffering.

Instead, Jesus walked away from the devil and his convoluted, self-serving promises. In fact, I believe that Jesus had *us* in mind. He still does. When He won the world back, like a ball, He tossed it to His blood-bought believers reinstating the promise of the Garden. "Here it is. Tend it. Make it fruitful. Multiply." What a Risk Taker! To win the earth back and then give it to a bunch of disciples who were running for their lives, discouraged, depressed, and defeated. Then, just to keep them and us from feeling totally overwhelmed with the weight of the world on our shoulders, He promised to be with us not just some of the time, but all of the time, and to give us greater power than He had on earth. If you don't believe me, check out John 14:12–14—"Very truly I tell you, whoever believes in me will do the works I have been doing, and they will do even greater things than these, because I am going to the Father. And I will do whatever you ask in my name, so that the Father may be glorified in the Son. You may ask me for anything in my name, and I will do it."

Then He told the disciples to get out there and announce a new day—that the Kingdom of Heaven had come to earth, that they could rule and reign over the earth with Him as He stood at the right hand of the Father praying for us. In fact, as we pray, we rule and reign with Him. Our part is to find the Mind of Christ, which will always be the will of the Father, and exercise our faith to bring His plans to earth—not just for us, but also for the world. Could it be that prayer might actually help change the world even as it changes us? Could it be that prayer, because it is the communication system that reaches from you to Christ, is a means of recovery and healing of your body, soul, and spirit?

I realize that your belief system is dependent on whether or not you accept the Bible as truth. I do want to add a point here, that even now, thousands and thousands of years after the Bible was spoken and the words written down, science is still discovering the truths in the Bible. We cannot conceive the wonders of His world and universe. Nor can we truly conceive the depths of prayer and what it can do for us and our broken world. However, if the enemy of this world can keep us busy at the shopping center, fighting over doctrines, and mesmerized with the "things of the world," he can keep us from praying. If he can keep our minds filled with "worthless," he can keep us from praying about the truly important. Thus, our perceptions of prayer can be reduced to simple shopping lists that we spin off in the few minutes set aside for "prayer." Or we don't pray until we are desperate. In order for the Lord to hear from us, we don't want desperation to be the signal to pray. Right now, however, desperation may be the flag you are waving.

Dr. Andrew Newberg, Director of the Center for Spirituality and the Mind at the University of Pennsylvania, found in laboratory tests that a *unique circuit in the brain that improves memory and cognition, reduces anxiety and depression, and enhances social awareness and empathy toward others* is activated in prayer and meditation. This response is not just limited to religious meditation.[7] However, Dr. Newberg and Dr. Mark Waldman, co-author of *How God Changes Your Brain,* say that if the meditation is religious and strengthens spiritual beliefs, there is a synergistic effect. The results improved.[8]

Even short and simple forms of prayer can produce effects in the mind and body as powerful neurotransmitters that increase clarity, consciousness, alertness, and peacefulness are up-regulated. Dr. Newberg says their research shows that the *more you engage in prayer with all parts of your being—your thoughts, emotions, perceptions, your social interactions and spiritual pursuits—the more it enhances your brain's function.*[9] He adds a caveat here, however, that these effects require a focus on love, forgiveness, and inclusiveness. Simple meditation practices and prayer can change the body, improve memory,[10] and change the soul.

Dr. Harold Koenig—Director of Duke University Center for Spirituality, Theology, and Health and author of many books on religion and healing including *Faith and Mental Health: Religious Resources for Healing* and his latest, *The Healing Power of Faith: Science Explores Medicine's Last Great Frontier*—is another outstanding scientist who is researching the power of faith and prayer in emotional health. He says that where there is a strong spiritual component, there is less depression, anxiety, greater well-being, and less drug and alcohol abuse. MRIs show that the structure of the brain is actually altered in brains of those at high risk for depression and there is a delay in loss of memory associated with aging as well as Alzheimer's.[11] He says that prayer and faith shows a lessening of severe depression by 81 percent.[12]

Why the interest in how prayer affects health? It's because people pray for themselves and for others in times of sickness. Some of these scientific studies have been on intercessory prayer—praying for others within proximity of touch and others miles away. Those prayed for close at hand as well as far away improved and recovered faster. For these people, those intercessory prayers, like an e-mail, went directly where intended. Even when the people prayed for and those praying did not know each other, the scientific results were there.[13] Some people are intentionally seeking physicians who believe in and practice prayer.

Dr. Koenig says that studies show prayer can prevent people from getting sick, and when they do get sick prayer can help them heal faster. One study showed remarkable improvement in visual and audio deficiencies.[14]

Dr. Herbert Benson, cardiovascular specialist at *Harvard Medical School*, refers to what he calls *the relaxation response* that occurs when we pray. The body's metabolism slows, heart rate slows, blood pressure goes down, and the breath becomes calmer and more regular. He says there are slower brain waves, tranquil alertness, feelings of control, and peace of mind. He also mentions that over half of doctor visits are prompted by high blood pressure, ulcers, migraines, and depression which can all be associated with high levels of stress.[15] One of his recent studies indicates that long-term daily spiritual practices can help to deactivate genes that cause inflammation and cellular death.[16] In short, there is a tranquilizing effect in the body and mind.

Consistent prayer and scriptural meditation can rebuild the brain, increasing the size of the frontal lobe and improving *executive function*.[17] This includes behaviors and processes that contribute to successful living and making healthy and wise decisions. In 2009, a clinical study on prayer at the University of Mississippi showed that direct prayer intervention over six weeks of one-hour sessions resulted in significant improvements in depression and anxiety.[18] A one-year follow-up of these same participants showed significantly less depression and anxiety, more optimism, and greater levels of spiritual experience than in the pre-prayer baseline measurements.[19]

Perhaps one of the first steps on the path to a new life is praying daily. Taking a dedicated time every day to talk to God, talking to Him during the day, and listening just in case He brings something to your heart or mind may make more difference than you can possibly know, not just in your mind but in the very cells of your body. In case you are at a point where you cannot pray, consider inviting someone trustworthy to pray with you until the words become your own. The sincere heart that longs for the Lord to come and take over will be heard. You may want to begin by talking to Him as if He were your best friend. After all, He is. His will and His plan are the best for you. Consider letting Him lead your life while you concentrate on changing your body so that you can change your future. Prayer may be the medicine you need for restoring your soul.

Often, when we are under stress and powerful emotions like regret and remorse plague us day and night, we awaken with anxiety. A sign of depression can be early morning awakenings and inability to go back to sleep, if you were able to go to sleep in the first place. Ending your day by pushing out those thoughts and emotions and replacing them with the old *counting your blessings* may increase your serotonin and melatonin enough to lull you to sleep. Then, by beginning your morning by inviting God into your day, asking Him to direct your path and keep you from evil, and speaking out personal gratitude to Him for who He is and for what He does can produce powerful changes in your brain and in your body. Adding some outside time with a good dose of the colors of dawn, the pinks and violets, can get you off to a good day.[20] While this may sound simplistic up against the problems you are facing, it's worth trying. Remember my shark pool story—when I reached for something to hold on to the first time, the stones were too slippery. My hands grabbed only algae. However, when I raised my body out of the water as best I could, I found something to hold on to. Prayer at its highest and at its most elemental is the same—it's talking to God. The cells in your body will join your mind in prayer. They will do what they are designed to do—when you pray.

Just as scientists figured out that our *gut* is a second brain, there is emerging science that says the heart is our *third* brain. In essence, their studies show the heart is a complex and organized system that maintains a "two-way dialogue" with the brain and the rest of the body, similar to that of the gut-brain connection. In *The HeartMath Solution*, Childre and Martin say that our feeling level influences our thinking level.[21] The Scriptures hold over 700 references to the heart as the center of emotion in our being. Can we, by persistent prayer that includes thankfulness and forgiveness of those who have wronged us, not only have a "change of heart" but also a *changed mind*, where emotional and mental illness no longer dominate the life? Proverbs 4:23 reads, "Above all else, guard your heart, for it is the wellspring of life." Guarding the heart through dedicated and spontaneous prayer may be good medicine for the soul. Jesus says to "Love the Lord your God with all your heart and with all your soul and with all your mind and with all your strength" (Mark 12:30). Perhaps this is physiology and psychology at its best, and perhaps this is the secret to wholeness in body, soul, and spirit.

CHAPTER 11

Redesigning Yourself: How Music Impacts Your Cells

When I was six, we moved to my father's homestead, a farm in southeast Georgia. My grandfather died and my father returned home to care for our grandmother and our beloved aunt, who was mentally impaired. When "cotton-picking time" arrived, I wanted to pick cotton along with everyone else. The cotton-pickers arrived early one morning. About twenty seasoned, experienced, and lightning-fast pickers piled out of the pickup truck. It was lawful to ride in the back of the truck in 1949. This was before cotton-picking machines, and farmers depended on the "pickers," just as many farms today are still harvested by migrant workers.

I was delighted to see several little girls who had come with their mother to pick. They had their bags slung over their shoulders and I showed off my bag. My mother had made it the night before. I knew absolutely nothing about picking cotton, so my father gave me a few pointers. The little girls' mother had assured my father she would teach me and I could pick with her girls. For some reason, everyone except for me was amused and exchanged glances and smiles. I was serious, however. I meant to pick that cotton.

It wasn't long, though, before my bag was heavy and I couldn't keep up. I was grateful when the dinner bell rang and we all went to the house for a large, Southern meal. It was customary to prepare a good, big meal for the pickers. After lunch we "sat a spell" under the big pecan trees in our yard. The pickers talked and chatted a while or took naps until the bright noonday sun lowered a bit in the skies. At some given time, the leader stood up and headed back to the fields. We all followed, my curly reddish-blond hair ballooning big on my head, due to the humidity, in the middle of twenty strong, robust African Americans. I was cared for and welcomed.

The afternoon was hot and humid. Fatigue began to set in. Ill tempers flared in the field, as one or the other accused the other of "picking my row." The workers were paid by the weight of the bag, so speed and agility meant more money at the end of the day. In the middle of the "fussing" from several rows over, I heard a voice began to sing softly. As her voice rose in the field, the other workers joined her, singing with the soul that mirrored their heritage, music, and faith. For the next few hours, until "quitting time," we sang. I watched moods change, laughter and smiles replaced frowns, and the hours passed quickly. The fatigue lifted.

Now, years later, I know what happened that day in the field. The singing changed their neurotransmitters, affecting brain waves positively and increasing endorphin release for tired muscles. The body is a beautiful mechanism; cells will do what they were designed to do unless hindered. Your mind, brain, and body are the vehicles to help you develop the life you want and a life worth living. Getting them into harmony with each other and with your conscious mind can and will bring healing.

Music was a part of working during my childhood. Often, I awakened on Saturday mornings to my mother's voice, humming and singing as she did her Saturday chores. When I was a teenager, I worked in "peaches." The local packing shed hired a busload of us every summer to pack peaches in bushel baskets to ship all over America, as Georgia peaches were famous. Our revered and beloved football coach was our boss. There were no discipline problems regardless of how fatigued we became. All he had to do was look at us. If we "slacked" and started talking, he would walk over and stand for a minute or two. We doubled our efforts. When we would get tired or bored in a hot packing shed with machines roaring and peach fuzz itching, we would sing. At the end of the day on the bus, we would sing. Singing was a natural part of our lives.

Those were the days before jam boxes, earplugs, and iPods. Technology has given us so much, but it has come with a significant cost. Much of our culture has changed. The body listens and responds to music videos differently than active singing. Yes, there is a neurotransmitter response to electronic music, but it's not the same as when the body is actively involved, singing, remembering the lyrics and melodies, harmonizing, using hands and feet in time with the music, or making motions with the music. The body's response to sounds is reciprocal to the level of listening and involvement.

Try this little test—go outside for a few minutes and just listen. Often when we go outside, we are on our way to the car and have our minds on many things. If the birds are singing, we don't notice. Go outside with the intention to listen to the sounds of the birds. In a few minutes, your body will feel different.

Using music to achieve results in the body goes back as far in time as we can go in history. Ancient instruments called people to war or to festival. Flutes, simple string instruments, drums, and trumpets were handcrafted in cultures as the people found their joy and repose in sounds that pleased the body and soul or, in case of war, increased passion, aggression, and hostility. In recent history, the trumpet is still used to summon for war and to bury the fallen. The Scottish bagpipes have frightened many in wartime to drop their weapons and flee. Yes, men wearing kilts with their bare legs could have an extraordinary effect, but it is the music from the pipes that stirs the emotions of both bravery and fear. The pipes are actually listed as "weapons of war"—many battle stories extoll where their sound carried the men to victory and survival.[1] Native Americans went on the warpath by rousing the tribes to fight by the use of drums and certain cadences.

Some of you will remember the rousing song from *Les Misérables* when Enjolras leads the people in passionately singing the lines, *When the beating of your heart echoes the beating of the drums.*[2] These words reflect the power of using music not only to mold the mind, but also to affect the very cells of the body.

Sounds move people. Sounds can also move matter. Sound waves can penetrate matter, going through walls and buildings. Sound waves can take down buildings. Most likely, the walls of Jericho fell because of sound waves—days of vibrations from marching feet, strategic trumpet blasts, and then a loud shout. Suddenly, the impenetrable walls of Jericho fell down. A miracle of revelation, obedience, and unity of action. The Lord had given Joshua an unusual strategy for taking the armed city of Jericho: *March around the city once with all the armed men. Do this for six days. Have seven priests carry trumpets of rams' horns in front of the ark. On the seventh day, march around the city seven times, with the priests blowing the trumpets. When you hear them sound a long blast on the trumpets, have the whole army give a loud shout; then the wall of the city will collapse* (see Josh. 6:3–5). Sound waves are powerful.

Can we harness some of this power to transform emotional, mental, and addictive disorders? Could it possibly be that Satan and his evil forces may know more about sound and music than we do? Could the being, whom many theologians and biblical scholars refer to as the *King of Tyre* in Ezekiel 28:13, "*the workmanship of thy tabrets and of thy pipes was prepared in thee in the day that thou wast created*" (KJV), use sound against us and harm us? Modern translations refer to *tabrets and pipes* as settings for jewels and stones. However, when these terms are used at other times in the Bible, it's clear the reference is to musical instruments. The earlier translators lived in a musical world where pipes and tambourine-type drums were more common. What if sounds do hold extraordinary power in our bodies and minds? Increasingly, science is using sound—ultrasound, sound waves, echocardiograms, sonar, etc. are commonplace. For example, you have seen ultrasound images of babies in the womb. Sound permeates all of our lives all of the time.

Have you noticed that every store seems to be playing music tracks? Did you know that marketing science is being used to cause us to spend more money due to the effects of the music on our persuasion? What about when you are *on hold*? The music track can make you slam the phone down or stay on the line—if it pleases your ear. The sound of music in the marketplace has drowned out silence and possibly had an effect on your pocketbook. Over four decades ago, Philip Kotler from

Northwestern University coined the term *atmospherics* in marketing. He predicted that there would be studies on the social and ethical implications of "man's growing power to create atmospheres to motivate purchase."[3] Present day marketing tests are sophisticated enough to know the type of music, beat, and level of sound needed to make us lose track of time, loiter in the store, and buy on impulse.

When I was working daily with teenagers, it was necessary for me to know a lot about their music in order to understand them better and the struggles they were facing. Eventually, I could guess their favorites by their mood and demeanor. I also knew that if I could not get them to give up certain music, I would have a very hard time helping them with their depression, harmful habits, and addictions, not to mention learning and behavior. The parents typically thought I was talking about lyrics. Those were bad enough, but it wasn't the lyrics; it was the tones, beat, and cadences combined together to create a potentially harmful effect on their mind and brain functions.

Heartbeat, blood pressure, and many cellular responses are affected by music.[4] A study from Washington State University in St. Louis, Missouri says that music affects the same neural pathways of reward and emotion that are affected by drugs, sex, and food. These include the dopamine, serotonin, and glutamate systems.[5] In addition, music affects emotional responses and memory. A recent study among older adults found that *music-evoked autobiographical memories* declined only a small amount after five decades. The music listened to at ages 15 to 24 was not only remembered, it actually evoked emotional responses in the brain.[6]

For centuries, oral traditions and history were passed down in song and sounds. People memorized and sang the cultural traditions, including long genealogies, healing remedies, and instructions for living. Those songs contained tribal histories for hundreds of years of migration and enabled the tribe to know their history. Nothing was lost because the words were set to music. Such is the power of music in the brain.

Dr. David Knauss, in his research on *music memorableness*, asked participants to rate what degree melody, harmony, rhythm patterns, phrases, musical form, tempo, timbre, and text influenced their musical memory. Participants reported that text and melody caused music to be remembered more than the other variables.[7]

Music tones and other music elements also affect emotion, emotional memory, language, and expression. We refer to music we "like" and music we don't like. Most likely, this is because music affects our emotions as well as our cells. Research is increasing on how music affects the brain, music therapy for brain injuries, stroke, behavior and learning, and how music affects emotional, mental, and addictive disorders.

Dr. Daniel Levitin, James McGill Professor of Psychology, Behavioral Neuroscience, and Music at McGill University, is a neuroscientist and composer. He claims music affects our entire brain, activating neurons in more regions of the brain than anything else we know of, and it causes the release of neurochemicals in the brain.[8] Dopamine production is increased when we even *approach* certain music that brings us pleasure; in other words, reaching for the CD or the iPod starts the process. Then, as the music progresses, our neurotransmitters respond to the musical patterns.[9]

We have millions of people struggling with emotional, mental, and addictive disorders. Many young people and adults walk a trapeze daily trying to keep thoughts and actions balanced. Many already have psychiatric diagnoses; others fear an evaluation because they don't want the labels. Often, a preteen searching for identity will attach to a particular singer or music group. That becomes their identity. How to talk, how to walk, and extremes of behavior, including following the lifestyle of a particular singer or group, become the preteen's goal in life.

When we look at large auditoriums and arenas filled for concerts, we cannot ignore that the "potion" in the air is music. They are attracted not just to the sound, but also to how music and the crowd make them feel, leaning into what the sound does in the mind and body. Do we have thousands of young people who already have dopamine inefficiencies (too low; too high; erratic and not stable) linked by a common neurotransmitter metabolic profile?

The Pied Piper, which tells the famous fairy tale of a piper who was hired to rid a town of rats, may be based on an element of truth. A town hired a piper to lure the rats away due to his renowned ability to play tones the rats followed. Now, for those of you who are raising your eyebrows, consider that pest control in many places is now ultrasonic—sound frequencies that humans can't hear. The piper was successful. The rats followed him right out of town. But the town refused to pay him. In retribution, he began to play, and all the children followed him out of town and into a deep cave where they were never seen again. Not a happy story. Symbolically, the tale could apply to many teens in our current culture.

I have often thought about the story while working with teens who locked themselves away into their music, closing their emotional doors behind them. Certain songs and tones expressed their anger, disappointment, angst, despair, and unresolved conflicts. Turning up the music to deafening levels helped to ease the pain, but also built an invisible refuge for them. Eventually, the parents would buy the teen earphones so they didn't have to listen to the loud music. Particular songs, now played as loud as possible, penetrated every cell in the body. Neurotransmitters would have reached abnormal levels; heart rate, blood pressure, brain waves, and cellular metabolism would all be affected. When the teen had finished his/her "dose" of music, their moods would reflect it. Who knows how many have been led into dark caves of depression as the tones skewed neurotransmitter levels. Solid research indicates that heavy metal music can lead to depression.[10]

When it comes to addiction, heavy metal music can also raise dopamine and adrenaline in the body, continuing and fueling addiction to dopamine and adrenaline (also called epinephrine). Simultaneously, though, other studies indicate listeners are less depressed after listening to heavy metal as the music helps them express those emotions.[11] But when it comes to calming emotions, clinical studies show that classical music—Mozart, in particular—has a soothing effect on the emotions, increasing serotonin and endorphins.[12]

The power of music has crossed all cultural and historical segments of time, and the influence of that power is well known to "mind-shapers."

A quote attributed to Napoleon says, *Give me control over he who shapes the music of a nation, and I care not who makes the laws.*[13] Music unites young people from all over the world. They may not speak the same language, but millions listen to the same songs. These songs—not just the words, but also the very music itself—shape culture as they shape individuals. No doubt you have been at a sports event or concert where a crowd was united and electrified by the joint singing of a song. In past generations, songs of patriotism united and fostered love of country and sense of duty to country. Dr. Karl Paulnack, Director of the Music Division, The Boston Conservatory of Music, says, "Music has a way of finding the big, invisible moving pieces inside our hearts and souls and helping us figure out the position of things inside us."[14]

Seemingly, what is emerging globally is a different kind of dedication, and that is to a global music culture that unites by age and generation. Some young people listen to between six to eight hours of music a day with their ear phones, successfully blocking out interaction with other people, especially their families. What will be the repercussions of this in the future? Isolation and lack of understanding already plague this generation. Can we expect to have solid character, responsibility, as well as compassion and empathy develop in isolation where there is a lack of molding relationships? What will our culture be like if developed from the music of the times?

Dr. Annett Schirmer says her studies suggest that rhythmic sound coordinates behavior and causes the mental processes of individuals in a group to become synchronized. Rhythmic sound synchronizes brain waves—within a few measures of music, brain waves start to get in sync with the rhythm.[15] Minds can be controlled and masses of people can be moved to negative or positive action by the rhythm of music. Could global counter culture be manipulated into following the wrong kinds of leaders due to the unity of rhythm and song? Are we contributing to the growing epidemic of emotional, mental, addictive, and learning and behavior disorders by distorting brain waves and neuron responses by certain rhythms? Do children have the wisdom to decide for themselves what is healthy listening? Is there a wide gap within families already over music?

According to Dr. John Diamond, research physician and psychiatrist, music with an *anapestic* beat is potentially harmful to the heart, blood pressure, and brain where it can interfere with signaling between hemispheres.[16] Especially concerning is new research that says the adolescent brain experiences rapid new neuron growth that is designed to prepare for adulthood. However, these neurons *lack order* and many must be *pruned* in order for the brain to develop judgment, sound thinking, as well as to acquire consistency in neuron patterns of learning. Certain music styles and syncopation can interfere with this pruning as new neurons may form as a response to discordant music.[17] The adolescent brain neurons are juggling—trying to find an ordered system of sounds.

In the past, young people between ages 15 to 24 were learning life skills—boys learned the father's trade; the girl, her mother's homemaking skills. Neural pathways developed in the brain, and practice honed these skills. This was also the time for choosing a mate, so all sorts of chemical changes would have developed as well, causing attraction to certain people. However, now with so many sounds affecting the brain, the pruning and development may not occur. Instead, the brain may not develop adequate acuity and judgment potential. Danger may not be realized, and risk taking can be common as the underdeveloped brain doesn't consider the consequences of actions any more than a much younger child would. Interestingly, classical music does just the opposite. Studies show that classical music and melodious music with sixty beats per minute affects the brain positively and engages both sides of the brain[18] helping to establish order in the neurons.

So, what does this say about the effect of music on our bodies and brain? King Saul experienced the effects of music on mood and dispositions. David, as a young shepherd, was proficient on his instrument, the lyre—a stringed instrument similar to a small harp. Saul's servants recommended that Saul allow them to find someone skilled on the lyre to play it to deliver the king from his distress and depression. First Samuel 16:16 says, "When the harmful spirit from God is upon you, he will play it, and you will be well" (ESV). Undoubtedly, it was well known that the sounds of a lyre could heal distressing mental and emotional conditions. First Samuel 16:23 says, "And whenever the harmful spirit from God was upon Saul, David took the lyre and played it with his hand. So Saul was refreshed and was well, and the harmful spirit departed from him" (ESV). In other words, the sounds of the lyre "cured" Saul.

Saul could have had hundreds of women with tambourines or flutes, so why was the lyre recommended? Dr. Knauss, who has studied the lyre and harp extensively, says these instruments hold an unusual ability to be resonant with the body. The harp is said to produce the same range of frequencies in an *acoustically sympathetic* manner as the human body. Putting all this together, when "correct" frequencies encounter "misaligned" ones, readjustments occur.[19] This explains why therapists playing harps in hospitals have reported healings happening through the use of music. The Mayo Clinic published a study in May, 2015 on therapeutic harp sounds. They report "strong positive effects."[20]

Dr. Ary Goldberger, Harvard Medical School, says that healthy heartbeats are similar to note patterns in classical music; and Dr. Abraham Kocheril, Carle Heart Center in Urbana, says that resonant vibrations from the harp may be effective in regulating heart rhythms. Dr. Mark J. Tramo, Massachusetts General Hospital, says, "There's nothing kooky about entrainment and using music in healing."[21] Entrainment happens when you place organisms and other matter in close proximity when the rhythm syncopates on its own accord. If you put clocks with pendulums swinging at different times in a room together, within a short time all of the clocks will syncopate. The same is true with metronomes swinging at different times together in a room.[22] All metronomes will *entrain*. This process also happens in humans and animals.

Dr. Knauss believes that the harp and its sound have great spiritual significance:

Since the human body, soul, and spirit are the image of God, the sameness of the harp and the body makes the harp a musical instrument that portrays the image of God. Also, God records in Scriptures that His voice is like a trumpet, roaring rushing waters, a loud peal of thunder, and many harps (Revelation 1:10; 14:2). First place among the four sounds is the harp, because there are two places in the Bible where God describes His voice as harps (Isaiah 30:31-32; Revelation 14:2). These principles have been known since ancient times.[23]

Every culture has its own music and sacred sounds. In Nepal, Tibet, and other parts of the East, bowls made out of bronze are used to produce sounds. The bowls are similar to bells that are upside down with no clapper. You have probably heard a bell choir with different sizes of bells produce lovely musical notes. Sounds and vibrations from bowls especially designed to play certain sounds are being used in cancer clinics in America, not for religious purposes, but for producing tones that affect the body. Dr. Mitchell Gaynor, M.D., a New York oncologist and Clinical Professor of Medicine at Weill Medical College of Cornell University, said, "There is no organ or system in the body that is not affected by sound, music, and vibration."[24]

Over thirty years ago, a French musician and acupuncturist, Fabian Maman, became interested in how sound affects human cells. He and Héléne Grimal, a senior researcher at the National Center for Scientific Research in Paris, began experimenting with the guitar, xylophone, gong, and the human voice. They found that when notes of the Ionic musical scale were played to cancer cells in test tubes, the cells would disintegrate within twenty-one minutes. When the human voice was used, the cells disintegrated within nine minutes. He said that the human voice carries something in its vibration that makes it more powerful than any musical instrument.[25] While this is an emerging field in psychiatric and medical fields, music therapists have been working with children and adults with mental and physical disorders for many years. Music therapy is becoming more mainstream in counseling as well as traditional medicine.

Should we be surprised that the human voice, made in the image of God, should be the most powerful in vibrational quality? According to Genesis, God created the world by speaking—"*And God said.*" Perhaps those sound waves, vibrations, frequencies, pitch are still moving through time and space. Perhaps He still speaks words of healing and regeneration today as millions will attest to His divine healing power that has come through the spoken word. We are to be His conduits and trust

His healing power in us and through us. He has used a bronze serpent, a fig poultice, the muddy water of the Jordan River, and mud in the eye to heal. Using music and sound are God's idea and God set these forces into being. It's true that many interest groups have drawn on these scientific principles. It's important for us, however, to remember that all truth comes from God, the Creator of the Universe. The law of gravity, for example, applies to all of us regardless of our religious beliefs. Should we be surprised if the powers of darkness attempt to counterfeit the Goodness of God in His healing gifts to mankind? The Good News is that Jesus took the keys! His best interest is your best interest and that is a better life for you. They are one and the same!

Sounds and vibrations are constant and all around us. If you stop and listen, you will hear sounds that you ignore—refrigerators humming, the air conditioner, the furnace, and also cosmic sounds we can't define. Stop and listen right now. Hear those sounds that you can't even recognize? Where do they come from? We listen "over" these sounds. However, the vibrations of these sounds pass into our cells just like an ultrasound can make an image inside a womb. Vibrations penetrate tissues. Cell phones, computers, electronics in general have frequencies, but these frequencies are not in sync with the frequencies in human cells.

Interestingly, the deaf "hear" music though vibrations. They don't actually "hear" the sounds, but the brain responds the same according to MRIs. They also show enhanced activity in the auditory cortex, which is usually only active during auditory stimulation.[26] Some of you will recall that Quasimodo, Victor Hugo's bell-toller in *The Hunchback of Notre Dame,* was deaf; he felt the vibrations of the bells in his body. Over four decades ago, Dr. Colin W.F. McClare, an Oxford University biophysicist, discovered that frequencies of vibrations are one hundred times more efficient in relaying information in our cells than hormones, neurotransmitters, other growth factors, and chemicals.[27] The deaf may not "hear" the music like others, but the effect is the same in the body and brain.

Music and sounds, vibrations, frequencies, and pitch can be used for health or they can lead to chronic mental and physical health problems.

As we sing and listen to music, we give our bodies a chance to respond to the vibrations of the music. If you play an instrument, you feel the vibrations. These vibrations affect your brain waves. It is said that Einstein played his violin when he needed to concentrate. When your mind is filled with repetitive thoughts, when you can't stop thinking about certain things that have happened, old wounds, and unresolved conflicts, music can be a catalyst to restore the neurotransmitters, brain waves, and neurons to a healthier way of reasoning. Music that is meaningful and songs that represent new life can replace those repetitive thoughts once your metabolism is balanced with the gut, neurotransmitters, and other functions corrected. Wholeness is body, soul, and spirit.

The path to healing may be quickened and enhanced by listening to sounds and music therapeutically designed to raise serotonin, for example. Changing your home and establishing a place for healing music to be playing in the background, as well as singing while you are working whenever possible, can be powerful in recovery. Singing also allows a full expression of emotions and will often bring forth buried anguish that needs to be spoken or even screamed. Certain songs can bring healing tears, triggering release of natural enzymes and hormones including *leucine-enkephalin,* which helps to control pain and prolactin. Crying also reduces manganese, a mineral that affects mood.[28] You may remember reading about manganese and soy formula from Chapter Nine. Crying lowers stress. Have you noticed that a baby or child is calmer after crying? Their pain has been lowered, whether physical or emotional, by their tears. The same is true with an adult. We are calmer after crying, whether in grief or anguish. When we suppress tears, we increase stress. While you are healing, let the tears come when they will.

Recovery and restoration from emotional, mental, and addictive disorders may be quickened and facilitated by making space for a "cry time." Ecclesiastes 3:4 says there is "a time to weep." Emotional abuse, whether physical or verbal; loss of loved ones; loss of limbs, mobility, finances, and fortunes; and a thousand other miserable experiences need to be mourned. If you are suppressing memories and emotions, it may be time to let the pain and expression of pain simply happen. It's healthy.

Cry your heart out. Scream your pain out. Refuse to keep the pain inside where it will continue to eat at you, little by little, hindering you from becoming the person you can be. Take off from work and maybe even from family and arrange a time to weep. A friend or counselor can help. Start at the beginning and talk until the tears begin to fall. Your tears are a great part of your recovery.

Could something as ordinary as music play a role in developing emotional, mental, and addictive disorders? Could it also potentially play a major role in changing your metabolism? In changing your brain, your mind, and the very cells of your body? I know a woman from an addictive family plagued with emotional and mental problems. When she was in her twenties, she began experiencing depression. She could find no cause or reason as she was happily teaching and changing young lives. She'd spoken to doctors and friends, but none could help her find a cause.

One day, while driving the long drive to where she taught, she asked the Lord why she was depressed. She'd prayed many times about the depression as it was deepening. This particular morning, she heard the words, "It's the music you are listening to." What? How could that be? A music lover, she kept the radio on as much as possible, listening to the "Top Forty." Since the eighth grade, when she got a radio for Christmas, she had listened almost around the clock to popular songs and knew almost every word to every song.

What else would she listen to? There were not a lot of choices in 1968, and she loved all the "hits." Plus, it kept the drive from being boring, especially at 6:30 in the morning. But she was convinced she had heard from the Lord. She obeyed as best she could and turned off the radio. The drive became prayer time and singing hymns as she drove. Within a few weeks, the depression was gone. It never returned. I can validate this story because I was the young woman.

Music can be strong medicine in your recovery. You may need to rid your room or your home of music that is negative, has discordant tones, unpredictable rhythms, and, in short, does not contribute to your mental health. Consider where the music takes you—does it spark old memories that need to be forgotten? Does it drum up feelings of aggression and hate? Does it put you so low you are down for days?

Changing what you listen to, learning to sing out your pain and distress, and letting go of pent-up and repressed emotions can free your body of deep cellular toxins and malfunctions. Join the birds in the morning by starting your day with a song. Close out the day with the evening insects like crickets, cicadas, and katydids serenading you. Their resonant chirps prepare your body for sleep. Keep attuned during the day to songs in your memory that keep you stable. Singing a song in your head has almost the same effect as singing out loud. Pick out a few songs that you transition to when an unhappy memory or mood surfaces.

Humming and rocking in a chair are powerfully effective, too, as resonance and vibrations that come from deep within your body change brain waves. While you are at it, add whistling to your prescription. Those various sounds of highs and lows cross a broad range of notes, frequencies, pitches, and vibrations. And put the earphones and ear buds away until you are on a plane and you need to block the dangerous sounds of jet engines. Becoming aware of "good" and "bad" sounds can go a long way in restoring your mind, will, and emotions.

CHAPTER 12

Corporate Redesign: How We Are Designed for Community Designing

As Christianity spread across England and Europe generations ago, impressive, massive, and imposing cathedrals were built in towns and villages. Vendors soon saw the economic opportunities, and outdoor markets for food, flowers, animals, and merchandise soon filled the surrounding streets. Cathedral bells marked the time of day, the news of the day—deaths, weddings, festivals—and they called the people to set times for prayer and worship at least three times a day. We can only imagine what it was like for a *barbarian*, as the Germanic wandering tribes were called, or a *pagan*, as those who followed Greek, Roman, or other polytheist religions were called, to walk into one of the cathedrals where the monks were chanting and singing the Psalms.

The tall vaulted ceilings would have enabled strong and powerful reverberations, causing the songs to echo while the monks were singing. The rich colors of the priestly robes, the oil burning lamps, the aromatherapy of the incense, the solemnity and sacred space away from the din outside added to the healing atmosphere. By the sixth century, stained glass windows were a part of cathedrals in Europe with vibrant reds, blues, violets, and green. Harvard research reports that red light can cut inflammatory chemicals in the blood as much as 3,400 percent in thirty minutes.[1] Blue, red, and green light therapies are being used today routinely. Gazing at the windows, surrounded by music that penetrated not only the cells of the body but also to the *inner man,* affecting the mind, will, and emotions, helped to span the bridge from curiosity and doubt to belief.

Awe can lead to mindful worship as a person's spirit is quieted enough from the disturbances inside to sit before the Lord, allowing the Holy Spirit to get their attention. Then, as now, the world demands our attention. Drawing apart to consider eternal matters is not a typical part of the day. Due to short attention spans and addictions to entertainment and leisure, getting the heart and mind "stayed" on the Lord is challenging, as the mind is often scattered and unable to concentrate. Considering that one of every four adults may have an emotional, mental, or addictive condition and the epidemic of learning and behavior problems, worship may have a hard time finding space in a person's life. Mindful worship, where the heart and mind is centered on the Lord, is experiential and powerful in healing the person and the surrounding community. When the heart learns to love God, loving people is a natural spillover. In fact, Jesus said the greatest commandment is this: "'Love the Lord your God with all your heart and with all your soul and with all your strength and with all your mind'; and, 'Love your neighbor as yourself'" (Luke 10:27).

History is clear that there were many "forced" conversions to Christianity—and this is grievous—but we cannot discount the fact that positive changes happened along the way. Going to church may have been mandatory, but the welcoming of Holy Spirit can't be forced; it has to be an individual invitation to surrender the old person and old life to a new covenant relationship with Holy God—Father, Son, and Holy Spirit. The evidence of real transformation in a community was the founding of hospitals, institutions of learning, and community design around the center of life—the cathedral—just as the synagogue and the temple were the center of the community in Jewish life and history.

In the atmosphere of the temple or cathedral, the body and the brain would have responded to the dictates of the music, vibrations, sound waves, and reverberations. Prayers, the reading and singing of Psalms and scriptures by the cantor and monks, would have added to the healing atmosphere. The tones of the chants and songs would have affected brain waves positively. Days later, the very sounds would have continued to linger in the brain, just as we experience a song we "can't get out of our head."

Much of the worship tradition of the early church came from Jewish traditional worship. This is not surprising because Jesus and the disciples were Jewish. Since the time of Ezra, the Hebrews were taught to pray at least three times daily, using ritual prayers that reminded them of God and their heritage of His faithfulness to them.[2] When they could not offer sacrifices in Babylon, three times a day they prayed. "We will offer the sacrifices of our lips" (Hos. 14:2 NKJV).

Before captivity, prayers and sacrifices were offered at set times throughout the day. Individuals were expected to offer prayers and sacrifices at other times as well. During the time of Solomon's temple, great fanfare accompanied the sacrifices of animals. Evening, morning, and afternoon, the priests offered sacrifices. Leviticus 3:16 gives careful instructions about these offerings, with a peculiar reminder that "all fat is the Lord's."

Now, why would the Lord want fat? The smoke from the sacrifice was to be a visual connecting point to God in Heaven. Smoke has been used in many cultures for communication; it was not a far stretch for the people to understand they could communicate with God; He was not far off—a smoke signal could reach Him. Fat produces a lot of smoke, but I think there is more here as it relates to the majesty of His love toward us in providing for our health. The fat in animals, including your own fat, is the major storage area in the body for toxins. Toxins produce inflammation in the body; inflammation leads to disease and chronic health problems mentally and physically. I believe, once again, the Lord had us in mind with these commands—eating the fat of animals means eating their toxins. With pork, toxins are stored in muscles, intestines, and throughout the body—not just in the fat. Without a rumen, what the pig eats is deposited rapidly into the body of the pig. If you know anything about pigs, you know they will eat anything. The Hebrews were commanded to not eat pork.

We continue to discover why the Lord gave certain rules and restrictions concerning food and hygiene. The Hebrews were promised health and none of the diseases of the Egyptians if they followed certain guidelines (see Exod. 15:26). When the Lord says "the fat is mine," I believe He simply didn't want us eating it for our own good. So the eating of fat was forbidden. Obedience does not demand that you understand why God said it; obedience is trusting He knows what He is talking about and always has our best interests in His plan and admonitions. I'm certainly not opposed to people eating pork, but I include this to show you once again how carefully we were designed and how God's rule book for health is still relevant.

Devout Jews still keep the three-times-a-day prayers that began during the time of Ezra. The prayers begin by acknowledging God as shield, refuge, all powerful, strong, holy, and the One who revives the dead. The prayers continue asking God for understanding, to cause repentance in the heart, forgiveness, redemption, and healing. The concluding prayers ask for good harvests, dew, and rain and that the expelled may be re-gathered and their judges and counselors would be restored. The final conclusion is a proclamation that God reigns over them and God alone.[3]

Some theologians believe that the three times a day Jewish prayer ritual was observed as Christianity grew by teaching new converts to pray the Lord's Prayer (see Matt. 6:9–13) three times daily. As you compare the ancient Hebrew prayers to the Lord's Prayer, it seems that Christ wasn't teaching a brand new prayer. Instead, He was making the complex personal and simple. It also indicates, once again, the emphasis Jesus placed on prayer in His life.

Many cultures and religions have chants and songs, and many world religions require specific times to pray and specific prayers. In particular, the Hebrews would have heard their sacred history chanted. It needed to be remembered. Psalms, Proverbs, various songs from deliverance would have been chanted, perhaps becoming more musically diverse when instruments, especially in the times of David and Solomon, were added. Reading the story of Solomon's temple with the musicians and singers describes a majestic, splendid display of colors, fragrances, music, chants, and participation. First Chronicles says there were 288 trained singers and 4,000 musicians divided into 24 groups (1 Chron. 23:5; 25:7). It was not just a ceremony of proclamation to God, Creator and Father, but also it would have been a cleansing of cells in body and brain. The cleansing was both spiritual and physical.

The Jews who knew Jesus as Messiah continued attending their synagogues until they were forbidden to attend, expelled, and eventually persecuted. Their chants and songs began to reflect this new journey and progression. At some time during the early Christian era, the Gregorian chant was developed. For centuries, the Gregorian chant was used to sing the Psalms for worship, prayer, and to teach congregants the faith. In the monastic orders, some monasteries were accustomed to six or more hours a day of the Gregorian chant.

A few years following the Second Vatican Council in 1959, Dr. Alfred Tomatis, M.D, a French physician, tells of being called to a Benedictine monastery to diagnose a strange malady among the monks. Instead of their usual energetic selves, praying and working and sleeping only a few hours every night, the monks were lethargic and sick. Other doctors had already changed their normal vegetarian diets to include meat, yet there was no improvement. The strange malady was sapping their strength.

During the early 1960s, many convents, monasteries, and churches saw major changes. This was true at this particular monastery where a new abbot had been appointed. He was anxious to implement the new changes, such as mass in the language of the people, less emphasis on vestments, and changes in the liturgy and music. Chanting was eliminated from the monks' daily schedule. When Dr. Tomatis encouraged the return to chanting of prayers and songs as before, within months the monks were restored and back to their rigorous schedules. They were treated solely with sound.[4]

Dr. Tomatis said that prayer demands extraordinary brain activity:

> Put yourself on your knees one day and try to pray, or try to
> meditate and you'll see how parasitic thoughts assail you—
> your vacation coming up, the friend who's displeased you, the
> letter you just received, the taxes you have to pay—thousands
> of things flood into the mind, to your subconscious, and you
> need to have an enormous cortical charge to overcome them.
> In the case of these monks, in giving them back their sounds,
> their stimuli, we succeeded in re-awakening them.[5]

Such is the power of sounds, vibrations, frequencies, and pitch
on the human body. The slow, melodious, one syllable sounds of the
Gregorian chant resonate with our cells, causing a very similar response
in our bodies as the room full of clocks with pendulums and a room of
metronomes. We are designed to resonate with the frequencies around
us. Because these can be measured electronically, it is not science fiction. Your cells respond to positive and negative ions in the atmosphere
around you. Your cells respond to sounds even if you can't hear them in
the atmosphere around you; the cells in your brain and body experience
them, especially the brain.

Recently, a group of monks who live in Norcia, Italy released an album
of Gregorian chants. In June 2015, it made number one on *Billboard's
Classical Music*, was the top overall seller at Barnes & Noble, number
two on Amazon, and in the Top 40 on iTunes.[6] About twenty years ago,
another album of Gregorian chants hit number one. Why the interest?
Obviously, this sort of response represents widespread purchasing, not
just by Catholics and Christian music fans. While most of us will readily
admit the music is beautiful and relaxing, is there more to the effects of
this music on body and soul?

Some of you may have heard of the effect that the music of Mozart
has on body and soul. Don Campbell has written extensively about what
Dr. Tomatis called *The Mozart Effect*. In addition to clinical studies that
show an increase in learning, Mozart's music affects the electrical signals
in the brain and may be effective in reducing epileptic seizures.[7]

If at least some of emotional, mental, and addictive disorders are the mind's response to broken systems in the body and an unordered world, these simple chants and structured music are filling a void and ministering on a deep level in the body. In the cacophony of noise, clatter, and discordant music that disturbs the cells in the body and disturbs the mind, these harmonic sounds strike a deep cord producing a rare thing in the world today—a feeling of peace, tranquility, and calm.

As the Protestant Reformation gained momentum, so did the hymns of the leaders and the people. Martin Luther began to write and sing of God's free grace, the wonder of knowing Christ, and expressions of love and gratitude to the Trinity. The people began singing these hymns and crowds gathered to hear street evangelists with hymns printed on leaflets. It's not a far stretch to say that the hymns did as much as the preaching to spread the Reformation as the songs, theology of the lyrics, and the message went deep into the hearts and minds of the people. By the time Luther died, there were sixty collections of hymns and numerous hymn writers.[8] The ensuing years produced hundreds of great hymns that taught not only deep theology, but also the love of Christ. There is no way to determine how many people learned in song what they could not learn in church, listening to even the best theologians.

We may be in danger in this present age of such watered down songs and melodies that we miss great opportunities. The cells of the body and brain will sync and resonate with those around us. Social activities cause us to synchronize and entrain with other people. Medical tests show that heartbeats, pulse rate, and brain waves syncopate, entraining with the people around us. While it is a physical and scientific response to frequencies, this response can be powerful for changing the lives in those with mental and addictive disorders. If you are around positive people, you tend to *catch* it; the same is true with negative people. Both are *contagious*. Being around people of compassion tends to increase compassion. Mercy is the same.

While these are intrinsic and can only be seen when expressed, the cells of the body and brain respond in measurable ways. Functional MRIs can show the areas of the brain that are activated with compassion, empathy, mercy, and generosity.[9] These scans show the areas of the brain that activate when a person receives a gift, revealing that the brain activates more intently when a person *gives* to another person.[10] But, you already knew that about giving, didn't you? You already know from experience that it truly is more blessed to give than to receive (see Acts 20:35).

Can you envision the power of healing that can emanate from within and without in a community of people worshiping God with heart and soul and might? Can you envision an ongoing daily ministry to those with emotional, mental, and addictive disorders? Can you imagine the power of faith in a community of believers to change people and to transform communities!

The power of a transformational community, as the church can be, offers the best opportunity when a church is resonating with people alive in Christ who are willing to encircle others with sincere love and transparency. Bathing the soul in music designed to heal and cure requires worship leaders to understand the powerful role they play in what happens, quite simply, to people who come to church. When the person with an emotional, mental, or addictive disorder "comes to church," there is opportunity for a new life to begin.

For the mind to understand and perceive, the heart needs preparation. A sense of well-being may be exchanged for a scattered, broken, disharmonic, discordant brain and body by worship music that extols our Maker, Great Physician, Savior, and Lord. On the contrary, music that is designed to stir up a sense of excitement or pep rally fever may cause the weary and brokenhearted to feel jaded and betrayed by the place where they had hoped to find repose. Sadly, I've had more than one counseling appointment with men who wept over fighting lust during the "worship music" due to how one or more of the leaders were dressed. The privilege and responsibility of leading people in worship is too wonderful and great to be trifled with clothes that lure.

Common sense as well as experience will confirm that many, if not most, people come to church needing refreshment and restoration. A week of stress from jobs, dysfunctional families, traffic, oxidative stress in the body, noise, and all sorts of other attacks on the body and soul beset and befuddle the normal person. Finding the right *sounds* for body and soul may be the most important preliminary to worship if a worship leader has the congregants in his/her heart. And lyrics, as wonderful and uplifting as they can be, are only a small part of sounds. It's the total combination that has potential to heal the sin-sick soul and brokenhearted. Well-being, the sense of *it is well with my soul,* is a good measuring stick when one leaves church—is there a sense of well-being with hope and strength rising up for the coming week? For emotional, mental, and addictive disorders, the Church should offer a place for healing and restoration. Perhaps even more important than counseling services offered by some churches could be rooms for silence, rooms to listen to healing chants that fix on Jesus and the Psalms, and rooms of music that causes the brain to begin the healing process. We cannot separate the body, brain, mind, and emotions.

In 1972, Dr. Candace Pert—Chief of the Section on Brain Biochemistry, Clinical Neuroscience Branch, at the National Institute of Mental Health (NIMH)—began to unravel how emotions affect the body. She said that emotions change the chemistry of every cell in the body and our emotions affect the people around us. She said that, "We send out a vibration to other people. We broadcast and receive." In Dr. Pert's book, *Molecules of Emotion,* she explains that neurotransmitters called *peptides* carry emotional messages: "As our feelings change, this mixture of peptides travels throughout your body and your brain." She goes on to explain that the way the brain is designed to make choices around things that please us and make us happy. The very highest, most intelligent part of our brain is drenched in receptors to make us use pleasure as a criterion for our decisions. She called those receptors "bliss receptors." These receptors are located in the part of the brain that makes evaluative and complex decisions. Dr. Pert indicated that she believes God designed us to utilize these "bliss receptors" for the bliss of our union with Divine Union. "God is good," she explains, "and it's okay to feel good."[11] This discovery was a breakthrough in how emotions affect the body and brain. In recent years, endorphins, dopamine, and serotonin have been identified as chemical messages that affect how a person views life.

If you are suffering with emotional, mental, and/or addictive disorders, can you imagine experiencing "bliss" that is a sacred experience with God and not a pharmaceutical counterfeit high, such as drugs can produce? Can you imagine feeling so good that your emotions not only change every cell in your body and brain, but also broadcast those happy *chemicals* to other people? Prayer, music, sounds, vibrations, frequencies, tones, and pitch affect the cells of the brain and body.

What about *glossolalia*, speaking in tongues? Does this spiritual experience have science to back it up, and could speaking in tongues be beneficial to those battling emotional, mental, and/or addictive disorders? Studies from England with almost 1,000 people indicate that those who speak in tongues showed more emotional stability and less depression than a control group.[12] Dr. Andrew Newberg, University of Pennsylvania, conducted a study on glossolalia about a decade ago that showed how glossolalia operates in the brain. Using a functional MRI, Dr. Newberg observed that activity in the frontal lobe of the brain decreased. The frontal lobe is used in mental activity, concentration, and language. The significance of the frontal lobe being inactive is "fascinating" according to Dr. Newberg.

An inactive frontal lobe means that the subjects being studied could not "make up" language or string syllables together without the frontal lobe being activated. In contrast, during vocalized prayer and meditation, the frontal lobe is activated. In addition, the region of the brain that is involved in self-consciousness was active, indicating the subjects were not in a trance. These findings indicate that while the subjects are in control, they do not have control over the flowing of speech.[13]

Yet another scientific study by Dr. Carl R. Peterson says that two chemicals produce a 35 to 40 percent boost to the immune system during speaking in tongues. He says that this secretion comes from a part of the brain that has no other apparent activity in humans and is only activated by "spirit led prayer and worship."[14] A study from the State University of New York at Albany says that glossolalia is associated with a reduction in stress in response to normal stressors, and it is significantly associated with positive mood and calmness. Cortisol was measured during speaking in tongues, and again on the following Monday. In contrast to control groups, those who used glossolalia had less stress when they began their workweek.[15] Some of you may have read of Jackie Pullinger's remarkable work that included using glossolalia to heal addiction.[16]

It is acknowledged that speaking in tongues has divided churches and remains a theological question. This is not a book about theology and doctrine. It is important regardless of what you believe to consider Paul's words in 1 Corinthians 14:4: "Anyone who speaks in a tongue edifies themselves." Corinth had become synonymous with corruption, sexual depravity, gross immorality, and drunkenness. It seems that even some of the church members were continuing in sexual depravity, fornication, and adultery. If televisions and computers had been available, for example, many of them would have probably watched pornography and immoral movies. In short, Corinth was a lot like America today—the church was not shining as a moral compass, nor was the church transforming society.

In 1 Corinthians 14:5, Paul says he wishes they all spoke in tongues. Did he see transformations in the sin-sick body and soul, perhaps, to a greater extent than in those who did not speak in tongues? I don't know the answer to that question, but in 1 Corinthians 14:18 he thanks God that he speaks in tongues more than any of them. Speaking in tongues may be especially edifying to those suffering with emotional, mental, and addictive disorders by helping them replace an embattled and/or embittered mind with sounds that refresh and heal.

With that in mind, what should we expect when a sanctuary is filled with congregants who join in singing together? Will just any old music do? Can we expect powerful changes in the mind and body with just any words and any tones? How can we, in an electronic age, with sound systems, microphones, earphones, and myriad varieties of music where the leader struggles to find a way to please everyone, find a way to use music to heal and restore people? Should we expect healing and restoration from our attendance at church? Or is church a place of instruction and fellowship, with a few songs tucked in here and there that support the message of the pastor? Should our places of worship be, like the early cathedrals, the center of community life with the poor and sick heading to the church to be helped? Should we be expecting the Shekinah cloud of glory to descend during one of our services so that the cloud is so thick we can't see each other? Is there a possibility that down through the ages, much has been lost? Could our doctrinal battles have caused a part of the sickness of the society around us?

Almost daily we are hearing or reading unimaginable events that are happening in America and around the world. Random killings. Atrocities. Murders followed by suicides. Juries often sentence to prison on the grounds of "mentally ill." Is this a disease that will go away by itself? Can the Church become the agent of transformation in communities to find and heal before something horrible happens? Just as the early Catholic Church began building hospitals, institutions of learning, convents, monasteries, and places of refuge, we must consider how the Church can rebuild society. Every church can become a center for the healing of emotional, mental, and addictive disorders.

For many years, we have depended on intellectual information to explain the Gospel. What do we do when the slavery of addiction is so powerful that the mind cannot engage with reason and explanations as to what the Gospel says and means? The power of the Holy Spirit can overcome even an injured brain. However, creating sacred space for awe-inspiring worship with transformational music could be a first step for many who cannot quiet the mind and soul enough to listen to sermons. Church should be pervading the community offering hope and real life solutions.

Cathedral bells were reminders of a sacred life to be lived in the midst of daily living. Enabling someone to transition from a life focused on carnality and worldliness will take more than cathedral bells. However, a church that "salts" and lights up the darkness of the encroaching age is a force to be reckoned with if that church is gaining ground on the darkness. If the church is walled up and ministers only to the attenders and those who fit the criteria, it is in danger of becoming ineffective, isolationist, and may indeed be "walked on" (see Matt. 5:13).

Longing for the presence of the Lord to pervade the Church is, at the same time, a longing for the Lord to pervade the community. He cannot be contained in the "church" because His own great love cannot resist the broken and fallen. If the Church is to be His voice and His arms, His hands and His feet at this crucial time in history, we must examine motives as well as expenditures. Can our huge, massive buildings built to bring thousands to an hour service on Sundays be used to transform the homeless, many of whom are emotionally and mentally ill and addictive? Could we, if we were to unite as churches in a city, provide for the fallen and broken in a way that the government cannot? Is it, after all, any of our business?

It is a rare week that I don't receive a call from a parent desperate for help for a child with ADHD, ADD, or Autism. My mention of physiological help as well as the few therapy centers I recommend is usually met with, "We just don't have the money." Quite often they have spent all of their resources on helping the child—or children—already. What's the Church to do about these children and adults whom Christ died to save? Often, parents with an autistic child are unable to attend church. If they cannot afford a baby sitter, one of the parents has to stay home. If it's a single parent home, attending church may be out of the question. Many rely on television for church, but they miss the transformation of what actually happens when we worship together.

When people who love God and who love people come together in holy assignment and worship, the building should be flooded with healing resources so strong that spontaneous healings of body and soul take place in the midst as powerful praise and worship fill both the "temples"—the physical building and our bodies. We were designed for praise and worship. Just as vibrations, frequencies, pitch, and sounds of music penetrate every cell and our neurotransmitters respond to what we see, hear, and feel, our entire being is designed to be restored as we worship.

However, it has to be the *real thing*. We have become dependent on our electronics to amplify the sounds of instruments and singing. It's the human voice and musical instruments that provide the healing to the cells. Filling the building with the sound of voices blending in harmony can be felt. Speaking the words of faith and belief, gratitude, trust, and love resonates with minds and hearts entraining with each other and with God. Worship. Solomon's temple was filled with harps and instruments, singing, and strong voices. To quote Charles Carrin, "a river of praise descended continually upon the city below. No wonder David wrote, 'the joy of the whole earth is Mount Zion.'"[17]

What would happen to our communities if the church, powerful in praise and worship, spilled over into the streets? Wouldn't this powerful experience show in our eyes and in how we live our lives? What hinders us, not only from the full expression of worship and praise, but also from the quiet awe that worship can bring to us?

What we bring to church is that which is un-crucified within ourselves. Holiness has become something to be mocked. Living a separate life is often scorned as legalism and misunderstood by a society that has been taught to conform to whatever is vogue. Yet what is offered to replace holiness? Losing the sense of "sacred" has been costly to our society. Is there anything holy anymore? Is there anything that is considered actual "sin" anymore? As James 3:12 says, "My brothers and sisters, can a fig tree bear olives, or a grapevine bear figs? Neither can a salt spring produce fresh water." We have a thirsty society that longs for fresh water. That longs for fresh bread. When they ask for bread, do we hand them a stone? (See Luke 11:11–13.) In the case of the emotionally ill, mentally ill, and addictive as well as those with learning and behavior problems, we may be doing just that. It's not our heart to shortchange these groups, but unfortunately it is our tradition and practice.

We are living in a very different time in history. With one of every four adults with an emotional or mental disorder; one out of every ten an addict; and one out every five children with an emotional, mental, learning, or behavior disorder, the Church must take action. If, indeed, there is an evil genius who knows how our bodies and brains are designed, who knows science, and who knows how easily we are lured into sickness and sin, could it be he has implemented a grand scheme to break us down within and without? Could he, as simplistic as it sounds, be behind the forces of greed at work in the marketplace and adverse daily habits that ruin our health and our minds?

Maybe so. However, the gates of hell can't prevail against the Church (see Matt. 16:18). Perhaps it is time for us to stop thinking about "our church" and start thinking about the Kingdom of God and our mandate to announce the Kingdom to those in captivity. The Church is to be an opportunity and authority for healing and restoration of body, soul, and spirit.

CHAPTER 13

Finding the Illusive:
Peace, Joy, and Quietness

At the very root of emotional, mental, and addictive disorders is the lack of peace. Real peace settles comfortably in the soul and body, bringing what medications and the world cannot give. Regardless of the reason for the emotional, mental, or addictive disorder, peace within the soul—the mind, will, and emotions—can bring healing and restoration. Often, the lack of peace in an emotionally wounded or agitated person is the reason they began taking medications or drugs in the first place. They could find no peace. Their days and their nights were tormented.

Peace holds a particular place in the Scriptures as well as in the tradition of the Church. For generations, many churches have used the tradition of *passing the peace,* a simple gesture of joining hands while pronouncing a blessing of peace to others in attendance. This ancient blessing was a way to encourage the people to be at peace with one another as well as to receive the good that peace brings. Those who are peacemakers, according to the Beatitudes in Matthew 5:9, will be called "the children of God." That's a powerful statement, when you look at it—children of God. Those listening were accustomed to thinking of themselves as "children of Abraham" and followers of the Law of Moses, which allowed retribution for offenses. Here, however, this is a graduation of enormous potential—children of God!

Finding peace in today's world is no easy matter and being a peacemaker is no easy matter. When the brain is diseased, reason and rationale are rarely enough to calm a person down. In addiction, the body has been taken over by drugs that overpower the brain, and the person may not know what they are doing. In those instances, it is best to call for help and keep them from hurting someone or themselves. Then, in ensuing weeks and months, steps can be taken for lasting change. The body and brain can be changed resulting in changes in behavior and thought processes. In Philippians 4:7, we read "the peace of God, which transcends all understanding, will guard your hearts and your minds in Christ Jesus." Guarding the heart and mind goes a long way in recovery. And in those instances of deep wounds and abuse, the coming of peace into a soul may be the only cure—because peace surpasses understanding. Setting the mind on the Spirit is life and peace—"The mind governed by the flesh is death, but the mind governed by the Spirit is life and peace" (Rom. 8:6).

Rearranging our day-to-day life is an integral part of healing, whether you are "religious" or not, and this simple book is designed to help you, whether you are religious or not. Peace, that treasure that is possible here on earth, may best be found in relationship to God, Maker of Heaven and earth.

We often use "peace and quiet" together when we are speaking of the mind's need for reflection, the body's need for relaxation, and the spirit's need for restoration. We were not designed to be around noise and activity all of the time. We, too, need to withdraw even as Christ did (see Luke 5:16) to give ourselves time to regroup. We are designed to integrate silence with the sounds of nature and conversations with people but not to be in noise all of the time. Centuries ago, even our last century, offered long periods of silence. There was time to be quiet and let the mind unravel its load of care. Time to consider creative pursuits; time to think. Many children are growing up in homes where there is no silence—not even while they are sleeping. Their exhausted bodies and brains adapt to sleeping in spite of noise, just as you do when you fall asleep on a plane or in front of a television. Without enough quietness, the brain cannot do its job as well.

A few years ago, a report from the Finnish Tourist Board made an astute statement: "In the future, people will be prepared to pay for the experience of silence." Retreat centers that offer silence are becoming well known; people pay thousands of dollars for a place and time to simply shut off noise.[1] Clinical trials report that silence calms our bodies, lowers blood pressure, and affects carbon dioxide and circulation in the brain. A two-minute silent pause proved more relaxing than music.[2]

Pam Grist, teacher and practitioner of Contemplative Prayer (pamgrist.wordpress.com) says, "One of the most precious commodities we have in our frenetic, noise-laden world today is *Silence*. Yet, as much as we long for and need it, we almost panic at the thought of it. For to travel into the depths of interior silence in purposeful, intentional contemplation is to risk uncovering our real desires, shadows, and gifts—in essence, our true selves. The practice of silence requires courage and persistence, but the rewards are exponential. Most importantly, we discover the essential realities of life—deep peace and equanimity. Gerald May says it best: "Contemplative moments…are glimpses of the way life yearns to be lived."

A study at Duke University revealed that two hours of silence per day prompted cell development in the hippocampus, the region of the brain that affects memory. New cells became functioning neurons during the silence, integrating them into proper neuron systems. Depression, schizophrenia, other psychiatric disorders, drug abuse[3] as well as ADD/ADHD and Autism,[4] dementia, and Alzheimer's are linked to the hippocampus.[5] So could two hours of silence everyday potentially bring about positive developments in the hippocampus, especially if this became regular and habitual?

Many with emotional, mental, and addictive disorders fight silence while others embrace it. That difference depends on the individual and the underlying causes of the struggle. Because the hippocampus is involved in forming memories, it can also "rerun" old memories when the brain is not engaged in another activity. Thus, a person may dread silence, may postpone trying to sleep, and may use loud music to drown out the thoughts, the "reruns," the mental recordings that cycle and seem unending.

One in four adults suffers from a diagnosable mental disorder—57.7 million people in the 2004 U.S. Census. Mental disorders are the leading cause of disability in the U.S. and Canada for ages 15 to 44; many are diagnosed with more than one mental disorder.[6] Victims of sexual abuse or simply bad sexual decisions, victims of violence, verbal abuse, and other mistreatment including traumatic births may be agitated during silence due to a desire to forget the pain as the brain clings to traumatic memories. PTSD is marked by an entire body and brain response to trauma.

Perhaps churches who desire to minister to one out of every four adults should consider places of imposed sacred silence, inside or outside in peaceful settings, to allow for quiet. In fact, it may prove to be more effective in personal and community transformation and design than coffee shops and physical fitness centers. These can be found in almost every shopping area; but where can one find quiet in a loud, noisy, and troubled world?

For those who cannot be alone and who cannot endure silence, sacred space and prayer rooms dedicated to spiritual songs and chants may be very effective if these are used in long sessions. Two hours seems to be the time needed. If indeed, as reported, the human voice has the most potential to reach the deep cells in the body, perhaps dedicated and personal prayers by people of faith, who are able to lift up holy hands and evidence of holy living, can pray with and for those who come and sit for long hours allowing the sounds, vibrations, reach the hurt places in the heart. This does not need to be rushed; when the person is ready for human help, they simply need to know it is there for them with no pressure and no performance.

Days of silence followed by days of the right sounds and personal singing is proven by science to affect the mind and the body. When the emotionally wounded are ready to voice the hurt, simple breathing in and then a long breathing out with the vocal cords adding sound may be enough to allow the emotions to respond. We use moans and groans, *uhhs, ahhs, uhm,* as well as laughter and other sounds naturally. When a person is expressing grief and loss, the sounds may be awful, but letting go of pent-up grief and sorrow is an important part of healing of the soul. Allowing the tones of the voice to express pain may begin softly and culminate in hysterical crying as the emptying of old memories surface. At those times, it would be good to have someone close by if the person needs support. When emotions have been stuffed for decades, when cellular memories are too deep to be consciously remembered, and when the mind is sick, the outpouring of grief is appropriate and necessary. This process does not need to be rushed.

However, counselors and ministers need to be able to recognize when a person needs medical care. There is a place and time for medicine and for hospitalization. When these are needed, it is best to use the care available. Healing can take months or years, but progress is knowing you are better this month than you were last month and that the path ahead is promising. Being a part of a community of faith with people who love God and who love people can make the difference in full recovery.

Without silence and mental rest away from noises, the mind cannot integrate the world inside and the world outside. The complexities of "making sense" of the world, family relationships, personal relationships, as well as major decisions take place when the mind is in "default" mode—it is not having to work on details at work or in school. Time to reflect is paramount in recovery of any brain or personality disorder. Sometimes physicians will put their patients in an imposed time of rest, even an induced coma, to allow the brain to rest so it can heal.

For those with emotional, mental, and addictive disorders that are physiological, caused by malfunction in the body, silence offers hope that as the physical disorders are corrected, the mind can be renewed. All too often, someone suffering with an emotional, mental, or addictive disorder has no idea as to the cause of the onset and why he or she is depressed. Often they began self-medication with alcohol, drugs, video games, movies, and television to bridge the gap when they are alone. Those who know the reasons for their illness or addiction may need a different path to healing from those who have physiological reasons.

We were not designed to run on alert all the time. Any body and brain will break down if there is not time for rest and change from normal activities. Rest is so important to our well-being that God instructed Moses to list it as number four in the Ten Commandments. Consider that. God counted keeping the Sabbath Day holy as important as not stealing, killing, and not committing adultery? Number four? Right up there after honoring God and before honoring parents?

Can you actually keep the Sabbath in today's busy world that continually spins on and on to the next thing? Is it that important, considering that Christ said the Sabbath was made for man, and not man for the Sabbath? Consider what keeping the Sabbath has meant in history—a poor laborer and slave could not be forced to work on the Sabbath; animals would have a day to rest; fathers and mothers, usually occupied with time sapping labor during the week, could take the time to be with their children. Time to be outside in nature; time to reflect; time for the brain to unload and the body to regroup. It wasn't that God was demanding "His" time; He was giving us "our" time.

Some studies indicate the Seventh-Day Adventists may be the healthiest people in America. They refrain from meat, alcohol, tobacco, and mild-altering substances.[7] And their founder, Ellen White, who instituted health reforms that were way beyond the common knowledge of the day, insisted on rigid adherence to keeping the Sabbath Day:

> Before the setting of the sun (on Friday) let all secular
> work be laid aside and all secular papers be put out of sight.
> Parents, explain your work and its purpose to your children,
> and let them share in your preparation to keep the Sabbath
> according to the commandment. There is another work that
> should receive attention on the preparation day. On this day
> all differences between brethren, whether in the family or in
> the church, should be put away. Let all bitterness and wrath

and malice be expelled from the soul. In a humble spirit, "confess your faults one to another, and pray one for another." Before the setting of the sun let the members of the family assemble to read God's Word, to sing and pray.[8]

Blue Zones Solution by Dan Buettner, a *National Geographic* explorer and author, lists Loma Linda, California as one of the top five places in the world where people live longer. Seventh-Day Adventists make up one third of the population there. The secret, Buettner says, is their diet and they take "the idea of Sabbath very seriously, so they're decompressing the stress."[9]

Another group recognized for good health is the Church of Jesus Christ of Latter-Day Saints. A recent address to Mormons from church leaders called for better observance of the Sabbath, pointing out how easy it is to become like the prevailing culture of Sunday as a business day.

What we hope is that the Sabbath will become a delight for people at home, that they'll love what happens in their homes on Sunday. It will be a time to draw apart from the world, to just give ourselves some rest from the things that are always before our eyes the other days of the week, with the work week, all the things we worry about. And then on the Sabbath we could think about the Savior.[10]

Since the earliest days of the Mormon faith, there has been and continues to be a recognition and observance of the Day of Rest. A study published a few years ago in *Prevention* magazine concluded that Mormons in California had the longest life expectancies ever documented in a well-defined U.S. study of a group of people. Devout Mormons live by a health code called the *Word of Wisdom* and keep strict observance of the Sabbath.[11] While diet and lifestyle are well accepted as keys to good physical and mental health, could it be that by trading the Sabbath for just another day in the daily grind has caused us to lose more than we gained?

I recall reading a study years ago regarding how long it takes for the body to recoup from labor—muscle recovery, mental stress, and fatigue. As you might guess, the scientists found that those subjects who rested every seven days scored highest on the lab results. Called *circaseptans* in science and medicine, it is known that our bodies seem to follow a seven-day pattern in heart, blood pressure, blood cells, other biological functions, including mood.[12] Increasingly, the circaseptan rhythm in plants, mice, and other organisms is being studied and validated.[13] If certain plants, animals, insects, and other organisms follow a set circaseptan rhythm, perhaps we should rethink the Sabbath. A return to "no work; no business" on the Sabbath as well as a "no electronics" could possibly not only change our health and work performance on the rest of the days of the week, but changing your actions on the Sabbath may also change your mind and health.

Every living thing needs some "downtime," and that includes your digestive system. In the Bible, Jesus says "when you fast" not "if" you fast (see Matt. 6:16–18). Fasting was to be expected in Old and New Testament times. Both Moses and Jesus fasted for forty days, going without food and water. Fasting crosses denominational and religious borders and is well proven in medical reports to be beneficial to many health disorders, including emotional, mental, and addictive disorders. In Mark 9:29 Jesus tells the disciples that the boy with seizures could only be delivered by prayer and fasting. Interestingly, in 2006 Johns Hopkins released a study indicating fasting improves epilepsy. Children who did not improve on a *ketonic*[14] diet improved significantly when they fasted on alternate days.[15] Studies on epilepsy have suggested an abnormal electrical signaling in the brain, which can also be found in several mental disorders. Gabriel Cousins, M.D. says he sees improvement in mental disorders though fasting. After four days, he reports improved concentration, expanded creative thinking, a lifting of depression, less anxiety, a more tranquil mind, no insomnia, and a natural joy begin to appear.[16] He attributes this to a cleansing of toxins from the brain.

Dr. Yuri Nikolayev of the Moscow Psychiatric Institute says the "hunger treatment" (as therapeutic fasting is called there) was used to treat over

10,000 patients with various neuropsychiatric disorders. Their cure rate was over 70 percent.[17] Should fasting be a regular part of your mental and physical health plan? Now, fasting doesn't include milkshakes and smoothies. Fasting is a lot more than just giving up three meals a day for another meal choice. It is a deeply moving and spiritual determination to move closer to God and a discipline to control the body and the flesh. Perhaps a church that desires to design a different community should include regular fasting in their planning. The International House of Prayer in Kansas City encourages consistent, weekly fasting for spiritual and physical benefits.[18,19] Begun just over fifteen years ago, IHOP has become internationally known and draws tens of thousands of people annually to events and attendance at the around-the-clock prayer services. CRU, formerly called Campus Crusade for Christ, has recommended fasting for over twenty years for spiritual strength. Bill Bright, one of the most respected Christian leaders of the 20th century, practiced a 40-day fast annually. His book, *7 Basic Steps to Successful Fasting and Prayer*, written over twenty years ago is still a landmark study for many who want to know more about fasting.

Could something as simple as refraining from food for certain hours retrain the brain? Could it break the power of addiction? Could it transform a soul as well as a community of believers? For those of us who are followers of Jesus, are we willing to stretch our "following" this far, to abstain from food for certain times of the day or days at a time? While it's wise to consult with your physician before you embark on an extended fast, missing a meal here and there most likely won't hurt you! For those who are fighting an emotional, mental, or addictive disorder, a supervised fast may break through years of delays in healing and bring about a quicker restoration.

When looking for solutions for emotional, mental, and addictive disorders, we can overlook a simple and profound means of improvement that is scientifically validated—laughter may truly be one of the best medicines for emotional distress. Author and counselor Catherine Rippenger Fenwick says, "Your body cannot heal without play. Your mind cannot heal without laughter. Your soul cannot heal without joy."[20]

Proverbs 17:22 tells us "A cheerful heart is good medicine, but a crushed spirit dries up the bones." (The bone marrow is greatly responsible for the immune system response in the body). But how can one laugh and be happy with an emotional, mental, or addictive disorder holding a person captive?

Turns out, the body can't tell the difference between "real" laughter and "fake" laughter. Remember how the body responds to "fake fear" on the television or in movies? The same thing happens with our subconscious mind—the body releases the same neurochemicals while you are watching a funny episode, listening to something humorous, and reading just plain old jokes. While there are many medical studies on the benefit of laughter in emotional and mental healing, a report published in 2010 says that laughter has psychological and quality-of-life benefits.

> Therapeutic efficacy of laughter is mainly derived from spontaneous laughter (triggered by external stimuli or positive emotions) and self-induced laughter (triggered by oneself at will), both occurring with or without humor. The brain is not able to distinguish between these types; therefore, it is assumed that similar benefits may be achieved with one or the other.[21]

Serotonin, dopamine, and endorphins are released when you smile. The eyes show it, and that smile is contagious.[22] So even if you don't really have anything to smile about or anything to laugh about, it's a good idea to find something. Instead of a movie filled with suspense, find a comedy if you are going to watch a movie. For those of you who are caregivers, keep a steady dose of humor going on in the house. It won't just help your family member who may be struggling; it will help you. I love the quote from Robert Frost that says, "If we couldn't laugh, we would all go insane."

On the path to rebuilding your body and soul, adding gratefulness to your life can make a difference in the neurotransmitters and cells of the body. That's right. Simply cultivating saying *thank you* to God and counting your blessings goes a long way. Making it a habit to thank God for every meal is a good way to keep those "happy" neurotransmitters climbing. Dr. P. Murali Doraiswamy, Director of Duke University Division of Biologic Psychology, says, "If thankfulness were a drug, it would be the world's best-selling product with a health maintenance indicator for every major organ system."[23] He says that mood neurotransmitters, serotonin, norepinephrine, oxytocin, cortisol, and dopamine are affected positively. On the other hand, he says that humans have a "negativity bias." When we think about the "bad stuff" in our lives, it outweighs the good by three to one.[24]

I have a dearly beloved friend who is 98 years old. I've known her now for almost fifty years and have seen her in the highs and lows of life, especially when she lost her son in his thirties. Throughout the hardships of pain in her heart and, in later years, the pain in her body, when she is asked, "How are you?" she always responds, "I am blessed." I've often told her, "Lois, when I grow up, I want to be like you!" We both laugh. At 72, I still have a long ways to go.

Finding the path to peace may mean you have to make changes in your life to introduce more laughter, joy, quietness, and pulling away from a troubled world to rest on the Sabbath, reflecting on your blessings and the faithfulness of God to help you heal body and soul, and keeping only one step ahead of troubles. However, just ahead around the bend you may find that you've grown stronger and more able every day. Mother Teresa, who saw so much suffering and offered so much love to the dying, said, "If we have no peace, it is because we have forgotten that we belong to each other."

CHAPTER 14

Finding Yourself: Is There Anyone Out There?

When you get an injury and the skin is broken, the wound needs to heal from the inside out and from the outside in. If the wound does not heal from the inside out, inflammation, pain, and infection will still be present even if the skin appears to be healed. If the wound does not heal on the outside, there will continue to be a painful gap in the skin, capable of more infection. When it comes to emotional, mental, and addictive disorders, the healing has to be both—inside out and outside in. With these disorders reaching epidemic proportions, we cannot keep our heads in the sand, hoping for some new medicine or some new therapy.

A recent study of Holocaust survivors reports that there are gene changes in their descendants born two generations later that can only be attributed to the traumatic experience of the victims. Our genes can be modified by the environment as "chemical tags" attach to DNA. These, in turn, are passed on through generations. The children of the Holocaust survivors have "epigenetic tags" which affect stress hormones that are known to be affected by trauma.[1] In another study on epigenetic tagging, scientists at Emory University in Atlanta showed startling parallels in a mouse study. Using the smell of cherry blossoms, they trained a group of mice to fear the smell by pairing the smell with an electric shock. Mice offspring were then afraid of the smell of cherry blossoms, too.[2] In contrast, this experiment gives strong credence to how aromatherapy may help with disassociation from hurtful memories as well.

These new findings add to growing evidence that what happened to our ancestors has a lot to do with our own personal lives. Called "epigenetic inheritance," science has unraveled enough to know that the effects of stress can be passed not only to the next generation, but also to at least the next two generations.[3] Several years ago, the University of Pennsylvania School of Medicine said that their studies discovered that anxiety or depression in an adult, teenager, or a child could cause lasting genetic changes in a man's sperm. This stress leads to a *blunted reaction to stress,* which is associated with emotional and mental disorders.[4]

The good news about epigenetic inheritance is that your genes don't dictate your life—nor your future. You did not choose your ancestors, but you can help to determine the genes of your descendants; you can change the functions of your body and your mind, will, and emotions.

For example, there are studies on how parenting affects genetic offspring. In mouse studies, mice raised by mothers who did not provide *tactile stimulation*—lots of physical touching of their little ones—developed lower levels of *glucocorticoid* receptors in the hippocampus, which affected their behavior. It seems the methylation of the genes for estrogen receptors are affected and that female mice born from the *inattentive* mothers were less attentive to their offspring. In humans, the same scientists found, in autopsies, that suicide victims who were abused in childhood showed the same "excess methylation" of genes in the hippocampus.[5] It seems that touch has much to do with the development of the hippocampus; attentive mothers who use "tactile"—lots of expressive and loving touch—send a major boost to a developing hippocampus; the wrong kind of touch does the opposite. Such is the power of touch.

But how can mothers and fathers be all their children need them to be? Many mothers and fathers are overly stressed. Jobs, commuting distances, hectic schedules, financial worries, marital discord, and lack of real restorative rest take a toll. All too often, "rest" is in front of electronic screens and stressful drama that further hinders the body's recovery.

The Old Testament had much to say about fathers and mothers. Numbers 14:18 says, "The Lord is slow to anger, abounding in love and forgiving sin and rebellion. Yet he does not leave the guilty unpunished; he punishes the children for the sin of the parents to the third and fourth generation." Wow. Just as the Lord had many scientific, hygienic, and flourishing health reasons behind what He told the Israelites, here the word "sin" takes on significant meaning. Sin was breaking the law, and the Israelites had many laws—laws about how to keep themselves clean, how garments were supposed to be made, cooking vessels, what to eat, and what not to eat. And they had laws about morality and relationships. The consequences of their everyday life and obedience to those laws, moral and scientific, are being validated by science. Our DNA proves the power of what happened to our ancestors, and the decisions they made affect us today.

In Malachi 4:6, we read a startling word: "He will turn the hearts of the parents to their children, and the hearts of the children to their parents; *or else I will come and strike the land with total destruction*." How we treat our children has something to do with the stability of nations and destruction. That's something very serious to think about. Then, as now, the parents struggled to make their children as important as they should be. While there may not have been as many indulgent parents who substituted material gifts for real love, there must have been parents who placed their affections somewhere else. I can tell the importance of children to their fathers when I watch the father's eyes. If they glow with love for his children, it shows. He simply can't hide it. If it is tolerance, it shows. If it's interference with what the father wants to do, it shows. When a father is dedicated to raising his children, it is his main focus— above his sports, leisure, and personal pursuits. Often, the only way a child can be with the father is if he is watching sports or TV with him. The dad is too busy, too preoccupied, too distant.

With mothers, all of the new gadgets that free up a mother's hands and arms may prove to be detrimental. Baby seats, carriers, swings, bouncers, etc. are all designed to have somewhere safe to put baby. However, if the scientific tests on mice are to be considered, it's the *feel* and *touch* of the mother's arms—her holding the baby; her carrying the baby with her. Unfortunately, many mothers, especially single mothers, have to drop their babies and children at day care centers where numbers of children are being cared for by a few caregivers. There are just not enough arms to go around. There's a lot more to a child's needs than just food, water, and a clean bottom. Most likely all of us have heard a child say to a parent, "Hold me." Holding a child, humming to the child, and rocking are science and love in wonderful combination.

It's a proven fact that hugging stimulates the release of neurotransmitters, including oxytocin that is linked to bonding and relationships. Hugs also increase release of dopamine. Procrastination and self-doubt accompany low dopamine and may regulate high dopamine. Serotonin and endorphins are released, and hugs balance out the nervous system and enhance the immune system.[6] Roy Spence, the amazing person and marketer, has a book called *The 10 Essential Hugs of Life*. Hugs are powerful transmitters of hope, strength, confidence, and so much more!

Mothers tend to fall into two groups—those with too much to do and those with too little to do. In describing a woman of noble character of excellence and virtue, Proverbs 31:27 says, "She looks well to the ways of her household, and does not eat the bread of idleness" (NASB). In a crumbling society where the home is threatened and where children are missing important attributes of diligence, perseverance, and achievement, mothers and fathers must put aside mindless shopping, personal pursuits of beauty and fitness, hours spent watching television and movies and reading novels to provide for their families homes of order, beauty, cleanliness, and peace.

All too often when I have visited homes of disturbed teenagers as well as disturbed adults, I found a home that reflected the problem. Often, the mother would explain she couldn't get anyone to help her, and I could believe that, but I also knew that the children had grown up in disarray and disorder and an unclean house. It became their norm. Working mothers have an especially hard time keeping order, but order and cleanliness goes a long way in establishing a "new hope" as disorders of the mind, will, and emotions are re-aligned. Sometimes, it is the opposite—the home is such a showcase of collections and decorative appointments that the family walks on eggshells so they won't upset their mother. Somewhere in the middle of these two worlds, there needs to be a place called "home" where the heart safely trusts that it will be loved and understood.

If science is correct and trauma, abuse, and painful relationships can "pass" to the next three and four generations, what hope is offered to the emotional, mental, and addictive person who wants to change the future, not just for themselves but for their future generations? The promise of Luke 1:17 says, "He will go on before the Lord, in the spirit and power of Elijah, to turn the hearts of the parents to their children and the disobedient to the wisdom of the righteous—to make ready a people prepared for the Lord." That means that as people are prepared for the Lord, *epigenetic inheritance* can be changed. Is it possible that cells, just like they can remember, can forget and be transformed? I believe they can. Psalms 105:8 assures us that "He remembers his covenant forever, the promise he made, for a thousand generations."

Those who have accepted Jesus Christ as Savior and Lord enter into the deepest of all covenants, one that allows the Father, Son, and Holy Spirit to exchange the former life of the individual—their past, present, and future—for a new life. It's a blood covenant. Now, to cut through the language barrier, what this means is that we get a new chance to start over as a newborn. Old things pass away; everything becomes new. Indeed, just as 2 Corinthians 5:17 says, "Therefore, if anyone is in Christ, the new creation has come." The old is gone, the new is here! That's really good news!

Your covenant means that the dregs of your life and that of your ancestors can be reprogramed in your body and soul; the DNA of body, soul, and spirit can be changed in the present and future. Remember those mice that had poor mothers? If baby mice of those mothers were given to a nurturing mother, the offspring could and did nurture their own. Just as you can change your body by following simple and consistent directions, you can change your mind, will, and emotions by following simple and consistent directions. Consider the possibilities for your descendants. It truly is a "whole new world," and you hold so much power over what you are, what you become, and the spiritual and physical inheritance of your descendants.

Likewise, a community of people who love God and who love people can change the community. It may sound too simplistic, but that's what Paul is talking about when he says love is greater than faith and teachings about faith, greater than charity and social justice, and greater than all the music, instruments, and sounds. Love is transformational in a life. If a person can't find love at the local church, they will find it somewhere. Some bars are warmer and friendlier than churches in the area. That's why many people go. Yes, for alcohol, but many go for human companionship, someone to talk to, and someone who at least appears interested in what they are experiencing in their lives.

Just as our deeds dictate much to our bodies and minds, our words and our thoughts play major roles in emotional, mental, and addictive disorders as well as daily life. Proverbs 23:7 says, "As he thinks in his heart, so is he" (NKJV). That's why changing what you think about yourself, other people, and your future has so much effect on you, including your DNA. Scientists are discovering so much about our words. You may have read the research on how positive and negative words can affect water.[7] You know by experience that words affect you. In fact, for some of you, that's what got you into where you are—someone's words may have been the beginning of your depression. Someone's words may also be the beginning of your healing and renewal.

You can change your mind about yourself by thinking and believing good and positive things about yourself. Looking at a blue sky changes your neurotransmitters; smiling releases all those good neurotransmitters too. Replacing those negative words cycling in your mind is such an important step on your new path. It's time to transition your life into a new life, and you can do it. The steps in this book can lead to a new and improved life for your body, soul, and spirit. You've got my word on it!

May God himself, the God of peace, sanctify you through and through. May your whole spirit, soul and body be kept blameless at the coming of our Lord Jesus Christ. The one who calls you is faithful, and he will do it (1 Thessalonians 5:23-24).

Notes

Chapter 1: Below the Surface: The Body and Brain Connection

1. R. Wickstrom, "Effects of Nicotine During Pregnancy: Human and Experimental Evidence," *Current Neuropharmacology CN* 5, no. 3 (2007): 213-222, doi:10.2174/157015907781695955.

2. Carl Sherman, "Impacts of Drugs on Neurotransmission," National Institute on Drug Abuse, October 01, 2007, http://www.drugabuse.gov/news-events/nida-notes/2007/10/impacts-drugs-neurotransmission.

3. Elizabeth Cohen, "No Alcohol during Pregnancy, Says Pediatricians Group," CNN, October 21, 2015, http://www.cnn.com/2015/10/21/health/aap-no-alcohol-during-pregnancy/.

4. Sarah Houlton, "Drug Maker Apologises for Thalidomide Tragedy," *Chemistry World*, September 4, 2012.

5. Susan Scutti, "Your Cell Phone Could Be Stunting Your Baby's Brain [VIDEO]," Medical Daily, June 03, 2014, http://www.medicaldaily.com/radiation-cell-phones-and-wireless-devices-harms-your-unborn-babys-brain-development-286170.

6. Meghan Holohan, "Unborn Babies Are Hearing You, Loud and Clear," NBC News, August 2013, http://www.nbcnews.com/health/unborn-babies-are-hearing-you-loud-clear-8C11005474.

7. Josh Clark, "Why Do We Remember Pain?" HowStuffWorks, October 11, 2010, http://science.howstuffworks.com/life/remember-pain.htm.

8. Clare Wilson, "Baby's First Gut Bacteria May Come from Mum's Mouth," *New Scientist* 222, no. 2971 (2014), doi:10.1016/s0262-4079(14)61046-0.

9. Dr. David Perlmutter, renowned neurologist, has published a new book, *Brain Maker*. While I have not read it, I still highly recommend it as his book, *Grain Brain*, has enabled many to understand the connections between diet and mental health.

10. Jessie Johnson-Cash, "The Human Microbiome: Considerations for Pregnancy, Birth and Early Mothering," MidwifeThinking, January 14, 2014, http://midwifethinking.com/2014/01/15/the-human-microbiome-considerations-for-pregnancy-birth-and-early-mothering/.

11. "The Infant Gut Microbiome: New Studies on Its Origins and How It's Knocked out of Balance," *Pediatrics Week*, May 30, 2015, https://www.highbeam.com/doc/1G1-416078279.html.

12. Joseph Mercola, "Abnormal Gut Flora May Hold Clues to Autism," Mercola.com, July 18, 2013, http://articles.mercola.com/sites/articles/archive/2013/07/18/autistic-children-gut-flora.aspx.

13. "NIH Human Microbiome Project Defines Normal Bacterial Makeup of the Body," *States News Service*, June 13, 2012, https://www.highbeam.com/doc/1G1-292995826.html.

14. Joseph Mercola, "Your Digestive System Dictates Whether You're Sick or Not," Mercola.com, January 2, 2013, http://articles.mercola.com/sites/articles/archive/2013/01/02/digestive-system-gut-flora.aspx.

15. Dr. Natasha Campbell-McBride, MD published *Gut and Psychology Syndrome* in 2010, a landmark compilation of information about how the gut is implicated in Autism, Dyspraxia, Dyslexia, ADD/ADHD, Depression, and Schizophrenia. I did not discover the book until several years ago. If you or a loved one have a mental, emotional, or addiction disorder, this is a valuable aid to understanding the larger picture of how the gut influences the brain.

16. Moheb Costandi, "Microbes on Your Mind," *Scientific American Mind* 23, no. 3 (2012), doi:10.1038/scientificamericanmind0712-32.

Chapter 2: Your Ecosystem: Changing Your Mind by Changing Your Diet

1. Adam Hadhazy, "Think Twice: How the Gut's 'Second Brain' Influences Mood and Well-Being," Scientific American, February 10, 2012, https://www.scientificamerican.com/article/gut-second-brain/.

2. Gabriella Kortsch, "Introducing Our Second and Third Brains: We Do Think with Our Heart and Instinct," Brain Health Community, May 22, 2009, http://www.wellsphere.com/brain-health-article/introducing-our-second-and-third-brains-we-do-think-with-our-heart-and-instinct/684591.

3. See Deuteronomy 23:10–13.

4. J.B. Furmess, W.A. Kunze, and N. Clerc, "Nutrient Tasting and Signaling Mechanisms in the Gut," *American Journal of Physiology*, November 1999, http://ajpgi.physiology.org/collection/nutrient-tasting-and-signaling-mechanisms-gut.

5. Joseph Mercola, "New Study Show How Bacteria Actually Synchronize Together to Harm You," Mercola.com, April 28, 2009, http://articles.mercola.com/sites/articles/archive/2009/04/28/New-Study-Show-How-Bacteria-Actually-Synchronize-Together-to-Harm-You.aspx.

6. Roddy Scheer and Doug Moss, "Dirt Poor: Have Fruits and Vegetables Become Less Nutritious?" Scientific American, April 27, 2011, http://www.scientificamerican.com/article/soil-depletion-and-nutrition-loss/.

7. Alexis Baden-Mayer, "15 Health Problems Linked to Monsanto's Roundup," EcoWatch, January 23, 2015, http://ecowatch.com/2015/01/23/health-problems-linked-to-monsanto-roundup/.

8. Tulane University has an easy-to-read tutorial on cell receptors at e.hormone.tulane.edu.

9. Shelly Guzman and Debra Boutin, "What Are Complementary Proteins, and How Do We Get Them?" Department of Nutrition and Exercise Science, May 1, 2011, http://www.bastyr.edu/news/health-tips/2011/09/what-are-complementary-proteins-and-how-do-we-get-them.

10. Hadhazy, "Think Twice."

11. I recommend that you not try to supplement yourself but seek a qualified health professional to interpret tests. The labs listed offer consultations and are reputable.

12. Medind Mohapatra, "Sertraline Induced Psychosis," *Delhi Psychiatry Journal* 16, no. 2 (October 2013).

13. Dr. Janet Starr Hull, "Phenylalanine—Aspartame," Sweetpoison.com, accessed January 01, 2016, http://www.sweetpoison.com/phenylalanine.html.

14. Joseph Mercola, "Aspartame: The Most Dangerous Substance on the Market," Mercola.com, November 6, 2011, http://articles.mercola.com/sites/articles/archive/2011/11/06/aspartame-most-dangerous-substance-added-to-food.aspx.

15. M.M. Perica and I. Delas, "Essential Fatty Acids and Psychiatric Disorders," *Nutrition in Clinical Practice* 26, no. 4 (2011): 409-425, doi:10.1177/0884533611411306.

Chapter 3: Emergence: When Mental Illness Is Not What It Seems

1. Over the past 50 years, I have read and collected data. I have known about this for years, but I have not been able to find the source.

2. Natasha Tracy, "History of Schizophrenia," HealthyPlace, April 20, 2012, http://www.healthyplace.com/thought-disorders/schizophrenia-information/history-of-schizophrenia/.

3. "Pellagra: Evidence Nutrient Deficiencies Produce Mental Symptoms," Orthomolecular Psychiatry Online, July 08, 2011, https://orthomolecularinfo.wordpress.com/history/nutrient-deficiencies-cause-mental-symptoms/.

4. Interview with Abram Hoffer, M.D., Ph.D. 2003.

5. Greg Newson, "Pyroluria," Vitality & Wellness Centre, accessed January 02, 2016, http://www.vitalityandwellness.com.au/pyroluria.

6. "Bill Wilson, Co-Founder of AA—The First Proponent of Orthomolecular Treatment for Alcoholism," Cure Alcoholism, January 22, 2013, http://curealcoholism.pro/bill-wilson.

7. Drew Ramsey, "Vitamin Deficiencies and Mental Health: How Are They Linked?" *Current Psychiatry* 12, no. 1 (January 2013).

8. Andrew Weil, "Organ Meats: Liver Lover?" Ask Dr. Weil, May 21, 2012, http://www.drweil.com/drw/u/QAA401116/Organ-Meats-Liver-Lover.html.

9. Walter Last, "Mental Illness," Health-science-spirit.com, accessed January 02, 2016, http://www.health-science-spirit.com/mentaldisease.html.

10. "Folate," Mental Health America, accessed January 02, 2016, http://www.mentalhealthamerica.net/folate.

11. Tamara Duker Freuman, "How Your Reflux Medication Affects Your Health," Usnews.com, October 30, 2012, http://health.usnews.com/health-news/blogs/eat-run/2012/10/30/how-your-reflux-medication-affects-your-health.

12. Kimberly Hartke, "Is Pellagra the Root Cause of Violent Shooting Rampages?" Hartke Is Online, August 24, 2012, http://hartkeisonline.com/2012/08/24/is-pellagra-the-root-cause-of-violent-shooting-rampages/.

13. Sahabeh Etebary and Sara Nikseresht, "Postpartum Depression and Role of Serum Trace Elements," *Iranian Journal of Psychiatry* 5, no. 2 (2010): 40–46, https://www.researchgate.net/publication/230805041_Postpartum_Depression_and_Role_of_Serum_Trace_Elements.

14. "Mental Illness" by Walter Last (http://www.health-science-spirit.com/mentaldisease.html) is a comprehensive study on how various vitamins and minerals and metals affect mental disorders. It's worth printing and keeping as a resource.

15. Ibid.

16. "MIT: Magnesium May Reverse Middle-age Memory Loss," MIT News, December 1, 2014, accessed January 02, 2016, http://news.mit.edu/2004/magnesium.

17. Robert A. Yokel and Patrick J. McNamara, "Aluminium Toxicokinetics: An Updated MiniReview," *Pharmacology & Toxicology* 88, no. 4 (2008): 159–167, doi:10.1111/j.1600-0773.2001.880401.x.

18. Last, "Mental Illness."

19. Joseph Mercola, "Kids Exposed to Mercury May Be at Risk for ADHD," Mercola.com, October 9, 2012, http://articles.mercola.com/sites/articles/archive/2012/10/09/mercury-in-seafood.aspx.

20. Barbara L. Gracious et al., "Vitamin D Deficiency and Psychotic Features in Mentally Ill Adolescents: A Cross-sectional Study," *BMC Psychiatry* 12, no. 1 (May 9, 2012): 38, doi:10.1186/1471-244x-12-38.

Chapter 4: A Gathering Storm: Why Pills Are Not a Cure

1. "Sigmund Freud Biography," Bio.com, accessed January 02, 2016, http://www.biography.com/people/sigmund-freud-9302400.

2. Edward Shorter, "The History of Lithium Therapy," *Bipolar Disorders Journal*, June 2009, 4–3. "Research Explains Lithium's Dual Anti-Manic/Anti-Depressive Effect," University of Wisconsin–Madison News, July 1, 1998, http://www.eurekalert.org/pub_releases/1998-07/UoW-RELD-070798.php.

3. "Research Explains Lithium's Dual Anti-Manic/Anti-Depressive Effect," University of Wisconsin–Madison News, July 1, 1998, news.wisc.edu.

4. Jill Andrews, "Natural Sources of Lithium," Livestrong.com, January 28, 2015, http://www.livestrong.com/article/327470-natural-sources-of-lithium.

5. Marcia Purse, "Did You Know Lithium Was the First Mood Stabilizer?" About.com Health, February 12, 2015, http://bipolar.about.com/od/lithium/a/010312_lithium1.htm.

6. Laura Fitzpatrick, "A Brief History of Antidepressants," Time, January 07, 2010, http://content.time.com/time/health/article/0,8599,1952143,00.html.

7. Joseph Goldberg, "Depression Medications (Antidepressants)," WebMD, January 14, 2015, http://www.webmd.com/depression/depression-medications-antidepressants.

8. Ann Tracy Blake, "Zoloft Doubled Then Tripled before Batman Shooting in Colorado," International Coalition for Drug Awareness, July 25, 2015, http://www.drugawareness.org/zoloft-doubled-then-tripled-before-batman-shooting-in-colorado.

9. "Problem," Integrative Mental Health for You, April 18, 2013, http://imhu.org/the-need/.

10. Joseph Mercola, "Why Are More than One in Ten Americans at Risk for Suicide?" Mercola.com, February 15, 2012, http://articles.mercola.com/sites/articles/archive/2012/02/15/why-are-more-than-one-in-ten-americans-at-risk-for-suicide.aspx.

11. Barbara Hollingsworth, "Army Psychologist: 'Direct Correlation' Between Military Suicides, Psychiatric Meds," CNS News, September 04, 2014, http://www.cnsnews.com/news/article/barbara-hollingsworth/army-psychologist-direct-correlation-between-military-suicides.

12. Joel H. Levitt, "Conquering Anxiety, Depression and Fatigue Without Drugs—the Role of Hypoglycemia," The Anxiety & Hypoglycemia Relief Institute, accessed January 03, 2016, http://www.alternativementalhealth.com/conquering-anxiety-depression-and-fatigue-without-drugs-the-role-of-hypoglycemia-2.

13. Russel Blaylock and Gallon Totheroh, "What's In That? How Food Affects Behavior," Christian Broadcasting Network, January 1, 2009, http://www.cbn.com/CBNnews/353246.aspx.

14. A.G. Awad, "The Thyroid and the Mind and Emotions/Thyroid Dysfunction and Mental Disorders," *Thyrobulletin* 7, no. 3, www.thyroid.ca/e10f.php.

15. Kathleen McCormick, "Hypothyroid Article," Women's International Pharmacy, June 2012, http://womensinternational.com/thyroid.html.

16. Dr. Sherwin Yen, "Estimate: 12 Million Americans Living with Undiagnosed Thyroid Disease," The Austin Diagnostic Clinic, January 15, 2015, https://www.adclinic.com/estimate-12-million-americans-living-undiagnosed-thyroid-disease.

17. Erik Stokstad, "Perchlorate Impacts Thyroid at Low Doses," AAAS, October 6, 2006, http://news.sciencemag.org/2006/10/perchlorate-impacts-thyroid-low-doses.

18. "Suspect Salads," EWG, April 28, 2003, http://www.ewg.org/research/suspect-salads.

19. Melinda Beck, "Confusing Medical Ailments with Mental Illness," The Wall Street Journal, August 9, 2011, http://www.wsj.com/articles/SB10001424053111904480904576496271983911668.

20. Mary Elizabeth Dallas, "Psychiatric Drugs More Often Prescribed in the South," Consumer HealthDay, January 2013, http://consumer.healthday.com/general-health-information-16/doctor-news-206/psychiatric-drugs-more-often-prescribed-in-the-south-672754.html.

Chapter 5: On the Surface: How the Mind Changes the Body

1. Dr. Nan Kathryn Fuchs, *Color Me Healthy* (Atlanta, GA: Soundview Publishing, LLC, 2005), 7.

2. Jun Li and Huda Akil, "Out of Sync with the World: Brain Study Shows Body Clocks of Depressed People Are Altered at Cell Level," University of Michigan, May 13, 2013, http://www.uofmhealth.org/news/archive/201305/out-sync-world-brain-study-shows-body-clocks-depressed.

3. Roxanne Dryden-Edwards, "What Is Seasonal Affective Disorder (SAD)?" MedicineNet, accessed January 03, 2016, http://www.medicinenet.com/seasonal_affective_disorder_sad/article.htm.

4. Jo Waters, "Tired, Grumpy, Always Hungry? Why Grey-skies Syndrome May Be to Blame," Mail Online, March 28, 2013, http://www.dailymail.co.uk/health/article-2299045/Winter-blues-Tired-grumpy-hungry-Why-grey-skies-syndrome-blame-.html.

5. "Seasonal Affective Disorder Treatment: Choosing a Light Box," Mayo Clinic, accessed January 03, 2016, http://www.mayoclinic.org/diseases-conditions/seasonal-affective-disorder/in-depth/seasonal-affective-disorder-treatment/ART-20048298.

6. Sue Penckofer et al., "Vitamin D and Depression: Where Is All the Sunshine?" *Issues in Mental Health Nursing Issues Ment Health Nurs* 31, no. 6 (2010): 385–393, doi:10.3109/01612840903437657.

7. "What Are Negative and Positive Ions?" Negative Ionizers, accessed January 07, 2016, http://negativeionizers.net/negative-and-positive-ions.

8. Joseph Mercola, "Heavy Cell Phone Use Can Quadruple Your Risk of Brain Cancer," Mercola.com, January 5, 2015, http://articles.mercola.com/sites/articles/archive/2015/01/06/cell-phone-use-brain-cancer-risk.aspx.

9. Ibid.

10. Daniel Stapleton, "Detailed Information about Negative Ions and Ionizers," Comtech Research, June 20, 1995, https://www.comtech-pcs.com/printable/details.html.

11. R.A. Duffee and R.H. Koontz, "Behavioral Effects of Ionized Air on Rats," *Psychophysiology* 1, no. 4 (1965): 1347–1359, doi:10.1111/j.1469-8986.1965.tb03267.x.

12. Stapleton, "Detailed Information about Negative Ions and Ionizers."

13. Ibid.

14. Connie Chung, CBS Evening News qtd. in Stapleton, "Detailed Information about Negative Ions and Ionizers."

15. Gianluca Rosso et al., "Glucose Metabolism Alterations in Patients with Bipolar Disorder," *Journal of Affective Disorders* 184 (2015): 293–298, doi:10.1016/j.jad.2015.06.006.

16. Phillip Zimbardo and Nikita Duncan, "'The Demise of Guys': How Video Games and Porn Are Ruining a Generation," CNN, May 24, 2012, http://www.cnn.com/2012/05/23/health/living-well/demise-of-guys/index.html.

17. "The Adrenal Glands," Endocrine Awareness Center for Health, accessed January 03, 2016, https://eaware.org/adrenal-glands/#The_Adrenal_Glands.

18. Dr. Una McCann, "Psychiatric Symptoms May Signal Brain Damage From Diet Pills," NIH News Release, August 1997, http://www.eurekalert.org/pub_releases/1997-08/NIoM-PSMS-270897.php.

19. Margo Harakas and Barbara Hijek, "Rx For Risks," Sun Sentinel, August 23, 1997, http://articles.sun-sentinel.com/1997-08-23/news/9708220531_1_phen-fen-fda.

20. Phillip Zimbardo, qtd. in Dannah Gresh, "Click Here for a Good Time (For a While Anyway)," Pure Freedom, accessed January 03, 2016, http://purefreedom.org/click-here-for-a-good-time-for-a-while-anyway/.

21. "Teen Sex Linked to Early Adult TV Content," UPI, accessed January 03, 2016, http://www.upi.com/Health_News/2009/05/09/Teen-sex-linked-to-early-adult-TV-content/61061241841883.

22. Christopher Berland, "Can Oxytocin Improve Brain Function in Children With Autism?" Psychology Today, December 4, 2013, https://www.psychologytoday.com/blog/the-athletes-way/201312/can-oxytocin-improve-brain-function-in-children-autism.

23. Maia Szalavitz, "How Oxytocin Makes Men (Almost) Monogamous," Time, November 27, 2013, http://healthland.time.com/2013/11/27/how-oxytocin-makes-men-almost-monogamous.

24. Helene Timpone, "Why Are Teen Girls Cutting?" Oxytocin Central, January 2, 2011, http://oxytocincentral.com/2011/01/why-are-teen-girls-cutting.

25. Szalavitz, "How Oxytocin Makes Men (Almost) Monogamous."

26. Melissa Healy, "Hormone May Help Protect Monogamous Relationships," Los Angeles Times, November 13, 2012, http://articles.latimes.com/2012/nov/13/science/la-sci-oxytocin-men-monogamy-20121114.

27. Teri Walsh, "New Finding: Too Much TV Linked to Depression," *Prevention*, February 1999, 34–36.

28. Victoria Dunckley, "Gray Matters: Too Much Screen Time Damages the Brain," Psychology Today, February 27, 2014, https://www.psychologytoday.com/blog/mental-wealth/201402/gray-matters-too-much-screen-time-damages-the-brain.

29. John Rosemond, "Limit Kids' PC Use Until They're Literate," *The Macon Telegraph* (Macon, GA), June 3, 2003.

30. Randy Dotinga, "" of Mother's Voice in Womb May Aid Fetal Brain Growth," *U.S. News & World Report*, February 23, 2015, http://www.highbeam.com/doc/1G1-402844679.html?refid=easy_hf.

31. "Cartoon-based Illness Mystifies Japan,"" CNN, December 17, 1997, http://www.cnn.com/WORLD/9712/17/japan.cartoon/index.html.

32. "TV Retards Your Child's Development," Consumers Association of Penang, accessed January 4, 2016, http://www.consumer.org.my/index.php/development/education/347-tv-retards-your-childs-development.

33. Jean Lotus, "It's Official: TV Linked to Attention Deficit," Whitedot.org, accessed January 04, 2016, http://www.whitedot.org/issue/iss_story.asp?slug=ADHD+Toddlers.

34. Jennifer A. Manganello and Catherine A. Taylor, "Television Exposure as a Risk Factor for Aggressive Behavior Among 3-Year-Old Children," *Archives of Pediatrics & Adolescent Medicine* 163, no. 11 (2009), doi:10.1001/archpediatrics.2009.193.

35. Robin Yapp, "Children Who Watch Too Much TV May Have 'Damaged Brain Structures'" Mail Online, January 10, 2014, http://www.dailymail.co.uk/health/article-2537240/Children-watch-TV-damaged-brain-structures.html.

Chapter 6: Beginning Today: You Control More Than You Think You Do

1. Beng-Choon Ho et al., "Long-term Antipsychotic Treatment and Brain Volumes," *Archives of General Psychiatry* 68, no. 2 (2011): 128, doi:10.1001/archgenpsychiatry.2010.199.

2. "Interview with Dr. Walsh, Nutritional Medicine Guru & Founder and President of the Walsh Research Institute, on Mental Disorders & Nutrition," Blooming Wellness, April 29, 2013, http://www.bloomingwellness.com/2013/04/interview-with-dr-walsh-nutritional-medicine-guru-founder-and-president-of-the-walsh-research-institute-on-mental-disorders-nutrition.

3. Tanya Lewis, "Virtual Reality Affects Brain's 'GPS Cells'" LiveScience, December 05, 2014, http://www.livescience.com/49021-virtual-reality-brain-maps.html.

4. "Late-night Teens 'Face Greater Depression Risk'" BBC News, January 02, 2010, http://news.bbc.co.uk/2/hi/health/8435955.stm.

5. Rachael Rettner, "Avoiding Depression: Sleeping in Dark Room May Help," LiveScience, November 17, 2010, http://www.livescience.com/9004-avoiding-depression-sleeping-dark-room.html.

6. "Insufficient Sleep Is a Public Health Problem," Centers for Disease Control and Prevention, September 03, 2015, http://www.cdc.gov/Features/dsSleep/index.html.

7. Yasmin Anwar, "Sleep Loss Linked to Psychiatric Disorders," Berkeley.edu, October 22, 2007, http://www.berkeley.edu/news/media/releases/2007/10/22_sleeploss.shtml.

8. Donald Hensrud, "Sleep and Weight Gain: What's the Connection?" Adult Health, April 16, 2015, http://www.mayoclinic.org/healthy-lifestyle/adult-health/expert-answers/sleep-and-weight-gain/faq-20058198.

9. Steven D. Ehrlich, "Melatonin," University of Maryland Medical Center, January 21, 2014, http://umm.edu/health/medical/altmed/supplement/melatonin.

10. Rich McManus, "Nedergaard Explores Why We Need Sleep," The NIH Record, April 10, 2015, http://nihrecord.nih.gov/newsletters/2015/04_10_2015/story1.htm.

11. Jochen Bauer et al., "Craving in Alcohol-Dependent Patients After Detoxification Is Related to Glutamatergic Dysfunction in the Nucleus Accumbens and the Anterior Cingulate Cortex," *Neuropsychopharmacology* 38, no. 8 (2013): 1401–1408, doi:10.1038/npp.2013.45.

12. Robert MacNeil, "Autism Now: Dr. Martha Herbert Extended Interview," PBS, April 20, 2011, http://www.pbs.org/newshour/bb/health-jan-june11-herbertext_04-20.

13. Felicity Ng et al., "Oxidative Stress in Psychiatric Disorders: Evidence Base and Therapeutic Implications," *The International Journal of Neuropsychopharmacology*, 11, no. 06 (2008), doi:10.1017/s1461145707008401.

14. Svetlana Dimova et al., "Acetaminophen Decreases Intracellular Glutathione Levels and Modulates Cytokine Production in Human Alveolar Macrophages and Type II Pneumocytes in Vitro," *The International Journal of Biochemistry & Cell Biology* 37, no. 8 (2005): 1727–1737, doi:10.1016/j.biocel.2005.03.005.

15. William Shaw, "Evidence That Increased Acetaminophen Use in Genetically Vulnerable Children Appears to Be a Major Cause of the Epidemics of Autism, Attention Deficit with Hyperactivity, and Asthma," *Journal of Restorative Medicine* 2, no. 1 (2013): 14-29, doi:10.14200/jrm.2013.2.0101.

16. CBC News, "'Good Night's Sleep' May Be Critical for Brain Health," CBC News, December 31, 2013, http://www.cbc.ca/news/health/good-nights-sleep-may-be-critical-for-brain-health-1.2480427.

Chapter 7: Finding Solutions: Developing a Healthy Mind

1. Joseph Mercola, "E-Motion: How Your Emotional Baggage May Be Sabotaging Your Health, and What to Do About It," Mercola.com, March 14, 2014, http://articles.mercola.com/sites/articles/archive/2015/03/14/trapped-emotional-energy.aspx.

2. Frans Pouwer, Nina Kupper, and Marcel C. Adriaanse, "Does Emotional Stress Cause Type 2 Diabetes Mellitus? A Review from the European Depression in Diabetes (EDID) Research Consortium," *Discovery Medicine* 9, no. 45 (February 2010): 112–118.

3. Cynthia V. Calkin et al., "The Relationship between Bipolar Disorder and Type 2 Diabetes: More than Just Co-morbid Disorders," *Annals of Medicine* 45, no. 2 (2013): 171–181, doi:10.3109/07853890.2012.687835.

4. Katie Wagner Lennon, "Metabolic Dysfunction Markers Found in Bipolar Patients," Clinical Psychiatry News, August 26, 2015, http://www.clinicalpsychiatrynews.com/specialty-focus/bipolar-disorder/single-article-page/metabolic-dysfunction-markers-found-in-bipolar-patients/137b332dcf899419eaf4633d34876cd3.html.

5. Puna Wai Ora Mind-Body Cancer Clinic, "Discover How Prolonged Chronic Stress Causes Cancer over 6 Interrelated Phases," Alternative Cancer Care, accessed January 05, 2016, http://www.alternative-cancer-care.com/the-12-step-cancer-survivor-program.html.

6. Andrew Schrepf, Kristian Markon, and Susan K. Lutgendorf, "From Childhood Trauma to Elevated C-Reactive Protein in Adulthood,"

Psychosomatic Medicine 76, no. 5 (2014): 327–336, doi:10.1097/psy.0000000000000072.

7. Lecia Bushak, "Can Powerful Emotions Kill You? The Negative Health Effects of Anger, Stress, Sadness, and Shock," Medical Daily, May 21, 2014, http://www.medicaldaily.com/can-powerful-emotions-kill-you-negative-health-effects-anger-stress-sadness-and-shock-283682.

8. Ibid.

9. Ibid.

10. Carnegie Mellon University, "How Stress Influences Disease: Study Reveals Inflammation as the Culprit," ScienceDaily, April 2, 2012, http://www.sciencedaily.com/releases/2012/04/120402162546.htm.

11. Christine Gorman, Alice Park, and Kristina Dell, "Cellular Inflammation: The Silent Killer," Inflammation Research Foundation, accessed January 05, 2016, http://www.inflammationresearchfoundation.org/inflammation-science/inflammation-details/time-cellular-inflammation-article.

12. Ljudmila Stojanovich and Dragomir Marisavljevich, "Stress as a Trigger of Autoimmune Disease," *Autoimmunity Reviews* 7, no. 3 (2008): 209–213, doi:10.1016/j.autrev.2007.11.007.

13. Sylvain-Jacques Desjardins, "Regrets? Study Examines How People Can Cope," Concordia News, March 1, 2011, http://www.concordia.ca/cunews/main/releases/2011/03/01/regrets-study-examines-how-people-can-cope.html.

14. Melissa Davey, "Chronic Depression Shrinks Brain's Memories and Emotions," The Guardian, June 30, 2015, http://www.theguardian.com/society/2015/jun/30/chronic-depression-shrinks-brains-memories-and-emotions.

15. Terry L. Davidson et al., "A Potential Role for the Hippocampus in Energy Intake and Body Weight Regulation," *Current Opinion in Pharmacology* 7, no. 6 (2007): 613–616, doi:10.1016/j.coph.2007.10.008.

16. Joseph Goldberg, "How Worrying Affects Your Body," WebMD, August 15, 2015, http://www.webmd.boots.com/anxiety-panic/guide/how-worrying-affects-your-body.

17. C. Brad Wilson et al., "Inflammation and Oxidative Stress Are Elevated in the Brain, Blood, and Adrenal Glands during the Progression of Post-Traumatic Stress Disorder in a Predator Exposure Animal Model," *PLOS ONE* 8, no. 10 (2013), doi:10.1371/journal.pone.0076146.

18. Andrzej J. Kuczmierczyk et al., "Serum Cholesterol Levels in Patients with Generalized Anxiety Disorder (GAD) and with GAD and Comorbid Major Depression," *Canadian Journal of Psychiatry* 41 (1996): 465–469.

19. Tahia Maimanee, "The Impact of Exams Anxiety on the Level of Triglycerides in University Female Students," *Journal of the Egyptian Society of Parasitology* 40, no. 1 (April 2010): 259–270, https://www.researchgate.

net/publication/44631369_The_impact_of_exams_anxiety_on_the_
level_of_triglycerides_in_university_female_students.

20. Harvard Women's Health Watch, "Anxiety and Physical Illness," Harvard
    Health, July 1, 2008, http://www.health.harvard.edu/staying-healthy/
    anxiety_and_physical_illness.

21. "Worry, Jealousy, Moodiness Linked to Higher Risk of Alzheimer's in
    Women," The American Academy of Neurology, October 1, 2014, https://
    www.aan.com/PressRoom/Home/PressRelease/1311.

22. Michael Linden, "Posttraumatic Embitterment Disorder," *Psychotherapy
    and Psychosomatics* 72, no. 4 (2003): 195–202, doi:10.1159/000070783.

23. Richard Alleyne, "Stress Could Cause Cancer Claim Scientists," The
    Telegraph, January 2010, http://www.telegraph.co.uk/news/health/
    news/6981222/Stress-could-cause-cancer-claim-scientists.html.

24. Alireza Farnam, "PH of Soul: How Does Acid-base Balance Affect Our
    Cognition?" Europe PubMed Central, July 2014, http://europepmc.org/
    articles/PMC4097972.

25. P. Geissler, "Psychosomatic Aspects of Gallstones: A Test Psychological
    Study of Female Gallstone Patients with Clinical Symptoms in Comparison
    with a Psychoanalytic Study of Gallstones," *Psychosomatic Medicine and
    Contemporary Psychoanalysis*, July 1981.

Chapter 8: Finding the Way Out: Understanding Addictions

1. Astrid K. Stoker and Athina Markou, "Neurobiological Bases of Cue- and
   Nicotine-induced Reinstatement of Nicotine Seeking: Implications for the
   Development of Smoking Cessation Medications," *The Neuropharmacology
   of Nicotine Dependence Current Topics in Behavioral Neurosciences* 10 (2015):
   125–154, doi:10.1007/978-3-319-13482-6_5.

2. Ibid.

3. Susan Scutti, "Your Parkinson's Is Gone, But Now You Can't Stop
   Gambling," Medical Daily, October 20, 2014, http://www.medicaldaily.
   com/addictive-personality-traits-may-result-dopamine-receptor-agonist-
   drugs-307492.

4. Jenny Hope, "How Cocaine Can Damage the Brain," Mail Online,
   October 11, 2015, http://www.dailymail.co.uk/health/article-153520/
   How-cocaine-damage-brain.html.

5. "How Drugs Affect Neurotransmitters," The Brain from Top to Bottom,
   accessed January 06, 2016, http://thebrain.mcgill.ca/flash/d/d_03/
   d_03_m/d_03_m_par/d_03_m_par.html.

6. Joseph Mercola, "OxyContin Addiction: The Hottest Selling Narcotic in
   History," Mercola.com, July 18, 2015, http://articles.mercola.com/sites/
   articles/archive/2015/07/18/oxycontin-addiction.aspx.

7. Ibid.

8. "How Drugs Affect Neurotransmitters."

9. Ibid.

10. Ibid.

11. Frederick Von Stieff, *Brain in Balance: Understanding the Genetics and Neurochemistry behind Addiction and Sobriety* (San Francisco: Canyon Hill Pub., 2011).

12. Ibid., 120.

13. Michael D. Lemonick and Alice Park, "The Science of Addiction," *Time*, July 16, 2007, 26–32.

14. Therese J. Borchard, "Why Sugar Is Dangerous to Depression," World of Psychology, July 13, 2011, http://psychcentral.com/blog/archives/2011/07/13/why-sugar-is-dangerous-to-depression.

15. Nicole M. Avena, Pedro Rada, and Bartley G. Hoebel, "Evidence for Sugar Addiction: Behavioral and Neurochemical Effects of Intermittent, Excessive Sugar Intake," *Neuroscience & Biobehavioral Reviews* 32, no. 1 (2008): 20–39, doi:10.1016/j.neubiorev.2007.04.019.

16. Magalie Lenoir et al., "Intense Sweetness Surpasses Cocaine Reward," *PLoS ONE* 2, no. 8 (2007), doi:10.1371/journal.pone.0000698.

17. Joseph Mercola, "Daily Candy in Childhood Linked to Violence in Adulthood," Mercola.com, October 24, 2009, http://articles.mercola.com/sites/articles/archive/2009/10/24/Daily-Candy-in-Childhood-Linked-to-Violence-in-Adulthood.aspx.

18. Ibid.

19. Ibid.

20. Russell Blaylock, "Reactive Hypoglycemia," Blaylock Health Channel, Episode 19, accessed January 06, 2016, http://www.blaylockhealthchannel.com/#!bhc-ep-19-reactive-hypoglycemia-/ce7q.

21. Michele La Merrill et al., "Toxicological Function of Adipose Tissue: Focus on Persistent Organic Pollutants," *Environmental Health Perspectives* 121, no. 2 (2012): 162–169, doi:10.1289/ehp.1205485.

22. Elliott Freeman, "Scientists: New GMO Wheat May 'Silence' Vital Human Genes," Health, October 09, 2012, http://www.digitaljournal.com/article/332822#ixzz40M8gRlMn.

23. "Genetically Engineered Food Alters Our Digestive Systems!" The Alliance for Natural Health, accessed January 06, 2016, http://www.anh-usa.org/genetically-engineered-food-alters-our-digestive-systems.

24. David Yeager, "Can GMOs Harm Digestive Health? A Controversial Animal Study Suggests GMOs May Cause Stomach Inflammation," *Today's Dietitian* 15, no. 12 (December 2013): 12.

25. Olivia Dean, Frank Giorlando, and Michael Berk, "N-acetylcysteine in

Psychiatry: Current Therapeutic Evidence and Potential Mechanisms of Action," *Journal of Psychiatry & Neuroscience* 36, no. 2 (2011): 78–86, doi:10.1503/jpn.100057.

26. Mark Hyman, "A New Era of Medicine Has Finally Arrived," Dr. Mark Hyman, August 26, 2010, http://drhyman.com/blog/2010/08/26/a-new-era-of-medicine-has-finally-arrived.

27. "Nutritional Values Plummet," U-Lite, accessed January 07, 2016, http://preventprediabetes.com/values.php.

28. When I found out about this supplement a few years ago, I enrolled with the company due to the science behind it. This is an acknowledgement I receive financial income from the company that markets this product. For more information, contact jacquelynsheppard.com.

29. Kalpana Velmurugan et al., "Synergistic Induction of Heme Oxygenase-1 by the Components of the Antioxidant Supplement Protandim," *Free Radical Biology and Medicine* 46, no. 3 (2009): 430–440, doi:10.1016/j.freeradbiomed.2008.10.050.

30. Kyeong-Ah Jung and Mi-Kyoung Kwak, "The Nrf2 System as a Potential Target for the Development of Indirect Antioxidants," *Molecules* 15, no. 10 (2010): 7266–7291, doi:10.3390/molecules15107266.

31. Andy Y. Shih et al., "Coordinate Regulation of Glutathione Biosynthesis and Release by Nrf2-Expressing Glia Potently Protects Neurons from Oxidative Stress," *The Journal of Neuroscience* 23, no. 8 (April 15, 2003): 3394–3406.

32. Ron Milo and Rob Phillips, "How Quickly Do Different Cells in the Body Replace Themselves?" Cell Biology by the Numbers, accessed January 07, 2016, http://book.bionumbers.org/how-quickly-do-different-cells-in-the-body-replace-themselves.

33. Regina Bailey, "Do Brain Cells Regenerate?" About.com Education, accessed January 07, 2016, http://biology.about.com/od/Brain/p/Regeneration-Of-Brain-Cells.htm.

34. Rob Waugh, "Internet Addiction Can Cause Physical Damage to the Brain, Just like Drugs, Say Researchers," Mail Online, January 12, 2012, http://www.dailymail.co.uk/sciencetech/article-2085369/Internet-addiction-cause-physical-damage-brain-just-like-drugs-say-researchers.html.

35. "US Shows Signs of Net Addiction," BBC News, October 18, 2006, http://news.bbc.co.uk/2/hi/technology/6062980.stm.

36. James Gallagher, "Computer Gamers' Brains 'Differ,'" BBC News, November 15, 2011, http://www.bbc.co.uk/news/health-15720178.

Chapter 9: Tough Questions: How Chemicals Change Your Life

1. Melanie Y. Gross-Sorokin, Stephen D. Roast, and Geoffrey C. Brighty, "Assessment of Feminization of Male Fish in English Rivers by the Environment Agency of England and Wales," *Environmental Health*

Perspectives 114, no. S-1 (2005): 147–151, doi:10.1289/ehp.8068.

2. Irma C. Willis, *Progress in Environmental Research* (New York: Nova Science Publishers, 2007), 176.

3. Gwynne Lyons, "Effects of Pollutants on the Reproductive Health of Male Vertebrate Wildlife—Males Under Threat," *ChemTrust,* December 2008, http://www.chemtrust.org.uk/wp-content/uploads/Male-Wildlife-Under-Threat-2008-full-report.pdf.

4. L. Barr et al., "Measurement of Paraben Concentrations in Human Breast Tissue at Serial Locations across the Breast from Axilla to Sternum," *Journal of Applied Toxicology* 32, no. 3 (2012): 219–232, doi:10.1002/jat.1786.

5. Ibid.

6. Joseph Mercola, "Worst Endocrine Disruptors Revealed, and They Could Be Raising Your Family's Cancer Risk," Mercola.com, November 13, 2013, http://articles.mercola.com/sites/articles/archive/2013/11/13/worst-endocrine-disruptors.aspx.

7. Chunyang Liao, Fang Liu, and Kurunthachalam Kannan, "Occurrence of and Dietary Exposure to Parabens in Foodstuffs from the United States," *Environmental Science & Technology* 47, no. 8 (2013): 3918–3925, doi:10.1021/es400724s.

8. Steven Gilbert, "Polybrominated Diphenyl Ethers (PBDEs)," Toxipedia, June 9, 2014, http://www.toxipedia.org/pages/viewpage.action?pageId=296.

9. Ernie Hood, "Endocrine Disruption and Flame-Retardant Chemicals: PBDE-99 Effects on Rat Sexual Development," *Environmental Health Perspectives* 114, no. 2 (2006), doi:10.1289/ehp.114-a112b.

10. "Dirty Dozen Endocrine Disruptors," EWG, October 28, 2013, http://www.ewg.org/research/dirty-dozen-list-endocrine-disruptors.

11. Joseph Mercola, "Documentary: The Disappearing Male," Mercola.com, August 21, 2013, http://articles.mercola.com/sites/articles/archive/2013/08/31/disappearing-male-documentary.aspx.

12. "Prenatal Phthalate Exposure Linked to Increased Risk of Childhood Asthma," Medical News Today, September 17, 2014, http://www.medicalnewstoday.com/articles/282688.php.

13. Joseph Mercola, "DEHP: One of the Top 6 Chemical Threats to Humans," Mercola.com, June 24, 2011, http://articles.mercola.com/sites/articles/archive/2011/06/24/europe-bans-penis-shrinking-chemical-america-does-not.aspx.

14. Tracey J. Woodruff, Ami R. Zota, and Jackie M. Schwartz, "Environmental Chemicals in Pregnant Women in the United States: NHANES 2003-2004," *Environmental Health Perspectives* 119, no. 6 (2011): 878–885, doi:10.1289/ehp.1002727.

15. Soria Eladak et al., "A New Chapter in the Bisphenol A Story: Bisphenol S and Bisphenol F Are Not Safe Alternatives to This Compound," *Fertility and Sterility* 103, no. 1 (2015): 11–21, doi:10.1016/j.fertnstert.2014.11.005.

16. Lisbeth Stigaard Kjeldsen and Eva Cecilie Bonefeld-Jorgensen, "Perfluorinated Compounds Affect the Function of Sex Hormone Receptors," *Toxicology Letters* 221 (2013), doi:10.1016/j.toxlet.2013.05.327.

17. James Hamblin, "The Toxins That Threaten Our Brains," The Atlantic, March 18, 2014, http://www.theatlantic.com/health/archive/2014/03/the-toxins-that-threaten-our-brains/284466.

18. Michael Connett, "Fluoride's Effect on the Male Reproductive System—In Vitro Studies," Fluoride Action Network, April 2012, http://fluoridealert.org/studies/fertility01.

19. T. Zhou et al., "Influence of Water Fluoride Exposure on Sex Hormone Binding Globulin and Testosterone in Adult Males," *Wei Sheng Yan Jiu* 42, no. 2 (March 2013): 241–244, doi:10.1016/j.chemosphere.2015.04.012.

20. Yongjiang Zhou et al., "Effects of Sodium Fluoride on Reproductive Function in Female Rats," *Food and Chemical Toxicology* 56 (2013): 297–303, doi:10.1016/j.fct.2013.02.026.

21. Joseph Mercola, "The Fluoride Deception Continues as US Government Ignores Fluoride's Role as Endocrine Disruptor," Mercola.com, June 20, 2015, http://articles.mercola.com/sites/articles/archive/2015/06/20/fluoride-deception-continues.aspx.

22. Ibid.

23. Switzerland, Office of the Swiss Federal Health Service, *Bulletin #28* (July 20, 1992).

24. Jonathan Cho, "Manganese in Soy Infant Formulas Linked to Brain Damage," Coalition to Govern America, November 29, 2013, http://governamerica.com/news/5988-manganese-in-soy-infant-formulas-linked-to-brain-damage.

25. Aviva Fattal-Valevski et al., "Delayed Language Development Due to Infantile Thiamine Deficiency," *Developmental Medicine & Child Neurology* 51, no. 8 (2009): 629–634, doi:10.1111/j.1469-8749.2008.03161.x.

26. Kenneth Setchell et al., "Exposure of Infants to Phyto-oestrogens from Soy-based Infant Formula," *The Lancet* 350, no. 9070 (1997): 23–27, doi:10.1016/s0140-6736(96)09480-9.

27. A. Wisniewski et al., "Perinatal Exposure to Genistein Alters Reproductive Development and Aggressive Behavior in Male Mice," *Physiology & Behavior* 84, no. 2 (2005): 327–334, doi:10.1016/j.physbeh.2004.12.008.

28. Chengjun Yu et al., "Maternal Exposure to Daidzein Alters Behaviour and Oestrogen Receptor α Expression in Adult Female Offspring," *Behavioural Pharmacology* 21, no. 4 (2010): 283–291, doi:10.1097/fbp.0b013e32833aec1a.

29. J. D. Sherrill et al., "Developmental Exposures of Male Rats to Soy Isoflavones Impact Leydig Cell Differentiation," *Biology of Reproduction* 83, no. 3 (2010): 488–501, doi:10.1095/biolreprod.109.082685.

30. S. V. Jargin, "Soy and Phytoestrogens: Possible Side Effects," *German Medical Science*, December 15, 2014, doi:10.3205/000203.

31. Heather B. Patisaul and Wendy Jefferson, "The Pros and Cons of Phytoestrogens," *Frontiers in Neuroendocrinology* 31, no. 4 (2010): 400–419, doi:10.1016/j.yfrne.2010.03.003.

32. "Phytoestrogen: Foods High in Phytoestrogens and Health Benefits," Cholesterol and Fat Database, June 7, 2014, http://www.dietaryfiberfood. com/phytoestrogen-hormones/phytoestrogen-food-sources.php.

33. Tom Dennen, "Over 100 Countries Ban US Milk from Cows Treated with Recombinant Bovine Growth Hormone," Before It's News, August 9, 2013, http://beforeitsnews.com/conspiracy-theories/2013/08/over-100-countries-ban-us-milk-from-cows-treated-with-recombinant-bovine-growth-hormone-yet-back-home-monsanto-milk-industry-do-not-clearly-label-milk-from-rbgh-treated-cows-isnt-2453644.html.

34. Jorge F. Rodriguez-Sierra, R. Sridaran, and Charles A. Blake, "Monosodium Glutamate Disruption of Behavioral and Endocrine Function in the Female Rat," *Neuroendocrinology* 31, no. 3 (1980): 228–235, doi:10.1159/000123079.

35. Becky Phillips, "Pesticide Linked to Three Generations of Disease," WSU News, July 24, 2014, https://news.wsu.edu/2014/07/24/pesticide-linked-to-three-generations-of-disease.

36. Mehmet Uzumcu, Hiroetsu Suzuki, and Michael K. Skinner, "Effect of the Anti-androgenic Endocrine Disruptor Vinclozolin on Embryonic Testis Cord Formation and Postnatal Testis Development and Function," *Reproductive Toxicology* 18, no. 6 (2004): 765–774, doi:10.1016/j. reprotox.2004.05.008.

37. "Pesticide Atrazine Can Turn Male Frogs into Females," ScienceDaily, March 1, 2010, http://www.sciencedaily.com/releases/2010/03/100301151927. htm.

38. Ibid.

39. Crystal Gammon, "Weed-Whacking Herbicide Proves Deadly to Human Cells," Scientific American, June 23, 2009, http://www.scientificamerican. com/article/weed-whacking-herbicide-p.

40. Ivan Petersen, "The Real Reason Wheat Is Toxic," *Nickel Mine Health Foods, LLC*, August 2015.

41. Leah Zerbe, "Roundup Red Alert! What You Need to Know about the Pesticide Poised to 'Push Us All Off of the Cliff,'" Rodale Wellness, February 03, 2011, http://www.rodalewellness.com/health/roundup.

42. Nick Meyer, "MIT Researcher's New Warning: At Today's Rate, Half of All U.S. Children Will Be Autistic (by 2025)," AltHealthWorkscom RSS2, June 11, 2014, http://althealthworks.com/2494/mit-researchers-new-warning-at -todays-rate-1-in-2-children-will-be-autistic-by-2025.

43. Vera Lúcia De Liz Oliveira Cavalli et al., "Roundup Disrupts Male Reproductive Functions by Triggering Calcium-mediated Cell Death in Rat Testis and Sertoli Cells," *Free Radical Biology and Medicine* 65 (2013): 335–346, doi:10.1016/j.freeradbiomed.2013.06.043.

44. Jeff Ritterman, "Monsanto's Roundup Linked to Cancer—Again," Truthout, October 6, 2014, http://www.truth-out.org/news/item/26614-monsanto-s-roundup-linked-to-cancer.

45. Youn K. Shim, Steven P. Mlynarek, and Edwin Van Wijngaarden, "Parental Exposure to Pesticides and Childhood Brain Cancer: U.S. Atlantic Coast Childhood Brain Cancer Study," *Environ Health Perspect Environmental Health Perspectives* 117, no. 6 (2009): 1002–1006, doi:10.1289/ehp.0800209.

46. "Arsenic in Your Food Investigated," Consumer Reports, November 2012, http://www.consumerreports.org/cro/magazine/2012/11/arsenic-in-your-food/index.htm.

47. "Endocrine Disruptor Screening Program (EDSP) Overview," EPA, October 1, 2015, http://www.epa.gov/endocrine-disruption/endocrine-disruptor-screening-program-edsp-overview.

Chapter 10: Getting Back to the Design: How Prayer Changes Your Body and Soul

1. Alex Knapp, "Martin Luther King, Jr. on Science and Religion," Forbes, January 20, 2014, http://www.forbes.com/sites/alexknapp/2014/01/20/martin-luther-king-jr-on-science-and-religion.

2. Dr. Francis Collins, "The Language of God," Point of Inquiry, August 31, 2007, http://www.pointofinquiry.org/dr_francis_collins_the_language_of_god.

3. Ryan Winter, "Can Your Religion Influence Your Treatment?" Soliant Health, January 13, 2010, http://blog.soliant.com/healthcare-news/can-your-religion-influence-your-treatment.

4. Andrew Newberg, "Research Questions: How Do Meditation and Prayer Change Our Brains?" Andrew Newberg, accessed January 08, 2016, http://www.andrewnewberg.com/research.

5. Andrew Newberg, "Strengthen Your Brain through the Power of Prayer," Full Gospel Businessmen's Training, accessed January 08, 2016, http://fgbt.org/Health-Tips/strengthen-your-brain-through-the-power-of-prayer.html.

6. Richard Schiffman, "Why People Who Pray Are Healthier Than Those Who Don't" The Huffington Post, January 18, 2012, http://www.huffingtonpost.com/richard-schiffman/why-people-who-pray-are-heathier_b_1197313.html.

7. Andrew Newberg, "Why Your Brain Needs God," OnFaith, March 27, 2009, http://www.faithstreet.com/onfaith/2009/03/27/faith-is-essential-for-your-brain/1746.

8. Ibid.

9. Ibid.

10. Ibid.

11. Beth Howard, "Prayer Is Good Medicine," Spirituality & Health Magazine, August 2014, http://spiritualityhealth.com/articles/prayer-good-medicine.

12. "Prayer Keeps You Healthy," *First for Women*, May 31, 1999, 45.

13. Randolph C. Byrd, "Positive Therapeutic Effects of Intercessory Prayer in a Coronary Care Unit Population," *Southern Medical Journal* 81, no. 7 (1988): 826–829, doi:10.1097/00007611-198807000-00005.

14. "Science Proves the Healing Power of Prayer," Newsmax, March 31, 2015, http://www.newsmax.com/Health/Headline/prayer-health-faith-medicine/2015/03/31/id/635623.

15. Schiffman, "Why People Who Pray Are Healthier."

16. Ibid.

17. Newberg, "Strengthen Your Brain through the Power of Prayer."

18. Peter A. Boelens et al., "A Randomized Trial of the Effect of Prayer on Depression and Anxiety," *The International Journal of Psychiatry in Medicine* 39, no. 4 (2009): 377–392, doi:10.2190/pm.39.4.c.

19. Peter A. Boelens et al., "The Effect of Prayer on Depression and Anxiety: Maintenance of Positive Influence One Year after Prayer Intervention," *The International Journal of Psychiatry in Medicine* 43, no. 1 (2012): 85–98, doi:10.2190/pm.43.1.f.

20. Lindsey Gruson, "Color Has a Powerful Effect on Behavior, Researchers Assert," The New York Times, October 18, 1982, http://www.nytimes.com/1982/10/19/science/color-has-a-powerful-effect-on-behavior-researchers-assert.html.

21. Kortsch, "Introducing Our Second and Third Brains."

Chapter 11: Redesigning Yourself: How Music Impacts Your Cells

1. Piperalpha, "Bagpipes Are a Weapon of War," Canada at War Forums, January 28, 2009, http://www.canadaatwar.ca/forums/showpost.php?p=3262&postcount=1.

2. Schönberg, Claude-Michael (Composer); Kretzmer, Herbert, (Lyricist). 1980.

3. Phillip Kotler, "Atmospherics as a Marketing Tool," *Journal of Retailing* 49, no. 4 (January 1974): 48–64.

4. Emma Baines, "Music and the Heart," *Circulation: European Perspectives in Cardiology* 116 (December 11, 2011): 139–140, doi:10.1161/CIRCULATIONAHA.107.187676.

5. A.J. Blood and R.J. Zatorre, "Intensely Pleasurable Responses to Music Correlate with Activity in Brain Regions Implicated in Reward and Emotion," *Proceedings of the National Academy of Sciences* 98, no. 20 (2001): 11818–11823, doi:10.1073/pnas.191355898.

6. Frederick Platz et al., "The Impact of Song-specific Age and Affective Qualities of Popular Songs on Music-evoked Autobiographical Memories (MEAMs)," *Musicae Scientiae* 19, no. 4 (2015): 327–349, doi:10.1177/1029864915597567.

7. David Knauss, PhD. *The Reported Influence of Multiple Variables on Memorableness of a Musical Selection*, Pennsylvania State University, March 2005, http://www.classroom-music.info/awards.htm.

8. "Daniel Levitin on Our Musical Brain," EarthSky, January 4, 2012, http://earthsky.org/human-world/daniel-levitin-on-our-musical-brain.

9. Valorie N. Salimpoor et al., "Anatomically Distinct Dopamine Release during Anticipation and Experience of Peak Emotion to Music," *Nature Neuroscience* 14, no. 2 (2011): 257–262, doi:10.1038/nn.2726.

10. Gavin Ryan Shafron and Mitchell P. Karno, "Heavy Metal Music and Emotional Dysphoria among Listeners," *Psychology of Popular Media Culture* 2, no. 2 (2013): 74–85, doi:10.1037/a0031722.

11. Leah Sharman and Genevieve A. Dingle, "Extreme Metal Music and Anger Processing," *Frontiers in Human Neuroscience Front. Hum. Neurosci.* 9 (2015), doi:10.3389/fnhum.2015.00272.

12. Silvia Francesca Maglione, "Effect of Classical Music on the Brain," Classical Forums, March 2, 2006, http://www.classicalforums.com/articles/Music_Brain.html.

13. James Myron Holland, *Singing Excellence and How to Achieve It* (Parowan, UT: Marjorie Montell Memorial Society, 2005).

14. Karl Paulnack, "Welcome Address given to Parents of Incoming Students" (address, Boston Conservatory of Music, September 1, 2004).

15. Douglas R. Fields, "The Power of Music: Mind Control by Rhythmic Sound," Scientific American, October 9, 2012, http://blogs.scientificamerican.com/guest-blog/the-power-of-music-mind-control-by-rhythmic-sound.

16. Laurence O'Donnell, "Music and the Brain," Cerebromente.org, 1999, accessed January 08, 2016, http://www.cerebromente.org.br/n15/mente/musica.html.

17. Roger W. Wicke, "Health Benefits of Music and Sound," Herbalist Review, June 28, 2008, http://www.rmhiherbal.org/review/2002-1.html.

18. O'Donnell, "Music and the Brain."

19. Knauss, David, PhD. Telephone interview, August 17, 2015.

20. Diane M. Schneider et al., "Application of Therapeutic Harp Sounds for Quality of Life Among Hospitalized Patients," *Journal of Pain and Symptom Management* 49, no. 5 (2015): 836–845, doi:10.1016/j.jpainsymman.2014.09.012.

21. Lindsey Tanner, "Harps' Healing Powers Strike a Chord with Physicians," *Los Angeles Times,* January 15, 2006, http://articles.latimes.com/2006/jan/15/news/adna-harps15.

22. "Portuguese Scientists Discover Why Pendulum Clocks Swing Together," The Guardian, July 24, 2015, http://www.theguardian.com/science/2015/jul/24/portuguese-scientists-discover-why-pendulum-clocks-swing-together.

23. Knauss. Op cit.

24. Mitchell L. Gaynor, *Sounds of Healing* (New York: Broadway Books, 1999).

25. Fabien Maman, *The Role of Music in the Twenty-First Century* (Redondo Beach, CA: Tama-Dō Press, 1997).

26. Walter Neary, "Brains of Deaf People Rewire to 'Hear' Music," UW Today, November 27, 2001, http://www.washington.edu/news/2001/11/27/brains-of-deaf-people-rewire-to-hear-music.

27. Bruce H. Lipton, *The Biology of Belief: Unleashing the Power of Consciousness, Matter and Miracles* (Santa Rosa, CA: Mountain of Love/Elite Books, 2005).

28. Jerry Bergman, "The Miracle of Tears," The Miracle of Tears, accessed January 08, 2016, http://creation.com/the-miracle-of-tears.

Chapter 12: Corporate Redesign: How We Are Designed for Community Designing

1. Shannon Hunt, "Harness the Healing Power of Color and Light," *Woman's World*, August 24, 2015, 20-21.

2. Nissan Mindel, "The Three Daily Prayers," Kehot Publication Society, accessed January 08, 2016, http://www.chabad.org/library/article_cdo/aid/682091/jewish/The-Three-Daily-Prayers.htm.

3. "Translation of the Weekday Amidah," Kehot Publication Society, accessed January 08, 2016, http://www.chabad.org/library/article_cdo/aid/867674/jewish/Translation.htm.

4. Anna Maria Galante, "Chant: The Healing Power of Voice and Ear," in *Music Physician for times to Come: An Anthology*, by Don G. Campbell (Wheaton, IL, U.S.A.: Theosophical Pub. House, 1991), August 28, 2014, http://singtoyourkids.ca/posts/chant-the-healing-power-of-voice-and-ear.

5. Ibid.

6. Leslie Miller, "Churches May Be in Decline, but Gregorian Chant Beats Secular Competition," Religion News Service, June 16, 2015, http://www.religionnews.com/2015/06/16/churches-may-decline-gregorian-chant-beats-secular-competition.

7. J.R. Hughes et al., "The 'Mozart Effect' on Epileptiform Activity," *Clinical EEG and Neuroscience* 29, no. 3 (1998): 109–119, doi:10.1177/155005949802900301.

8. "The Hymn Writers of the Reformation," Christian Classics Ethereal Library, accessed January 08, 2016, http://www.ccel.org/ccel/ryden/hymnstory.p2.c7.html.

9. M.H. Immordino-Yang et al., "Neural Correlates of Admiration and Compassion," *Proceedings of the National Academy of Sciences* 106, no. 19 (2009): 8021–8026, doi:10.1073/pnas.0810363106.

10. Elizabeth Svoboda, "Hard-Wired for Giving," WSJ, August 31, 2013, http://www.wsj.com/articles/SB10001424127887324009304579041231971683854.

11. Joshua Freedman, "The Physics of Emotion: Candace Pert on Feeling Go(o)d," Six Seconds, January 26, 2007, http://www.6seconds.org/2007/01/26/the-physics-of-emotion-candace-pert-on-feeling-good.

12. Leslie J. Francis and Mandy Robbins, "Personality and Glossolalia: A Study Among Male Evangelical Clergy," *Pastoral Psychology* 51, no. 5 (May 2003): 391–396.

13. Andrew B. Newberg et al., "The Measurement of Regional Cerebral Blood Flow during Glossolalia: A Preliminary SPECT Study," *Psychiatry Research: Neuroimaging* 148, no. 1 (2006): 67–71, doi:10.1016/j.pscychresns.2006.07.001.

14. Carl R. Peterson, "Medical Facts about Speaking in Tongues," Being Part of the New Covenant, June 13, 2011, https://beingunderthenewcovenant.wordpress.com/2011/06/14/medical-facts-about-speaking-in-tongues-%e2%80%93-carl-r-peterson-m-d.

15. Christopher Dana. Lynn, *Glossolalia Influences on Stress Response among Apostolic Pentecostals* (State University of New York at Albany, 2009).

16. Jackie Pullinger and Andrew Quicke, *Chasing the Dragon: One Woman's Struggle against the Darkness of Hong Kong's Drug Dens* (Ventura, CA: Regal, 2006).

17. Charles Carrin, "The Church's 3,000 Year Old Model for Worship," Charles Carrin Ministries, July 21, 2015, http://www.charlescarrinministries.com/newsletter/the-church%E2%80%99s-3-000-year-old-model-for-worship.

Chapter 13: Finding the Illusive: Peace, Joy, and Quietness

1. Daniel A. Gross, "This Is Your Brain on Silence," Nautilus, August 21, 2014, http://nautil.us/issue/16/nothingness/this-is-your-brain-on-silence.

2. P.D. Larsen, "The Sound of Silence Is Music to the Heart," *Heart* 92, no. 4 (2005): 433–434, doi:10.1136/hrt.2005.071902.

3. By Jennifer Welsh, "Child Abuse Leaves Mark on Brain," LiveScience, February 13, 2012, http://www.livescience.com/18453-child-abuse-brain.html.

4. G. Robert Delong, "Autism, Amnesia, Hippocampus, and Learning," *Neuroscience & Biobehavioral Reviews* 16, no. 1 (1992): 63–70, doi:10.1016/s0149-7634(05)80052-1.

5. Chris Zarow et al., "Correlates of Hippocampal Neuron Number in Alzheimer's Disease and Ischemic Vascular Dementia," *Annals of Neurology* 57, no. 6 (2005): 896–903, doi:10.1002/ana.20503.

6. "Mental Disorders in America," Mental Illness Statistics, accessed January 09, 2016, http://www.thekimfoundation.org/html/about_mental_ill/statistics.html.

7. Emily Esfahani Smith, "The Lovely Hill: Where People Live Longer and Happier," The Atlantic, February 04, 2013, http://www.theatlantic.com/health/archive/2013/02/the-lovely-hill-where-people-live-longer-and-happier/272798.

8. Ellen G. White, "Preparing for the Holy Day," Our Father Cares, accessed January 09, 2016, http://www.whiteestate .org/devotional/ofc/03_02.asp.

9. Ryan Buxton, "What Seventh-Day Adventists Get Right That Lengthens Their Life Expectancy," The Huffington Post, July 31, 2013, http://www.huffingtonpost.com/2014/07/31/seventh-day-adventists-life-expectancy_n_5638098.html.

10. "Church Leaders Call for Better Observance of Sabbath Day," Newsroom, June 30, 2015, http://www.mormonnewsroom.org/article/church-leaders-call-for-better-observance-of-sabbath-day.

11. James E. Enstrom and Lester Breslow, "Lifestyle and Reduced Mortality among Active California Mormons, 1980–2004," *Preventive Medicine* 46, no. 2 (2008): 133–136, doi:10.1016/j.ypmed.2007.07.030.

12. F. Halberg et al., "Spectral Resolution of Low-Frequency, Small-Amplitude Rhythms in Excreted 17-Ketosteroids; Probable Androgen-Induced Circaseptan Desynchronization," *European Journal of Endocrinology* 50, no. 4 Suppl (1965), doi:10.1530/acta.0.050s0005.

13. Bruce Miller, *Your Life in Rhythm* (Carol Stream, IL: Tyndale House Publishers, 2009), 133-134.

14. David Perlmutter, "New Study Validates Ketogenic Diet for Epilepsy Treatment in Adults," David Perlmutter MD, accessed January 13, 2016, http://www.drperlmutter.com/new-study-validates-ketogenic-diet-epilepsy-treatment-adults.

15. Ekaterina Pesheva, "Study: Fasting May Benefit Patients with Epilepsy," Johns Hopkins Children's Center, December 6, 2012, http://www.hopkinschildrens.org/Fasting-May-Benefit-Patients-with-Epilepsy.aspx.

16. Allan Cott, Jerome Agel, and Eugene Boe, *Fasting: The Ultimate Diet* (Toronto: Bantam, 1975).

17. "Caloric Restriction," LifeExtension.com, accessed January 13, 2016, http://www.lifeextension.com/protocols/lifestyle-longevity/caloric-restriction/Page-01.

18. Mike Bickle and Dana Candler, *The Rewards of Fasting: Experiencing the Power and Affections of God* (Kansas City, MO: Forerunner Books, 2005).

19. "Fasting Guidelines and Information," About IHOPKC, accessed January 13, 2016, http://www.ihopkc.org/about/fasting-guidelines-and-information.

20. Carol Whipple and Susan Calvert, "The Connection between Laughter, Humor, and Good Health," *University of Kentucky Co-operative Extension Service*, May 2008, 1–4, doi:10.1201/b16307-2.

21. Ramon Mora-Ripoli, "The Therapeutic Value of Laughter in Medicine," *Alternative Therapies in Health and Medicine* 16, no. 6 (November/December 2010): 56–64, http://psycdweeb.weebly.com/uploads/3/5/2/0/3520924/therapeutic_value_of_laughter_in_medicine.pdf.

22. Richard D. Lane, Lynn Nadel, and Geoffrey Ahern, "Neural Correlates of Conscious Emotional Experience," in *Cognitive Neuroscience of Emotion* (New York: Oxford University Press, 2000), 345–370.

23. Mikaela Conley, "Thankfulness Linked to Positive Changes in Brain And Body," ABC News Radio, November 23, 2011, http://abcnewsradioonline.com/health-news/thankfulness-linked-to-positive-changes-in-brain-and-body.html.

24. Ibid.

Chapter 14: Finding Yourself: Is There Anyone Out There?

1. Helen Thomson, "Study of Holocaust Survivors Finds Trauma Passed on to Children's Genes," The Guardian, August 21, 2015, http://www.theguardian.com/science/2015/aug/21/study-of-holocaust-survivors-finds-trauma-passed-on-to-childrens-genes.

2. Ibid.

3. Andy Coghlan, "Stress Can Affect Future Generations' Genes," New Scientist, January 25, 2013, https://www.newscientist.com/article/dn23109-stress-can-affect-future-generations-genes.

4. Suzannah Hills, "Stress Can Cause Permanent Damage to a Man's Sperm—and Affect the Mental Health of His Children," Mail Online, June 13, 2013, http://www.dailymail.co.uk/health/article-2341121/Stress-cause-permanent-damage-mans-sperm–affect-mental-health-children.html.

5. Dan Hurley, "Grandma's Experiences Leave a Mark on Your Genes," Discover Magazine, June 25, 2015, http://discovermagazine.com/2013/may/13-grandmas-experiences-leave-epigenetic-mark-on-your-genes.

6. Eddie L, "8 Ways Science Reveals That Hugging Creates a Physiological Response Equivalent to Drugs," World Truth.TV, June 29, 2015, http://worldtruth.tv/8-ways-science-reveals-that-hugging-creates-a-physiological-response-equivalent-to-drugs.

7. Masaru Emoto, *The Hidden Messages in Water* (Hillsboro, OR: Beyond Words Pub., 2004).

About Jacquelyn Sheppard

Jacquelyn Sheppard is a mother, grandmother, educator and writer. She and her husband, Glenn, live in Missouri on a ten-acre farm where they raise sheep and goats and spoil their eight grandchildren, who come to visit from Boston, Kansas City and Northern Ireland. She loves working with the new born lambs and kids and working in her small organic garden of raised beds and heirloom seeds. But, her favorite moments are with the grandchildren.

A native Georgian, she graduated from Perry High School and attended Tift College in Forsyth. She received the B.A. degree from Mercer University in Macon, GA and has additional graduate study. She is the founder of a private high school, a former journalist and photographer, and the co-founder of International Prayer Ministries. Her husband, Glenn Sheppard, is a well-known minister and speaker as are her children, Tre' (Tori), Krista (Mark) Harris, and Trent (Bronwyn) Sheppard.

For the past 50 years, her extensive research, experience, and concepts concerning the body and the brain have enabled many to live better lives. She lives a busy life, juggling phone calls, appointments, and speaking nationally and internationally on physical and mental health.

Mrs. Sheppard, or just "Jackie" to most, she is just beginning to enter the world of social media and is launching a blog, called Ancient Wisdom and Common Sense. Find her on Facebook at Jacquelyn Sheppard and on her website, JacquelynSheppard.com or at Ancient Wisdom and CommonSense.com.